# JESUS AND THE POLITICS OF INTERPRETATION

# J E S U S

## AND THE POLITICS

## OF INTERPRETATION

*Elisabeth Schüssler Fiorenza*

CONTINUUM NEW YORK LONDON

2001

The Continuum International Publishing Group Inc
370 Lexington Avenue, New York, NY 10017

The Continuum International Publishing Group Ltd
The Tower Building, 11 York Road, London SE1 7NX

Printed in the United States of America

Library of Congress Cataloging-in-Publication Data

Schüssler Fiorenza, Elisabeth, 1938–
    Jesus and the politics of interpretation / Elisabeth Schüssler Fiorenza.
        p.   cm.
    Includes bibliographical references and index.
    ISBN 0-8264-1366-8
        1. Jesus Christ—Historicity—History of doctrines.   2. Feminist
    theology.   I. Title.

BT303.2 .S33 2000
232.9'08—dc21                                                    00-056986

To Francis

*Ubi caritas et amor*
*Ibi Sophia est.*

# CONTENTS

# PREFACE

TO RETHINK BIBLICAL STUDIES AS RHETORICAL PRACTICE AND AN ethics of interpretation requires that one critically investigate not only the meaning of the Bible but also the meaning-making of biblical studies. Hence, I am not concerned here to present one more sophisticated variation of the story of Jesus. Rather I want to investigate how such Jesus research is produced.

With this book I hope to assist students, colleagues, and the wider public interested in Historical-Jesus research to sort out the academic and popular meaning-making about Jesus and its moral and religious implications. I do not see the problem as such in the rich proliferation of Jesus images. Rather, I see it in the scholarly claim to have produced a history or biography of the "real" Jesus that, unlike theological-religious images of Jesus, is a truly scientific account of Jesus as he "really" was.

Thus, the problem that I want to investigate in these pages is not so much one of "data." Rather, the rich array of Historical-Jesus reconstructions calls for a critical epistemological inquiry into the politics of Historical-Jesus discourses, probing how they can say what they say and for whom and to what ends scholars produce Historical-Jesus research. Such a critical discussion seeks to explore the nexus between rhetorical reconstructions of the Historical-Jesus and those theoretical, historical, cultural, and political conceptual frameworks that shape Historical-Jesus discourses.

In short, in this book I seek to inquire into the rhetoricity and politics of Historical-Jesus interpretation as a rhetorical process of meaning-making. In so doing one cannot avoid discussing and evaluating critically theses and proposals especially of those colleagues whose work one respects and appreciates greatly. Such critical engagement must therefore not be personalized but must be seen for what it is: a critical assessment and debate that seeks to make salient epistemological points.

The chapters of this book have been shaped and refined by many discussions and debates with colleagues in biblical and theological studies. I want to thank Professors Marcus Borg and Paula Fredriksen for giving me the opportunity to discuss my book *Jesus: Miriam's Child, Sophia's Prophet* with other Historical-Jesus scholars in the Jesus and Theology Seminar at the annual meeting of the Society of Biblical Literature in 1995. The panel on "Women and the Search for the Historical Jesus" sponsored by the Wo/men in the Biblical World section was the beginning of the present fourth chapter. It was one of the many such panels that sought critically to raise into consciousness the pernicious anti-Judaism continuing to stalk even feminist work. Some of the points of chapter 4 were also presented at a symposium on Christian–Jewish dialogue in Basel. I want to thank Professors Ekkehard Stegemann and Jane Schaberg, the previous chair of the Wo/men in the Biblical World section, for their invitation to participate in these important discussions on Historical-Jesus scholarship and anti-Judaism.

A substantive part of chapter 2 was presented at a symposium on the occasion of the seventieth birthday of my colleague Helmut Koester and was subsequently published in a different form in *Harvard Theological Review*. I want to thank my colleague François Bovon for organizing this symposium. In a more rudimentary form, chapter 1 was presented in the European New Testament Seminar at the International Meeting of the Society of Biblical Literature in 1999 in Helsinki. The questions of chapter 3 were conceptualized in preparation for an Akademietagung in Tutzing, where European social-historical and American social-scientific biblical scholars met for the first time to explore methodological and epistemological issues in sociohistorical scientific Jesus research. Again I am grateful to Dr. Michael Labahn and Pfarrer Andreas Schmitt as well as to Professors Gerd Theissen and Wolfgang Stegemann for inviting me to be part of the conversation. Both chapters will be published in a very different form. Finally, chapter 5 testifies to a different converstaion. A large part of it was written for and published in the Festschrift for Letty Russell edited by Margaret Farley and Serene Jones. I thank them for their expertise and engagement.

Needless to say, the publication of a book, like all intellectual work, always owes its existence to teamwork and much labor. I am once again grateful to my research assistants Lyn Miller, for polishing my English and for giving me critical substantive feedback, and Emily Neill, for tirelessly supporting the research for this book. My faculty assistant, Hilary Muzingo, deserves special thanks for cheerfully answering letters and phone calls and keeping the office on target. As always, I am thankful to Chris Schüssler Fiorenza for numerous probing conversations.

Justus George Lawler of Continuum Publishing Group enthusiastically supported this project, and I am grateful for his interest in my work over the years. I am also indebted to Frank Oveis of Continuum and to Maurya Horgan of The HK Scriptorium, Inc., for faithfully shepherding the manuscript through the production process, and to Rachel Connelly for designing the cover. Finally, I want to thank the Association of Theological Schools in the United States and in Canada for supporting my research for one semester with a Lilly Faculty Research Grant.

This book is dedicated to Francis Schüssler Fiorenza in celebration of thirty-five years of unfailing companionship, love, and friendship. When we first met we got into a heated theological discussion, and we have never stopped arguing about theological matters. This book is a token of my appreciation and of my hope that we will be able to continue our passionate debates in the years to come. *Ad multos annos!*

# INTRODUCTION

## The Historical-Jesus and the Politics of Meaning

A RABBINIC STORY TELLS US THAT THE DISTINGUISHED RABBI Akivah was renowned and celebrated not only in Israel but also by the angelic hosts for his Torah interpretation. Moses, the great prophet and founder, became curious and decided to visit Rabbi Akivah's academy. Sitting in the back of the classroom, Moses listened in wonder as Akivah with great eloquence, exegetical skill, and intellectual breadth expounded the unfathomable mysteries of the Torah. When Moses asked, amazed, who had written such great things about which he had never heard, Rabbi Akiva answered: "These are the words of the Torah given by G*d[1] to Moses at Mount Sinai."

If Jesus, like Moses, were to return to earth, read all his biographies, and attend the Jesus Seminar or the Society of Biblical Literature annual meeting, he also would marvel and ask with amazement: "Who is this person they are talking about?" Is it Jesus, the apocalyptic prophet, the Cynic peasant, the millenarian seer, the magician, the wisdom teacher, or the witch doctor? But, unlike Moses, Jesus might not just marvel at the rich diversity of meanings ascribed to him by distinguished scholars. Rather, most likely he would have an identity crisis and fall into deep depression. He rightly would ask: "Who am I if I take seriously what they say?" As my grandmother—who, like Jesus, would have been seen as a peasant wo/man by many of these scholars, but herself would have rejected such a label—used to say whenever she heard of atrocities committed in Jesus' name: "Poor Jesus, he would turn over in his grave if he were still there!"

---

[1] Similarly to orthodox Jewish custom, I write G*d in this broken way to emphasize the inadequacy of language to speak about the divine.

1

To complicate the story further: What if Miriam had accompanied her brother Moses to Rabbi Akivah's academy and cried out in protest, hearing him expound her story? Would she have been punished again with leprosy for speaking out? Or what would Mary of Magdala—who, like Jesus, was a member of the emancipatory *basileia* movement of Divine Wisdom for the well-being of all—have to say? Would she not be puzzled that scholars attribute only to Jesus and not to his companions a movement that they had together envisioned—an egalitarian movement of Divine Wisdom for the healing of the downtrodden, an inclusive community of those who are powerless in the eyes of the mighty? Hearing that she was a whore and repentant sinner who was rescued by Jesus, the great man, would she not laugh at such nonsense, or would she break out in tears over such slanderous silencing? Or would both Mary—realizing that she was one of the "disappeared" in history—and Jesus, suffering from overexposure to elite scholarly imagination,[2] sneak together out of the "Jesus Seminar" and go to the beach for a swim? One is tempted to ask such and similar questions when reading recent scholarship on the Historical-Jesus.[3]

This book is indeed about an identity crisis, but not about that of Jesus or Mary of Magdala. Rather, it seeks to foster an identity crisis in the scientific self-understanding of Historical-Jesus scholarship[4] and its reception in theology and in the media.[5] It wants to assist students and the wider public interested in Historical-Jesus research to sort out the academic meaning-making and politics of Jesus research and its moral and religious implications. I do not see the problem as such in the rich proliferation of Jesus images. Rather, it lies in the scholarly claim to have produced a his-

---

[2] I do not want to argue here that the commodification of Mary of Magdala should become equal to that of Jesus, since the commercialization of the feminist rediscovery of Mary of Magdala has already begun. For a comprehensive discussion of the cultural discourses on the Historical-Mary-of-Magdala, see Susan Haskins, *Mary Magdalen: Myth and Metaphor* (New York: Harcourt, Brace, 1993).

[3] I have adopted this form of writing in order to indicate that the Historical-Jesus is a scholarly construct.

[4] See Werner Kelber, "The Quest for the Historical Jesus: From the Perspectives of Medieval, Modern, and Post-Enlightenment Readings, and in View of Ancient Oral Esthetics," in *The Jesus Controversy,* ed. Werner Kelber (Harrisburg, Pa.: Trinity Press International, 1999); and Marcus J. Borg, *Jesus in Contemporary Scholarship* (Valley Forge, Pa.: Trinity Press International, 1994).

[5] See, e.g., *Jesus von Nazareth und das Christentum: Braucht die pluralistische Gesellschaft ein neues Jesusbild?* ed. Sigmund M. Daecke and Peter R. S. Sahm (Neukirchen-Vluyn: Neukirchener Verlag, 2000).

tory or biography of the "real" Jesus that, unlike theological-religious images of Jesus, is a truly scientific account of Jesus as he "really" was. From the outset I want to state that I see the problem to be investigated in these pages not as one of "data" but as one of epistemology, that is, as how scholars make meaning out of the "data." It is epistemological not so much with respect to whether and how one can establish scientific proof that Jesus said this or did that, but rather with respect to how scientific Historical-Jesus discourses authorize their reconstructions as "true," "scientific," and "reliable." In other words, the rich array of Historical-Jesus reconstructions calls for a critical epistemological inquiry not only into the authority but also into the rhetoricity of Historical-Jesus discourses, probing how they can say what they say and for whom and to what ends scholars produce Historical-Jesus research. Such a critical discussion seeks to explore the nexus between reconstructions of Jesus and those theoretical, historical, cultural, and political conceptual frameworks that shape male-stream[6] biblical as well as feminist academic Historical-Jesus discourses. In short, in this book I seek to inquire into the politics of Historical-Jesus interpretation as a rhetorical process of meaning-making.

## THE POLITICS OF HISTORICAL-JESUS RESEARCH

A politics of meaning contends that just like other studies in Bible, history, and theology, Jesus research[7] is of significance not only for religious com-

[6] I use this term in a descriptive way to indicate that scripture, tradition, church, and society have been and still are determined and dominated by elite educated white men.
[7] To mention just a view additional references: Marcus J. Borg, "Portraits of Jesus in Contemporary North American Scholarship," *Harvard Theological Review* 84, no. 1 (1991): 1–22; James H. Charlesworth, "Annotated Bibliography," in *Jesus' Jewishness: Exploring the Place of Jesus within Early Judaism,* ed. Marcus J. Borg (New York: Crossroad/The American Interfaith Institute, 1991); John F. O'Grady, "The Present State of Christology," *Chicago Studies* 32, no. 1 (April 1993): 77–91; Werner G. Kümmel, "Jesusforschung seit 1981," *Theologische Rundschau* N.F. 53 (1988): 229–49; 54 (1989): 1–53; Dieter Georgi, "The Interest in Life of Jesus Theology as a Paradigm for the Social History of Biblical Criticism," *Harvard Theological Review* 85, no. 1 (1992): 51–83; Daniel Kosch, "Neue Jesusliteratur," *Bibel und Kirche* 48 (1993): 40–44; Ferdinand Hahn, "Umstrittenes Jesusbild?" *Münchener Theologische Zeitschrift* 44 (1993): 95–107; *Jesus and Faith: A Conversation on the Work of John Dominic Crossan, Author of the Historical Jesus,* ed. Jeffrey Carlson and Robert A. Ludwig (Maryknoll, N.Y.: Orbis Books, 1994); *Images of Jesus Today,* ed. James H. Charlesworth and Walter P. Weaver (Valley Forge, Pa.: Trinity Press International, 1994); Luke T. Johnson, *The*

munities. As a master narrative of Western cultures, it is always already implicated in structures of domination. Historical-Jesus discourses collude with the production and maintenance of systems of knowledge that either foster exploitation and oppression or contribute to a vision and praxis of emancipation and liberation. Hence, a politics of meaning must open up to critical inquiry the contesting political interests and theoretical frameworks that determine the articulations of malestream and feminist Jesus research.

The sociopolitical context in which feminist as well as malestream Jesus research takes place is constituted by the resurgence of the religious Right, which claims the power of naming and of defining the true nature of religion.[8] Well-financed, right-wing think tanks are supported by reactionary political and financial institutions that seek to defend patriarchal capitalism.[9] The interconnection between religious antidemocratic arguments and the debate with regard to wo/men's[10] place and role is not accidental

---

*Real Jesus: The Misguided Quest for the Historical Jesus and the Truth of the Traditional Gospels* (San Francisco: Harper & Row, 1966); Robert W. Funk, *Honest to Jesus: Jesus for a New Millennium* (San Francisco: HarperCollins 1996).

[8] See the varied contributions in *Fundamentalism as an Ecumenical Challenge*, ed. Hans Küng and Jürgen Moltmann (Concilium; London: SCM Press, 1992).

[9] For an excellent critical analysis of the involvement of religion in this global struggle, see especially the work of the late Penny Lernoux, *Cry of the People* (New York: Penguin, 1982); eadem, *In Banks We Trust* (New York: Penguin, 1986); and her last book before her untimely death, *People of God: The Struggle for World Catholicism* (New York: Penguin, 1989); Robert B. Reich, *The Work of Nations* (New York: Vintage Books, 1992); Joan Smith, "The Creation of the World We Know: The World-Economy and the Re-Creation of Gendered Identities," in *Identity Politics & Women: Cultural Reassertions and Feminisms in International Perspective*, ed. Valentine M. Moghadam (Boulder, Colo.: Westview Press, 1994), 27–41; see also Diana L. Eck, *Encountering God: A Spiritual Journey from Bozeman to Banaras* (Boston: Beacon Press, 1993), 176, who writes: "A new wave of exclusivism is cresting around the world today. Expressed in social and political life, exclusivism becomes ethnic or religious chauvinism, described in South Asia as communalism. . . . As we have observed, identity-based politics is on the rise because it is found to be a successful way of arousing political energy."

[10] I write wo/men in this way in order not only to indicate the instability in the meaning of the term but also to signal that when I say wo/men I also mean to include subordinated men. For the problematic meaning of the term woman/women, see Denise Riley, *"Am I That Name?" Feminism and the Category of Women in History* (Minneapolis: University of Minnesota Press, 1988); Judith Butler, *Gender Trouble: Feminism and the Subversion of Identity* (New York: Routledge, 1990). My way of writing wo/men seeks to underscore not only the ambiguous character of the term "wo/man or wo/men" but also to retain the expression "wo/men" as a political category. Since this designation is often read as referring to white women only, my unorthodox writing of the term seeks to draw to the attention of readers

or of merely intratheological significance. In the past decade or so right-wing movements around the globe have insisted on the figuration of emancipated wo/men as signifiers of Western decadence and of modern atheistic secularism, and they have presented masculine power as the expression of divine power.[11]

In this rhetorical context of struggle over meaning, the proliferation of Historical-Jesus books for popular and scientific consumption by male-stream biblical and theological studies seems to function as the reverse side of the fundamentalist literalist coin. In and through a literalist dogmatic reading, fundamentalist christologies seek to "fix" the pluriform expressions of Christian scriptures and traditions, and to consolidate the variegated texts and ambiguous metaphors of Jesus Christ into a single, definite discourse of meaning.

In response to such reifying fundamentalist theological readings, Historical-Jesus scholarship insists on the scientific character of its production of knowledge as factual and historical, stressing its objectivity and detachment from all theological interests. Just like fundamentalist readings, Historical-Jesus books are concerned with authority. However, they assert not theological revelatory positivism but historical positivism in order to shore up the scholarly authority and scientific truth of their research portrayals of Jesus.[12] Hence, the proliferation of "new" Jesus books does not undermine and undo but rather reinforces the literalist desire of religious fundamentalists for an "accurate," reliable biography of Jesus.

The refusal of much of Historical-Jesus scholarship to lay open for crit-

---

that those kyriarchal structures which determine wo/men's lives and status also impact the lives and status of men of subordinated race, classes, countries, and religions, albeit in different ways. The expression "wo/men" must therefore be understood as inclusive rather than as an exclusive universalized gender term.

[11] See especially the declaration of the Division for the Advancement of Women on "International Standards of Equality and Religious Freedom: Implications for the Status of Women," in *Identity Politics & Women*, ed. Moghadam, 425–38; Rebecca E. Klatch, "Women of the New Right in the United States: Family, Feminism, and Politics," ibid., 367–88. Most of the contributions in *Identity Politics & Women* are on women and Islam in different parts of the world. However, see Sucheta Mazumdar, "Moving Away from a Secular Vision? Women, Nation, and the Cultural Construction of Hindu India" (pp. 243–73), and Radha Kumar, "Identity Politics and the Contemporary Indian Feminist Movement" (pp. 274–92).

[12] See the critical review of N. T. Wright, "Taking the Text with Her Pleasure: A Post-Post-Modernist Response to J. Dominic Crossan's *The Historical Jesus: The Life of a Mediterranean Jewish Peasant* (With apologies to A. A. Milne, St. Paul and James Joyce)," *Theology* 96, no. 112 (1993): 303–10, from the perspective of a critical realistic reading. It is regrettable, however, that Wright's critical essay resorts to sexist "figuration."

ical reflection and discussion its own ideological or theological interests, together with the restoration of historical positivism,[13] corresponds to political conservatism. The emphasis on the *realia* and "facts" of history[14] serves to promote scientific fundamentalism since the Third Quest for the Historical-Jesus generally does not sufficiently problematize the fact that scholars not only select and interpret archaeological artifacts and textual evidence but also make sense of these so-called data by framing them in terms of a scientific model and by rearranging them in a new narrative framework of meaning.[15]

Whether they imagine Jesus as an existentialist religious thinker, a rabbinic teacher, an apocalyptic prophet, a pious Hasid, a revolutionary peasant, a wandering Cynic, a Greco-Roman magician, a healing witch doctor, a nationalist anti-Temple Galilean revolutionary, or a wo/man-identified man, the present flood of Historical-Jesus books and articles documents that despite their scientific positivistic rhetoric of facts and historical realism, scholars inescapably fashion the Historical-Jesus in their own image and likeness.

At best one can glimpse his historical shadow-image or negative, but how one develops this picture will always depend on the chemicals one uses, that is, the kind of reconstructive methods and models one adopts. The earliest portrayals of Jesus in the canonical and extracanonical early Christian literature owe their existence to the same process of selection and reframing of traditions. Any presentation of Jesus—scientific or otherwise—must therefore acknowledge that it is a "reconstruction" and open up its critical methods, rhetorical interests, and reconstructive models to critical inspection and public scrutiny.

Scientific reconstructive historical-theoretical models must be scrutinized not only for how much they can account for our textual and archaeological information on the Historical-Jesus and his sociopolitical contexts but also for how much they are able to inquire into the rhetorical interests, theological functions, and politics of meaning that produce his-

---

[13] See my critique of positivism in biblical studies in "Text and Reality—Reality as Text: The Problem of a Feminist Social and Historical Reconstruction on the Basis of Texts," *Studia Theologica* 43 (1989): 19–34, and *But She Said: Feminist Practices of Biblical Interpretation* (Boston: Beacon Press, 1992), 79–101.

[14] James H. Charlesworth, ed., *Jews and Christians: Exploring the Past, Present and Future* (New York: Crossroad, 1990).

[15] See James H. Charlesworth, "From Barren Mazes to Gentle Rappings: The Emergence of Jesus Research," *Princeton Seminary Bulletin* 7, no. 3 (1986): 221–30, with annotated bibliography.

torical knowledge about Jesus. Moreover, the ethics of interpretation[16] requires that such reconstructive models and analytic categories be tested for whether they inculcate mind-sets of discrimination and exclusion. For, not just hegemonic but even feminist Jesus studies have reinscribed the modern-cultural or orthodox-theological discourses of domination.

In order to avoid the liberal-historical or orthodox-theological hegemonic framework of Historical-Jesus research that focuses on Jesus the great charismatic leader or divine man, I have suggested in my own work that Historical-Jesus research should replace this "realist" narrative of the Historical-Jesus as the great charismatic individual with the category of memory. This category of memory includes that of history making, but it is much more comprehensive and more adequate to our source texts. While the canonical and extracanonical gospels all focus on Jesus, they do so from the perspective of their own time and place. They are interested not in antiquarian documentation but in the politics of meaning-making for their own audiences.

The gospel transmitters and writers were not concerned with simply writing down what Jesus said and did; rather, they attempted to comprehend what Jesus meant to his first followers and what meaning his life and ministry had for their own time and communities. Most importantly, they had to come to terms with the historical event of his execution by the Romans as an insurrectionist. As a result, what we can learn from the process of their transmission and redaction is that Jesus—as we can still know him—must be remembered, discussed, interpreted, critiqued, accepted, or rejected if one wants to comprehend the impulse and importance of his life. The gospels center on the life-praxis of Jesus and the movement carrying his name, which they sought to preserve as either a "dangerous" or a "status quo" memory.[17]

Most recently, Paula Fredriksen has proposed a similar move in interpretation. However, she insists on developing her interpretation in a historical-positivist framework. She concedes that no historical reconstruction of the Historical-Jesus can be proven correct and that the best

---

[16] Elisabeth Schüssler Fiorenza, "The Ethics of Interpretation: Decentering Biblical Scholarship: SBL Presidential Address," *Journal of Biblical Literature* 107 (1988): 3–17, now reprinted in Elisabeth Schüssler Fiorenza, *Rhetoric and Ethic: The Politics of Biblical Studies* (Minneapolis: Fortress Press, 1999).

[17] See Elisabeth Schüssler Fiorenza, *In Memory of Her: A Feminist Theological Reconstruction of Christian Origins* (New York: Crossroad, 1983; 10th Anniversary Edition With a New Introduction, 1994), 102; and eadem, *Bread Not Stone: The Challenge of Feminist Biblical Interpretation* (Boston: Beacon Press, 1984; 10th Anniversary Edition 1995), 114–15.

one can do is to ensure that one's reconstruction is plausible and persuasive within the social-historical context in which Jesus lived. Pointing to the great variety in scholarly Historical-Jesus reconstructions, she nevertheless insists:

> But all narratives are not created equal, and the reasons for choosing between them, for deciding which is persuasive, are not arbitrary. This is so because, even if the focus of a historical narrative is an individual, that individual, be it Jesus or anyone else, lived in a social context. This historical context is the historian's critical promontory.
>
> This means that the search for the historical Jesus must be, of necessity, a search for his first-century audience, too. . . . [A]ll the information in our sources actually speaks more directly about them than about him, for Jesus left us no writings.[18]

Hence, the challenge for Historical-Jesus research is to find a first-century Jesus whose words and worlds would have made sense to his contemporary audience. However, rather than dismantling the modern liberal or orthodox Historical-Jesus research framework and program, Fredriksen wants just to refine it. She insists that to view Jesus from the perspective of his own time and place requires that scholars acknowledge the "facts" of history and respect the distance between now and then, the present and the past, between Jesus' concerns and our own. That this is her central hermeneutical concern comes to the fore in the following concluding statement of the book:

> To regard Jesus historically requires releasing him from modern concerns or confessional identity. . . . It means allowing him the irreducible otherness of his own antiquity, the strangeness Schweitzer captured in his closing description: "He comes to us as One unknown, without a name, as of old, by the lakeside."[19] It is when we renounce the false familiarity proffered by the dark [sic] angels of Relevance and Anachronism that we see Jesus, his contemporaries, and perhaps even ourselves, more clearly in our common humanity.[20]

I could not agree more with Fredriksen's shift from focusing on Jesus, the individual, to focusing on his context and the gospels' rhetorical world, situation, and audience. Moreover, I agree with her that in the final analy-

---

[18] Paula Fredriksen, *Jesus of Nazareth, King of the Jews: A Jewish Life and the Emergence of Christianity* (New York: Alfred A. Knopf, 1999), 267–68.

[19] This is also a favorite quotation of John Dominic Crossan.

[20] Fredriksen, *Jesus*, 270.

sis Historical-Jesus research is about seeing more clearly the "common humanity" shared by Jesus, his contemporaries, and Historical-Jesus scholars. I would argue, however, that Fredriksen does not problematize her understanding of humanity in light of the insight of feminist theory that both the modern-liberal and the confessional-orthodox Historical-Jesus research frameworks have unquestioningly relied on the Western definition of humanity as elite, white, educated masculinity.

This book therefore asks to be read (and taught) in tandem with *Jesus: Miriam's Child, Sophia's Prophet* because the two works function as two sides of the same argumentative coin. *Miriam's Child* sought to intervene in the feminist discussions on Jesus, the Christ, whose maleness has been foregrounded in Western modernity and has become the center of feminist attention. Whereas in the nineteenth-century wo/men's movement the question of wo/man's sinfulness and the attendant need for redemption was central, today feminist christological discourses circle around the problem of Jesus' maleness. This problem, which was succinctly formulated by Rosemary Radford Ruether in the question "Can a male savior save wo/men?" is not just a theoretical problem but has its setting in life in the struggles of wo/men for public speaking, full citizenship, theological education, and ministerial ordination. It also permeates Historical-Jesus research. Ironically, Jesus, like wo/man, is seen as totally different from wo/man, as a being of a totally different kind, the ideal of (feminine) purity and love.

To understand the thematizing and valorizing of Jesus' maleness in modernity it is necessary to understand the emergence of the ideology of gender dualism upon which that thematizing depends. Anthropologists have pointed out that not all cultures and languages know of only two sexes/genders, and historians of gender have argued that even in Western cultures, the dual sex/gender system is of modern origin. Like the grammatical, the social classification of gendered humanity does not always correspond to the biological classification of sex. Thomas Laqueur, for instance, has shown that a decisive shift took place in modernity from the ancient one-sex model to the present dichotomous two-sex model.[21] For thousands of years it was considered to be commonplace that women had the same sex and genitals as men except that they were inside their bodies, whereas men's were outside. The vagina was understood as an interior

---

[21] Thomas Laqueur, *Making Sex: Body and Gender from the Greeks to Freud* (Cambridge, Mass.: Harvard University Press, 1990).

penis, the labia as foreskin, the uterus as scrotum, and the ovaries as testicles.

Not sex but gender as a cultural category was primary and part of the order of things. What it meant to be a man or a woman was determined by social rank and by one's place in society, not by sexual organs. As man or woman one had to perform a cultural role according to one's *social* status, rather than to be organically one of two incommensurable sexes. The social status of the elite propertied male heads of household determined superior gender status. The ancients did not need the facts of sexual difference to support their claim that wo/men were inferior to men and therefore subordinate beings.

Beginning with the Enlightenment, the two-sex model—the notion that there are two stable, incommensurable, opposite sexes—emerges. Now, it is held that the economic, political, and cultural lives of wo/men and men, their gender roles, are based on these two incommensurable sexes which are biologically given. Just as in antiquity the body was seen as reflecting the cosmological order, so in modernity the body and sexuality are seen as representing and legitimating the social-political order. Social and political changes wrought by the Enlightenment produced the change from the one-sex to the two-sex model.

Since the democratic universalistic claims for human liberty and equality theoretically included but de facto excluded freeborn wo/men, slave wo/men, and wo/men of lower status from full citizenship, arguments had to be fashioned for elite men to justify their dominance of the public domain whose difference from the private world of wo/men was figured in terms of sexual difference.

Moreover, the promise of democracy that wo/men and disenfranchised men could achieve civic and personal liberties generated a new kind of antifeminist argument on the basis of nature, physiology, and science. Those, for instance, who opposed the democratic participation of freeborn wo/men generated evidence for wo/men's mental and physical unsuitability for the public sphere and argued that their bodies and biology made them unfit for it. The doctrine of separate spheres for men and wo/men thus engendered the dual-sex model.

In the antifeminist and feminist discourses of modernity, wo/man is construed no longer *as lesser man* but as totally different from man, as a being of a "purer race," an "angelic species" less affected by sexual drives and desires. Since wo/men have to be excluded from the new civil society and the ground for this exclusion is their biology, catalogues of physical and moral differences needed to be made in order to ensure that the sexes do not to resemble each other in mind any more than in looks. Two incommensurable sexes are the result of these discursive exclusionary practices.

Similar arguments were put forward for excluding the so-called darker races and uncivilized savages from assuming civic responsibilities and powers. The distinction between biological sex and cultural gender as well as between biological and cultural race and ethnicity that has become common sense even in feminist discourses is a product and process of anti-feminist as well as emancipatory Enlightenment discourses that have located differences within the dualistic framework of the modern sex-gender system.

Such a critical understanding not only of gender and its operation but also of race, class, and imperialism is necessary if one does not want to reinscribe the cultural patterns and stereotypes of domination in the process of reconstructing the Historical-Jesus. Whereas in *Jesus: Miriam's Child, Sophia's Prophet* I sought to critically engage feminist discourses on Jesus, in this book I therefore have a different audience and goal in mind. I enter into conversation not so much with other feminist proposals as with my colleagues in the biblical Historical-Jesus academy, and I do so—as always—from a critical feminist political perspective. I seek to reflect on the presuppositions, implications, and ramifications of Historical-Jesus research and the proliferation of popular and scholarly works about Jesus which scientifically reinscribe the modern understanding of Jesus, the great man and charismatic leader. In pointing out the theoretical drawbacks of leading Jesus scholarship, I am not interested in polemics for the sake of polemics. Nor am I interested in the academic scientific game of critically picking apart the scholarly narratives of others in order to show that my own interpretation is the correct and superior one. Instead, I seek to render problematic academic biblical discourses on Jesus and to interrogate them as to whether they support or do not support the rhetorics and structures of domination.

Feminist studies have shown that androcentric languages and cultures not only place elite Man in the center of historical scientific discourses but also relegate wo/men to the margins or silently pass them over altogether. Hence wo/men belong to the "disappeared" in history. A reconstruction of the Historical-Jesus that sees him as a great charismatic leader and heroic or divine man therefore reinforces the ideological power of androcentrism and the immasculation (Judith Fetterly) of wo/men. Even if it concedes that wo/men were disciples of Jesus, it still does not break through the linguistic-cultural androcentric or, better, kyriocentric (lord/master/father/husband-centered) framework of Historical-Jesus studies insofar as it still places Jesus, the charismatic male leader, into the center and positions wo/men in relation to him.

It is easy to see from the multiplicity of divergent Historical-Jesus reconstructions that scholars tend to find their image and likeness mirrored in the well of their sources. However, an often unconscious self-identification with the male hero and great individual of the Jesus story is possible only for male readers, not for wo/men readers, because it is taken as a "commonsense" fact that Jesus was male and that wo/men are the other to maleness. Such a process of self-identification is a complex one insofar as Historical-Jesus scholars, who for the most part are still elite educated white males, distance Jesus as the totally other and at the same time project either their idealized or their negative-Other image onto him.

In this syntax of gender, wo/men readers can only situate themselves in relation to Him. They can idealize Him as the great man and charismatic leader or feminize Him, typically by projecting the kyriarchal cultural values of true womanhood onto Him. In any case, both interpretive strategies reinforce the linguistic-ideological structure of andro/kyriocentrism. To elaborate Jesus not just with feminine qualities but to picture him as a wo/man goes against all "common sense" and all that is considered normal and natural, since Jesus is "evidently" a male. A scholarly elaboration of Jesus as wo/man would be seen as slightly crazy and definitely not as scholarship to be taken seriously.

Yet, while picturing Jesus as a wo/man is jarring, a white reading public is not jarred in the same way—even does not notice it—when scholars picture the Historical-Jesus as a white European male with blue eyes and blond hair. Whether Jesus is portrayed as a marginal Jew, a devout Jew, a trickster Jew, or a Jewish seer, his primary identification in a modern Christian context is not Jewish but male. Whether Jesus is seen as a Jewish prophet or Greco-Roman Cynic, his maleness is always tacitly presupposed because of the modern sex-gender framework that is all-pervasive in Christian cultures.

Whereas medieval Christianity turned Jesus into a sovereign king and noble ruler, when he clearly had not been one historically, modernity stresses the maleness of Jesus, although our sources do not elaborate his masculinity. A dualistic gender lens thus provides the unquestioned modern framework of Historical-Jesus research, a lens and framework that are not adequate to the understanding of individuals in antiquity who are shaped by the single-sex framework and by status expectations.

This book centers on the thesis that the boom in Historical-Jesus publications is not so much about history as about identity. This was already recognized by Albert Schweitzer at the end of the first scientific Quest for the Historical-Jesus. He observed even then that scholars inevitably fashion Jesus in their own image and likeness. What Schweitzer did not recognize, however, is that scholars who create Jesus in their own image and likeness on scientific grounds then tend to displace this image by projecting it onto the "Other." In a romantic vein, Jesus becomes the same in the disguise of the other—the peasant, the revolutionary, the magician, the ascetic, the lover, the Hasid, or the incarnation of the feminine, to mention a few of such scholarly creations—and then functions as a commodity for cultural or religious edification.

Since the 1960s, for example, much ink has been spilled to prove that Jesus was not a political revolutionary and had nothing whatever to do with the Zealots, a militant movement of his time. Nevertheless, in the last decade a sea change in Historical-Jesus studies seems to have taken place. Now Jesus is imagined as a figure concerned with the broader issues of politics. He has become a peasant leader and social-religious reformer who was executed by the Romans for sedition. Hence, scholars assert that they do not make the Historical-Jesus in their own image and likeness because they are obviously neither marginal nor itinerant, neither peasants nor seers, but their subtext is still male. Thus the Historical-Jesus becomes an object of scholarly projection both as the same and as the idealized or disparaged *other*. These projections become culturally reified and thus lose any potential and power for changing relations of domination.[22]

In sum, this is not just another scientific Historical-Jesus book. Rather it is a sustained rhetorical inquiry into the scholarly discourses that produce the Historical-Jesus as an article of trade and an object of spiritual consumption in the global neocapitalist market. In the past decade numerous scholarly volumes have appeared promising to tell us everything we want to know about the "real" Jesus. By claiming to produce knowledge about the "real" Jesus, malestream as well as wo/men scholars deny the rhetoricity of their research and obfuscate the fact that their reconstructive cultural models and theological interests are not able to *produce* the *real* Jesus but only creative *images* of him. Hence, a critical inquiry into the politics of Historical-Jesus research is called for, a politics of meaning that

---

[22] In an editorial comment Lyn Miller observes: "I'm also often struck that these scholarly identificatory posturings as revolutionary, or otherwise politically heroic and pertinent, as in the romance not just with Jesus but with the martyred Benjamin, or the starved Weil, or the imprisoned Gramsci, or the soldier-saint Che, etc. are ludic constructions that serve to legitimate irrelevant (i.e. pernicious) conservative scholarship."

interrupts the elitist, anti-Jewish, colonialist, racist, and anti-feminist tendencies of positivist Historical-Jesus scholarship.

The answer to the commodification of Jesus, I argue, is not the rejection and abandonment of critical inquiry but an investigation of Historical-Jesus discourses in terms of ideological criticism and ethics. It is no accident that scholars in the North American academy and Europe have rediscovered the Historical-Jesus at a time when feminist studies, critical theory, interreligious dialogue, postcolonial criticism, and liberation theologies have pointed to the interconnections of knowledge and power at work in academic and popular discourses. It is also no accident that such an explosion of Historical-Jesus books has occurred at a time when the media have discovered the "angry white male" syndrome that fuels white-supremacist, antifeminist, anti-Semitic, and anti-immigrant, antipeasant, neo-fascist movements. Hence, this book calls for an ethics of interpretation that explores a scholarly politics of meaning rather than just continuing ideological discourses on Jesus that are fraught with ideologies of domination.

## HISTORICAL-JESUS RESEARCH AS A DISCOURSE

Historical-Jesus discourse is characterized by a paradoxical rhetoric that stresses the capability of its scientific method to produce a reliable account of the "real" Historical-Jesus. Yet this rhetoric has been proven to be wrong because Historical-Jesus research has produced a host of different and often competing images of Jesus. Since the multiplicity and variety of Historical-Jesus images and approaches are not a controvertible but a scientifically verifiable "fact," it is necessary, I argue here, to look more closely at Historical-Jesus research and its social-scientific rhetoric[23] as well as to study Historical-Jesus research as a discursive formation.

The dictionary definition of the term "discourse" stresses that the general sense of this word is "to speak, talk, converse, discuss." It can also mean "speech" and "treatise." However, such a generalized definition suppresses that, at least since Michel Foucault, discourse and discursivity must be understood as related to context and power.[24] Discourses do more than

---

[23] For the historical context of this rhetoric, see Roy A. Harrisville and Walter Sundberg, *The Bible in Modern Culture: Theology and Historical-Critical Method from Spinoza to Käsemann* (Grand Rapids: Eerdmans, 1995).

[24] Michel Foucault, *Power/Knowledge: Selected Interviews and Other Writings, 1972–1977*

just designate things; they are practices "that systematically form the objects of which they speak."[25] The notion of discourse allows one to attend to the processes that govern the construction of discourse. The task is to understand how power, which is ubiquitous, is at work in numerous practices and operates in specific methods and categories. Power is something that is exercised and dispersed in language rather than something that is simply possessed.[26]

Historical-Jesus research can be studied as a discursive formation. One can investigate how it manufactures the Historical-Jesus as a symbolic scholarly construct and as an ideologically produced subject position that elite men are able to inhabit and in relation to which wo/men always are positioned in and through practices of subordination and/or romance. Hence Historical-Jesus research, if it aims to be scientific, must always engage not only in ideological construction but also in ideological criticism. By ideology I do not mean simply "false consciousness" or misrepresentation and mystification of reality. Rather, I understand ideology first in the broader sense as a practice and politics of meaning-making.

Feminist ideology critique, then, is a mode of investigation that recognizes the contesting interests at stake in the construction of the Historical-Jesus. It conducts its investigation from a committed position within a social analytic whose legitimacy is argued for not on the grounds of its scientific Truth but on the basis of its explanatory power and its commitment to emancipatory social change.[27] Conceptualizing Historical-Jesus discourses as ideology, that is, as meaning-making under certain sociopolitical and religious conditions, allows one to investigate feminist "history making" as a critical practice that is always already an intervention in the interest of emancipatory social and religious change.

The generative discursive problem to be overcome or fruitfully transformed by Historical-Jesus research is the simple fact that the Christian canon has not one but four gospels—that is, four quite different narratives about Jesus. It is this hermeneutical problem posed by the multiplicity of the gospels that has spawned, then and now, attempts to reduce the pluriform gospels to one uniform gospel message. Moreover, the linguistic turn

---

(Brighton: Harvester, 1980); idem, *The Archaeology of Knowledge* (London: Routledge, 1972).

[25] Michèle Barrett, *The Politics of Truth: From Marx to Foucault* (Stanford: Stanford University Press, 1991), 130.

[26] Ibid., 135.

[27] Rosemary Hennessy, *Materialist Feminism and the Politics of Discourse* (New York: Routledge, 1993), 15.

in biblical studies has driven home that texts do not have a single, definite meaning and a "final solution."[28] The rhetoricity of discourse understands the textuality of texts as a construct rather than as a mirror reflecting pre-existing reality. Language is not a mere vehicle for the transmission of social and historical context but the producer of meaning.

Archival and other sources, therefore, are not just quarries for factual information but are producers of historical meaning. In short, the textuality of the gospels poses the rhetorical problem that Historical-Jesus research seeks to overcome. Such an understanding of text and language as rhetorical and constructive challenges the epistemological dichotomy between scientific and creative writing, between fact and fiction. In light of the linguistic turn to rhetoric, the Third Quest for the Historical-Jesus seems to be a step backwards from the methodological achievement of redaction and narrative criticism, since it appears to be less apt to do justice to the textuality and rhetoricity of the canonical and extracanonical gospels.

Characteristic of the Historical-Jesus Quest is its insistence on the scientific character of its research, which it seeks to establish in terms of the quantitative method of stratigraphy with its segmentation of the text and its reassembly in vast data bases. It also adopts social-scientific models derived from cultural anthropology or quantitative sociology for authorizing its scientificity. In claiming to be a scientific discourse, Historical-Jesus research also takes over the theoretical assumptions that have shaped and governed scientific discourse. It is well known that biblical studies in general and Historical-Jesus discourses in particular emerged on the scene together with other disciplines in the humanities that sought to articulate their discourses as scientific practices in analogy to the natural sciences. Sandra Harding has pointed to a three-stage process in the emergence of science shaping and determining scholarly discourses, their presuppositions and intellectual frameworks.

The *first* stage, according to Harding, consisted in the breakdown of feudal labor divisions and slave relations. This breakdown made the scientific method of experimental observation possible. The traditional division between intellectuals and landed aristocracy, and those who worked with their hands, no longer pertained. New groups of workers such as artisans, shipbuilders, miners, mariners, foundrymen, and carpenters invented the compass and guns, introduced machines into mining, and manipulated

---

[28] See, e.g., Alicia Suskin Ostriker, *Feminist Revision and the Bible* (Cambridge: Blackwell, 1993).

observational technologies. Harding observes: "Science's new way of seeing the world developed from the perspective of the new kind of social labor of artisans and the inventors of modern technology."[29]

The *second* stage is exemplified in the New Science movement of the seventeenth century, which flourished in Puritan England and brought forth a new political self-consciousness with radical social goals. "Science's progressiveness was perceived to lie not in method alone but in its mutually supportive relationship to progressive tendencies in the larger society."[30] Scientific knowledge was to serve the people and to be used for redistributing knowledge and wealth. The radical goals of this New Science movement are summed up in the following statement:

> The Baconian reform movement linked and identified the New Learning with moral, educational, and social aspects. In all the social utopias of the period, the learned societies of the new philosophy . . . are regarded as the basis for a reconstruction of social life. . . . Reflection upon the effects of science is part of a condition for science itself.[31]

The *third* stage produced the notion of purely technical and value-neutral science. The progress that science represents is based entirely on scientific method. The emergence of this third stage in the development of science also spelled the end of the collaboration between science and social, political, or educational reform—a price paid for institutionalization and political protection. The institutionalization of science meant the separation of science's cognitive and political aims and the restriction of true science and scientists to the former.

Pure science, according to Harding, was characterized by *atomism*, the claim that nature's fundamental units are separate with no intrinsic connection. This model goes hand in hand with the political assertion that people are not bound to the group in which they are born but are autonomous individuals who form alliances by contract. It also goes hand in hand with value-neutrality, which captures what is real through impersonal, quantitative language, and *method*, understood as norms, rules, procedures, and scientific technologies, which are assumed to follow nature's

---

[29] Sandra Harding, *The Science Question in Feminism* (Ithaca, N.Y.: Cornell University Press, 1986), 218, with reference to Edgar Zilsel, "The Sociological Roots of Science," *American Journal of Sociology* 47 (1942).

[30] Harding, *Science Question*, 219.

[31] Wolfgang van den Daele, "The Social Construction of Science," in *The Social Production of Scientific Knowledge*, ed. Everett Mendelsohn, Peter Weingart, Richard Whitley (Dordrecht: Reidel, 1977), 38.

rule by impartial law. Scientific values are transhistorical human values; they are not particularistic, local, partial, or political. Historically and culturally specific values, emotions, and interests must be kept separated from depoliticized transcendental scientific practices. Abstract thinking, mathematical intelligibility, and mechanistic metaphors become the hallmarks of true science.

The Quest for the Historical-Jesus is located at this third scientific stage, which constructs a sharp dualism between science and theology, or scientific discourse and ideology, in order to prove itself as scientific. A series of structuring dualisms[32] and dichotomies between science and politics, history and theology, knowledge and fiction, past and present, rationality and faith, male and female, white and black, Caucasian and Asian, and so on, determine the Western scientific worldview. Historical-Jesus discourses reinscribe such structuring dualisms as a series of methodological dichotomies and oppositions between historical Jesus and kerygmatic Christ, Mediterranean culture and U.S. society, itinerant prophets and sedentary householders, Jesus and Judaism, or Jesus and wo/men. As a scientific discourse, Historical-Jesus research thus participates in the discourses of domination that were produced by science.

It is also at this third stage of the development of academic scientific disciplines that the discourses of domination—racism, heterosexism, colonialism, class privilege, ageism—also were articulated as "scientific" discourses.[33] While previously discourses of colonization were developed on the grounds of Christian religion, now science takes the place of religion and continues its work of hegemonic legitimization. The discourses of domination were formed as elite discourses that justified relations of ruling. Hence, "soft" academic disciplines such as history, sociology, and anthropology, in their formative stage, developed discourses of domination in order to prove that they also belonged to the "hard" sciences.

---

[32] For such structuring dualisms in Q research, see the forthcoming dissertation of Melanie Johnson-DeBaufre. For a comprehensive interpretation of Q scholarship, see, e.g., Richard Horsley, *Whoever Hears You Hears Me: Prophets, Performance and Tradition in Q* (Harrisburg, Pa.: Trinity Press International, 1999); and Burton L. Mack, *The Lost Gospel: The Book of Q and Christian Origins* (San Francisco: HarperCollins, 1993).

[33] See Ronald T. Takaki, "Aesclepius Was a White Man: Race and the Cult of True Womanhood," in *The "Racial" Economy of Science: Toward a Democratic Future*, ed. Sandra Harding (Indianapolis: Indiana University Press, 1993), 201–9; Nancy Leys Stepan and Sander L. Gilman, "Appropriating the Idioms of Science: The Rejection of Scientific Racism," ibid., 170–93; and Nancy Leys Stepan, "Race and Gender: The Role of Analogy in Science," ibid., 369–76.

Thereby academic social-science disciplines supported European colonialism and capitalist industrial development.

For instance, the nineteenth-century professionalization of history fostered scientific practices advocating commitment to an objectivity above the critical scrutiny of such categories as class and gender, along with strict use of evidence, less rhetorical style, the development of archives, libraries, peer reviews, and professional education. Scientific historical discourses created an intellectual space inhabited by an "invisible and neutered I" which was considered to be a "gender- and race-free" community of scholars. At the same time science was producing discourses of exclusion such as racism, heterosexism, and colonialism barring wo/men from the professions and turning them into objects of research.

> Using women as the sign both of gender in its entirety (i.e., women as the gendered other to the neutral man) and of all that was outside of history, the new scholars created a fantasy world of the Real, that is, of history. It was a world purged of gender (as well as class [and race]), sufficient unto itself in charting and defining significant human experience in the past, and redolent of the power such claims generated.[34]

American sociology in its formative years exhibited the same symptoms as scientific historiography. It was influenced by European anthropological discourses that emerged with imperialism and understood colonized peoples as "primitives" who were considered to be more natural, sexual, untouched by civilization, and inferior because of their innate biological differences—for instance, their allegedly smaller brains. In the United States, Indian Americans and African Americans were those who represented the "primitive" in sociological and anthropological scientific discourses. They were construed to be either violent or childlike or both. People who were Not-white and Not-male were praised as "noble savages" or feared as "bloodthirsty cannibals" on biological and cultural grounds.

Blacks and white women were viewed as childlike, a factor used to explain their supposedly inferior intelligence.

> White women and Blacks were also seen as more embodied, "natural," and controlled by their physical, biological essences. Both were viewed as having an inherent "nature" of some sort—for blacks violence, for White women passivity. Collectively, these comparisons generated a situation in which

---

[34] Bonnie G. Smith, "Gender, Objectivity, and the Rise of Scientific History," in *Objectivity and Its Other,* ed. Wolfgang Natter, Theodore R. Schatzki, and John Paul Jones III (New York: Guilford Press, 1995), 59.

race and gender gained meaning from another, situated within economic class hierarchies that drew upon these ideas. . . . Remaining in the private sphere of home and caring for the family would protect middle-class White women from the dangers of the public sphere that, with urbanization and industrialization, was increasingly populated by poor people, immigrants, Black people, and "fallen" women. . . . Thus social processes that created these categories in the first place, namely, restricting wo/men to the private sphere and racially segregating African-Americans, could largely be taken for granted.[35]

The rhetoric of Historical-Jesus discourses, I argue, belongs to this third stage of the history of science. As Dieter Georgi and Kwok Pui-Lan have argued convincingly, Historical-Jesus research participated in fashioning and legitimating the cultural-scientific discourses of domination that were conditioned on the absence of wo/men who were non-elite, non-white, and non-male.[36] Thus Historical-Jesus research as a scientific discourse shares in the dualistic rhetoric of the discourses of prejudice, racism, sexism, heterosexism, elitism, ethnocentrism, and other discourses of domination.

Hence, it is important to critically scrutinize Historical-Jesus research, especially that of the Third Quest with its emphasis on scientific method and objectivist reconstructive models, and to interrogate its rhetoric as a discursive formation. At the same time, it is necessary to explore the construction of an alternative Historical-Jesus discourse, one that focuses not on Jesus, the individual heroic man and charismatic leader, as point of origin, but one that concentrates on a critical reconstruction and analysis of the values and visions embodied in Historical-Jesus scholarship.

## CONSTRUCTING AN ALTERNATIVE
## HISTORICAL-JESUS DISCOURSE

If emancipatory knowledge has the task of fostering the self-definition and self-determination of subaltern wo/men, then feminist scholars may not

[35] Patricia Hill Collins, *Fighting Words: Black Women and the Search for Justice* (Minneapolis: University of Minnesota Press, 1998), 100–101.

[36] Georgi, "Interest in Life of Jesus Theology"; Kwok Pui-Lan, "Jesus/the Native: Biblical Studies from a Postcolonial Perspective," in *Teaching the Bible: The Discourses and Politics of Biblical Pedagogy,* ed. Fernando F. Segovia and Mary Ann Tolbert (Maryknoll, N.Y.: Orbis Books, 1998).

just engage in the play of unending deconstruction but must also participate in reconstructing and reenvisioning Historical-Jesus discourse as an
alternative discourse to domination. They must do so in a global context
not only of market commodification and positivist science but also of
emancipation. If Historical-Jesus discourses are to position themselves not
in the spaces of domination but in the critical alternative spaces of emancipation, I argue, they need to shift their theoretical focus and frame of
reference away from the Historical-Jesus, the exceptional man and charismatic leader, to the emancipatory Divine Wisdom movement of which he
was a part and whose values and visions decisively shaped him.

Such a shift in research focus would require that Historical-Jesus studies articulate an alternative scientific ethos of biblical inquiry for transforming the scientific discourses of domination, rather than uncritically
incorporating them. It calls for a redefinition of science and research in the
interest of emancipation. The following areas of change, I suggest, are crucial for such a revolutionary paradigm shift (Thomas Kuhn).

*First:* Since Historical-Jesus research, especially the Third Quest for the
Historical-Jesus, stresses the scientific character of its discourses, it must
learn to take notice of and analyze the discourses of domination produced
by Western science as an integral part of its research project. Such discourses of domination are engendered by the logic of difference or the
logic of "othering." This logic of difference as domination understands the
other always as a "not" (e.g., not-white, not-male, not-civilized) who lacks
the valued qualities of hegemonic society and whose humanity becomes
the opposite of that of those who are elite and in power.

The others (wo/men, innocent children, nature, noble savages) become
the object of negative projection as well as of romantic desire. Either the
"others" are seen only in a pejorative vein as lazy, irrational, backward,
emotional, gossipy, or sex hungry, or they are idealized and romanticized
("The eternal feminine draws us heavenwards" [Goethe]), and thereby
made into a repository of all that elite white educated males are not. In and
through such a logic and politics of domination, the dehumanized or glo-
rified "other" is transformed into an object of study and ceases to be a subject of history. According to Edward Said, the European construction of
the Orient [and I would add here of the Mediterranean] as its "other," for
example, is an outgrowth of its will to power. "Orientalism" is a "Western
strategy for dominating, restructuring, and having authority over the
Orient."[37]

[37] Edward Said, *Orientalism* (New York: Vintage Press, 1978), 3.

Such a logic and politics of "othering" is at work in Historical-Jesus studies in various ways. It comes to the fore in interpretations that reconstruct the Historical-Jesus as the other, for example, as a fanatic millenarianist, a Mediterranean peasant, or a magician and witch doctor.[38] Such a politics and rhetoric of "othering" inform especially the social-scientific constructions of Mediterranean culture as totally other from European and North American Western cultures. In the last analysis, this politics of "othering" is at work in critical-biblical studies on the whole, because of their tendency to construe the past as an artifact and alien, separated through the chasm of time and culture from the present. Rather than see both the differences and the commonalities between past and present, between Mediterranean and contemporary democratic societies, the scientific discourses of domination seek to control the "other" of past societies by objectifying and making them totally alien. Thereby they obfuscate common structures of domination across history.

*Second:* The logic and politics of "othering" determining the scientific discourses of domination is the "necessary precondition, then, for the creation of the transcendent rational subject who could persuade himself that he existed outside time and space and power relations."[39] Donna Haraway has dubbed this foundational scientific assumption of Western philosophical discourses the "god-trick"[40] that produced the subject of scientific discourse as the "invisible I" that can see everything from nowhere. This "god's-eye-view" standpoint has shaped the scientific ethos, insisting that only disembodied reason can produce accurate and objective accounts of the world. Nancy Hartsock summarizes this epistemological position as follows:

> Through reason the philosopher could escape the limits of the body, time, and space to contemplate the eternal problems related to man as knower. Finally, as a result of all this, Enlightenment political thought was characterized by a denial of the importance of power to knowledge and concomitantly a denial of the centrality of systematic domination in human societies. The subject/individual and power were said to be distinct.[41]

---

[38] Bruce J. Malina and Jerome H. Neyrey, *Calling Jesus Names: The Social Value of Labels in Matthew* (Sonoma, Calif.: Polebridge Press, 1988).

[39] Nancy C. M. Hartsock, *The Feminist Standpoint Revisited & Other Essays* (Boulder, Colo.: Westview Press, 1998), 207.

[40] Donna Haraway, "Situated Knowledges: The Science Question in Feminism and the Privilege of Partial Perspective," *Feminist Studies* 14 (1988): 575–99.

[41] Hartsock, *Feminist Standpoint Revisited*, 206f.

In opposition to this modern scientific epistemology of abstraction and the "god's-eye-view," emancipatory movements and theories insist that what we see depends on where we stand. There is no "god's-eye-view" position outside of power relations. Hence, in order to deconstruct and transform the scientific ethos of the "Man of Reason,"[42] Historical-Jesus scholars must begin their inquiry by critically reflecting on their own social location in the kyriarchal structures of domination. This does not mean that we should engage in confessional litanies of biographical self-mirroring such as "I am a white, middle-class, European, immigrant wo/man scholar at an Ivy League institution in the United States"—litanies that ritually list biographical information without analyzing their function in the discourses of domination. Rather, it means that we must learn to understand social location not in terms of individual but in terms of group identity. Such a sociocultural group identity is determined both by struggles for liberation and by the kyriarchal pyramid of domination—that is, by the intersecting discourses of gender, race, class, ethnicity, and imperialism.[43]

To contextualize the subject of scientific Historical-Jesus discourses not in terms of individual biography but in terms of group assignation compels one to acknowledge the significance of power relations for producing knowledge and truth, which are always situated and perspectival. To locate Historical-Jesus discourses in relation to the specific historical conditions and relations of domination in which they emerge, can productively recognize that what constitutes knowledge and truth is markedly changed when sociopolitical context is taken into account. Such a recognition, however, presupposes that scholars adopt and articulate a systemic analytic of the kyriarchal relations of domination that have produced the scientific discourses of dehumanization.

*Third:* An explicit contextualization of Historical-Jesus research in terms of sociopolitical and religious-cultural location, I suggest, would enable the discipline to free itself from the unreflected compulsion to reconstruct the Historical-Jesus in the likeness and desire of the individual Historical-Jesus scholar. If scientific Historical-Jesus research does not

---

[42] Genevieve Lloyd, *The Man of Reason: Male and Female in Western Philosophy* (2nd ed.; London: Routledge, 1993).

[43] For the theoretical conceptualization and discussion of kyriarchy as replacing the more common patriarchy, see especially my books *But She Said; Jesus, Miriam's Child, Sophia's Prophet: Critical Issues in Feminist Christology* (New York: Continuum, 1999); and *Rhetoric and Ethic.*

want to continue its reinscription of the liberal or orthodox understandings of Jesus either as the great heroic man and charismatic leader or as the Divine Man and G*d striding over the earth (Käsemann), it needs to develop a reconstructive model that is social rather than individual. Such a collective social emancipatory model is provided by the "new social movements" that seek to change the scientific discourses and social-political structures of domination.

Yet while there are many studies on modern social movements for change, there are almost no studies on such movements in antiquity. Although there are, for instance, references to the Jewish movements mentioned by Josephus or to philosophical movements such as Cynicism, these are usually conceptualized as schools gathered around a great teacher or charismatic leader—who naturally is always male. Moreover, we lack sustained studies of slave movements, peasant movements, or national liberation movements in antiquity that could develop a reconstructive model inspired by the "new social movements." Instead, much work has been done on "honor and shame" culture or the patron–client social system—reconstructive historical models embodying the dominant kyriarchal structures of Greco-Roman society and culture.

While it is important to study the cultures and institutions of domination, it is equally important to analyze the social movements and cultural-religious values of those who envisioned and fought for a different society and culture. Jewish apocalypticism, for instance, has been recognized as a social movement, but Historical-Jesus scholars have not focused carefully on its collective emancipatory aspects. Instead they have centered on the imminent end of the world and on millenarianism, a Christian doctrinal term taken over and rendered "scientific" by cultural and social anthropologists. If Historical-Jesus scholars would understand the apocalypticism of the Jesus traditions in terms of social movement and motivating vision, they might be able to articulate an emancipatory rhetoric and politics of meaning that functions no longer to support the status quo but to energize movements for justice and transformation.

*Fourth:* In order to become more rather than less scientific, Historical-Jesus research that understands itself in terms of an emancipatory ethos of science must become engaged in a critical discussion of social theory. Rather than simply taking over anthropological and sociological models because they are allegedly scientific, Historical-Jesus research must investigate their understandings of the social world and of human beings within it as well as the values they advocate. This is necessary because the discourses of domination that decisively shaped scientific method and imagination as academic disciplines have manufactured scientific justification and consent to racism, heterosexism, class prejudice, and colonialism. The African American feminist sociologist Patricia Hill Collins has articulated three epistemological criteria for adjudicating social theory.[44] They can be equally applied to the social theory utilized by Historical-Jesus discourses because even social theories that claim value detachment and eschew politics of all kinds imply a theory of society and religion that is either emancipatory or supports the status quo. Such criteria can be translated into the following questions:

Does this social theory or theology speak the truth to people about their lives? What counts as knowledge? Whose knowledge is reckoned with, whose is discredited, and which statements count?

What is a social theory's or theology's stance toward freedom? What is its vision of emancipation and what kind of pragmatic strategies does it support for realizing this vision? Does this social theory equip people to resist oppression, and is it functional as a tool for social transformation?

Does this social theory or theology move people to struggle for self-definition and self-determination? What is the ethical foundation and vision of this social theory, and what is its relation to the discourses of domination and the struggles for emancipation and justice? These and other critical methodological questions must be asked in such an attempt to construct an alternative discourse of Historical-Jesus research.

## DECONSTRUCTING AND RESHAPING
## HISTORICAL-JESUS DISCOURSES

In the following chapters I therefore seek to investigate Historical-Jesus discourses from a critical feminist perspective committed to grass-roots wo/men's struggles and movements for survival and well-being. I ask how Historical-Jesus research is constructed, who is doing so and for whom, and I look at such discursive constructions from different theoretical and methodological angles. My argument is not linear-progressive but topical-cumulative and spiral. In pursuing it, I want it to be understood that I am

---

[44] Hill Collins, *Fighting Words*, 198–99.

not arguing for Historical-Jesus research to abandon the canons of science for those of religion. Religious and Christian theological discourses have equally participated in legitimating the order of domination and exclusion with its structural prejudices against people who are not elite white and elite male. Rather, I am arguing that the discipline of Historical-Jesus studies must become more conscious of its kyriarchal rhetoric of scientificity and its ideological functions in the regimes of dehumanization. Thus, one must deconstruct the intellectual frameworks and arguments that determine Historical-Jesus research and show how they participate in discourses of domination that seek to create an elite intellectual space free from all wo/men who are not white and not male.

The first chapter addresses the paradox that one finds numerous publications on Jesus and Wo/men but no feminist book-length reconstruction of the Historical-Jesus.[45] In order to explore this contradiction I review the discrete periods of "Historical-Jesus and women" research and look at the boundaries set by its scientific theoretical frameworks. Insofar as the Third Quest for the Historical-Jesus relies heavily on the rhetoric of quantitative method and the criterion of plausibility, it has "common sense" as its touchstone, common sense being understood as "ultimately a rationalization of (a) culture's power relations."[46] Hence, I conclude that it is not possible to write a critical feminist Historical-Jesus work within the research framework of the Third Quest because its scientific method and intellectual framework are andro/kyriocentric and support the status quo.

The second chapter looks at the same problem but this time not through the lenses of a reconstructive genealogy but through focusing on two quite different Historical-Jesus discourses. The liberal scientific discourse is exemplified here by the work of John Dominic Crossan, while the neo-orthodox theological Historical-Jesus discourse is represented by the work of Luke Timothy Johnson. After having critically discussed these scholars'

---

[45] Despite its title's alluding to redaction criticism, the book by Helga Melzer Keller, *Jesus und die Frauen: Eine Verhältnisbestimmung nach den synoptischen Evangelien* (Freiburg: Herder, 1997), utilizes the framework and methods of the Third Quest but is not feminist. Although it claims to be so, its analyses are determined and co-opted by the constraints of a doctoral thesis requirement that owes its inspiration (or compulsion) to the positivistic framework of its Doktorvater rather than to a stringent critical feminist impulse and inquiry. It sadly exemplifies the co-optation of the creativity, intelligence, and self-interests of wo/men by the malestream kyriarchal academy.

[46] James Arnt Aune, "Cultures of Discourse: Marxism and Rhetorical Theory," in *Contemporary Rhetorical Theory: A Reader,* ed. John Louis Lucaites, Celeste Michelle Condit, and Sally Caudill (New York: Guilford Press, 1999), 548.

arguments, I conclude that neither the framework of the liberal nor that of the neo-orthodox Historical-Jesus discourse suffices for constructing a critical feminist interpretation for liberation because both unwittingly reinscribe a cultural and/or religious image of Jesus that fosters relations of domination. The liberal Historical-Jesus discourse does so by reasserting the "Jesus-the-man and great charismatic leader" image, whereas the neo-orthodox one does so by reproducing the kyriocentric and anti-Jewish frameworks of the gospels.

The third chapter questions once more the positivist rhetoric and reifying tendencies of social-scientific Historical-Jesus research. This rhetoric of scientific positivism stressing methodological control, and its conservative framework of cultural anthropology with its proliferating dichotomies and stress on Mediterranean "commonsense" notions, produces a dualistic rhetorical discourse that is constructed not over and against Western neo-capitalist societies but over and against a democratic ethos and social movements for change. Instead of engaging in such a dualistic conservative rhetoric and instead of celebrating Jesus as the "charismatic leader" and "great man," I argue that the Third Quest must develop a reconstructive social-scientific model patterned after grass-roots social movements for change if it will do justice to its own scientific emancipatory impulses and to feminist and other emancipatory critical requirements for a radical democratic society and religion.

In the fourth chapter I turn to feminist Historical-Jesus discourses and specifically address the continuing debate on Christian anti-Judaism in feminist historical reconstruction. While I appreciate the passion for justice that imbues this debate, I also observe some jockeying for position when scholars indict the work of others but do not critically discuss their own mostly unconscious impregnation with anti-Jewish or racist assumptions. I am worried about the tendencies in malestream and feminist Historical-Jesus research to reinscribe either anti-Judaism or antifeminism by unwittingly reinscribing the discourse of the "white lady."

This cultural-religious discourse, which in the nineteenth century was dubbed the cult of "true womanhood," and which I have renamed the discourse of the "white lady," stresses not only the intellectual "innocence" and "purity" of elite wo/men but also their function to culturally mediate the andro/kyriocentric discourses from which elite wo/men's "indirect power" derives. This ideology of the "white lady" promises that if elite wo/men prove that they are "loyal to civilization," to quote Adrienne Rich, and "faithful" to the kyriarchal interests of their (Doktor)fathers and (spiritual) masters, they will be protected from (the other man's) violence (cf.

the practice of lynching), the fate of their intellectual and spiritual "mothers," and be rewarded with security and high status.

Finally, in the fifth chapter, in dialogue with critical feminist work, I sketch out a reconstructive model of the Jesus movement(s) as Jewish emancipatory *basileia* movement(s). I retain the Greek word *basileia* as a tensive symbol because I have not found a good translation of its radical egalitarian subversive horizon of meaning that would adequately communicate its politics of meaning. Such a reconstructive model is fashioned after and derives its inspiration from contemporary grass-roots wo/men's movements[47] and their struggles for change and the well-being of all.

Since, however, the historical-experiential contexts of meaning of *basileia* also have been the kyriarchal household structures of subordination and the Greco-Roman imperial structures of domination, the translation of the term as "kingship, kingly rule, and kingdom" has become so much "common sense" that any other translation sounds wrong and inappropriate. In using the tensive symbol *basileia*, I am well aware that this key symbol of the Jesus movement(s) harbors in it the seeds of imperialism and domination that have engendered European colonization and the virulent anti-Semitism that climaxed in the Holocaust.

In conclusion, the different theoretical moves and critical analyses of Historical-Jesus research in each chapter are not interested in producing a *feminist Historical-Jesus*. Rather, they seek to investigate Historical-Jesus research as a sociopolitical and scientific-religious discourse. I cannot stress enough that I am interested not in engaging in a polemic against individual scholars but rather in investigating Historical-Jesus discourse as an elite discourse. For, as Patricia Hill Collins points out:

> Elite discourses present a view of social reality that elevates the ideas and actions of highly educated White men as normative and superior. Thus elite discourses measure everyone else's accomplishments in light of how much they deviate from the ideal.[48]

Hence, a critical social theory, not market research techniques and "plausibility" arguments, is called for in Historical-Jesus studies. Historical-Jesus research has to become, I argue, a critical emancipatory scientific discourse that stands publicly accountable for its Historical-Jesus productions. Such

[47] See the literature in *Democratization and Women's Grassroots Movements,* ed. Jill M. Bystydzienski and Joti Sekhon (Indianapolis: Indiana University Press, 1999).

[48] Hill Collins, *Fighting Words,* 45.

an alternative model of reconstruction must be formulated in dialogue with critical emancipatory feminist discourses.

Rather than relinquishing Historical-Jesus research or fixing and reifying its proliferating discourses with a rhetoric of scientific authority and unquestionability, Historical-Jesus studies, I argue throughout, must engage in a progressive and emancipatory politics of interpretation that ceases to maintain scientific discourses of domination. This book challenges Historical-Jesus scholarship to raise critical questions and to transform its scientific horizons. Because millions of wo/men still subscribe to the authority of both science and/or the Bible even when they have long given up on the authority of religion, feminist and other liberation scholars must become involved in reshaping hegemonic Historical-Jesus discourses. They must seek to encourage scientific Historical-Jesus studies to spell out such a "revolutionary paradigm change" of the discipline by articulating the interests at work in the meaning-making about the Historical-Jesus and by reconceptualizing the movement that carries Jesus' name in analogy to contemporary social movements for justice and well-being.

# 1

# WHO DO THEY SAY I AM?
## The Quest for the Historical-Jesus

IN THE PAST DECADE A HOST OF HISTORICAL-JESUS BOOKS
have appeared which range from the very scholarly to the very popular.[1]
The Newest, or Third, Quest for the Historical-Jesus seems to end up with
many different results, although it claims scientific method as its bench-
mark of objectivity. In 1992 N. T. Wright succinctly summed up this
dilemma of pluralist relativism in Historical-Jesus research: "The current
wave of books about Jesus offers a bewildering range of competing
hypotheses. There is no unifying theological agenda; no final agreement
about method; certainly no common set of results."[2]

One would think that the great disparity in the results of Historical-
Jesus research would have persuaded scholars a long time ago to abandon
their quest for the Historical-Jesus produced by the disciplined use of historical methods, in favor of more fruitful endeavors. Yet this has not been
the case. Rather, the opposite seems to be true: the flood of Jesus publications has dramatically increased in the past decade. Both the wide variety
of Historical-Jesus studies, books, and articles and the scholarly claim to
scientific objectivity in and through the controlled use of method can be
understood if one looks at Historical-Jesus research as a discursive practice
and productive site of struggle over the meaning of Jesus.

---

[1] It would be too much to list them here. For the discussion of the literature, see my
book *Jesus: Miriam's Child, Sophia's Prophet: Critical Issues in Feminist Christology* (New
York: Continuum, 1994).

[2] N. T. Wright, "The Quest for the Historical Jesus," in *The Anchor Bible Dictionary,* ed.
D. N. Freedman (New York: Doubleday, 1992), 3:800.

Books and articles on "Jesus and women" equally continue to proliferate and seek to intervene in this struggle over the meaning of Jesus. Hence, the Historical-Jesus is also widely discussed not only in popular Christian publications but also in feminist theological studies.[3] However, while there are plenty of scholarly articles and popular books on Jesus' relationship to wo/men, no book-length feminist study on the Historical-Jesus has been published.[4] The leading Historical-Jesus scholar John Dominic Crossan has pointed to this lack of feminist interest in the most recent Quest for the Historical-Jesus.

> But there is a special problem with "feminist sources" on the historical Jesus. Where are they? Why are so few women interested in that area of research? ... Why are so few Christian feminists focusing on the historical Jesus or on questions of inventory, stratigraphy, and attestation, on, that is, the precise cartography of Christianity's earliest re-oppression of women?[5]

These rhetorical questions are a sweeping gesture to declare critical feminist historical work on Jesus and early Christian beginnings nonexistent because it has adopted neither the Third Quest's theoretical framework with its stress on the scientific methods of inventory, stratigraphy, and attestation, nor its liberal understanding of Jesus as the great man and popular hero. Since despite his protestations to the contrary, Crossan still operates out of this scientific positivist paradigm of Historical-Jesus research with its emphasis on controllable method,[6] he cannot recognize

[3] For instance, Jaquelyn Grant, *White Women's Christ and Black Women's Jesus: Feminist Christology and Womanist Response* (Atlanta: Scholars Press, 1989); Maryanne Stevens, ed., *Reconstructing the Christ Symbol: Essays in Feminist Christology* (New York: Paulist Press, 1993); Kelly Brown Douglas, *The Black Christ* (Maryknoll, N.Y.: Orbis Books, 1994). See also the works by Chung Hyun Kyung, Rita Nakashima Brock, Rosemary Radford Ruether, Susan Brooks Thistlethwaite, Elizabeth Johnson, Verena Wodtke, Doris Strahm, and others.

[4] Although black theology and African, Latin American, or Asian liberation theologies always have focused on Jesus, they have not joined in the production of Historical-Jesus discourses.

[5] In *Jesus and Faith: A Conversation on the Work of John Dominic Crossan, Author of the Historical Jesus,* ed. Jeffrey Carlson and Robert A. Ludwig (Maryknoll, N.Y.: Orbis Books, 1994), 151.

[6] See also the positivist rhetoric of the Jesus Seminar, which was founded in 1985 and is led by Robert Funk and John Dominic Crossan. Since the Jesus Seminar wants to intervene in public discourses, it has described its work from the beginning in positivist terms. According to Mark Allan Powell, the Jesus Seminar is "claiming to offer 'the assured results of historical-critical scholarship.' To some this conveys a false impression of 'objective' scholarship, according to which evidence is impartially weighed by academics who had no

the affinities between his own model of historical reconstruction and my feminist one.

Although the Historical-Jesus reconstructions of Third-Quest scholars such as Crossan, Marcus Borg, and Richard Horsley characterize certain aspects of the Jesus movement (e.g., equality, commensality, marginals, prophets, eschatology, and political death) similarly to what I had done in *In Memory of Her*, such dependency is generally not acknowledged. However, even though I have pioneered such a reconstructive approach, I have not been and I am not interested in writing a tome about the Historical-Jesus because I want to avoid the trap of liberal Jesus research that elaborates Jesus the charismatic leader and great hero. Whereas I have tried to bypass this trap by focusing on the movement to which Jesus belonged and its expansion and modification in the cities of the Roman empire, Historical-Jesus books continue to reconstruct Jesus as unequaled individual[7] and charismatic leader.[8]

Jane Schaberg has responded to the query of Crossan as to why there are no feminist sources on the Historical-Jesus and pointed to the studied "ignoring, censoring, dismissing, silencing and trivializing of feminist scholarship, as well as its appropriation without attribution, which is a form of silencing" by malestream Historical-Jesus studies as a crucial reason for such an alleged lack of feminist scholarship.[9] She argues that one would have expected that, for instance, my work, particularly *In Memory of Her*,[10] would have made a difference or been a serious dialogue partner for most of the Historical-Jesus studies of the past decade but that it is not mentioned in most of them. She then goes on

> to raise the question of the effect this studied ignorance or dismissal of [Schüssler Fiorenza's] work –that of the most eminent feminist NT critic — has on the field, especially what impact it has on other feminist critics. State of the art discussions in other fields such as psychology, literature and his-

---

vested interest in the outcome. This was not the case" (*Jesus as a Future in History: How Modern Historians View the Man from Galilee* [Louisville: Westminster John Knox Press, 1998], 80).

[7] See chapter 2 for further elaboration.

[8] To my knowledge the first scholar to do so was Gerd Theissen.

[9] Jane Schaberg, "A Feminist Experience of Historical-Jesus Scholarship," in *Whose Historical Jesus?* ed. William Arnal and Michel Desjardins, Studies in Christianity and Judaism 7 (Waterloo, Ont.: Wilfrid Laurier University Press, 1997), 146.

[10] Elisabeth Schüssler Fiorenza, *In Memory of Her: A Feminist Theological Reconstruction of Christian Origins* (New York: Crossroad, 1983; 10th Anniversary Edition With New Introduction, 1994).

tory usually feature analyses of how feminist studies have changed them. Why have they not changed this field?[11]

In what follows I would like to explore more fully this last question raised by Schaberg: Why has feminist work not been able to become at least a scholarly approach to be seriously discussed if not an agent able to change the field of Historical-Jesus studies? It is interesting to note that even after Schaberg raised this question in a talk given to the Canadian Society of Biblical Studies in 1993, the taxonomies and surveys of the field[12]—with the exception of that by Edith Humphrey[13]—which were presented at a follow-up meeting in 1994 still do not mention feminist work in general and *In Memory of Her* in particular. This blatant disregard for feminist work, I argue, is engendered not only by the social location and rhetorical situation of Historical-Jesus research and its positivist and empiricist discursive construction; it is also due to the continuing refusal of the discipline to critically reflect on and take responsibility for the public political implications of its research program.[14]

By raising once more the question of theory, hermeneutics, and epistemology in the face of an adamantly positivist scientific ethos in biblical studies,[15] I will approach Historical-Jesus research as a scholarly discourse that constitutes the Historical-Jesus as its subject while at the same time claiming to derive this "reality" from the extant sources. It does so by re-arranging the extant information in a reconstructive model that, consciously or not, is determined by the experience and interests of the scholar at work. It thereby overlooks that "[t]exts do more and less than represent: they configure what they point to, and they are configured by it. To the

---

[11] Schaberg, "Feminist Experience," 147.

[12] E.g., Halvor Moxnes, "The Theological Importance of the 'Third Quest' for the Historical Jesus," in *Whose Historical Jesus?* ed. Arnal and Desjardins, 118–31; Larry W. Hurtado, "A Taxonomy of Recent Historical-Jesus Work," ibid., 272–95; and Peter Richardson, "Enduring Concerns: Desiderata for Future Historical-Jesus Research," ibid., 296–307.

[13] Edith M. Humphrey, "Will the Reader Understand? Apocalypse as Veil or Vision in Recent Historical-Jesus Research," in *Whose Historical Jesus?* ed. Arnal and Desjardins, 215–37.

[14] See my book *Rhetoric and Ethic: The Politics of Biblical Studies* (Minneapolis: Fortress Press, 1999).

[15] See, e.g., Robert W. Funk, Roy W. Hoover, and the Jesus Seminar, *The Five Gospels: The Search for the Authentic Words of Jesus* (New York: Macmillan, 1993), 34–35: "the Fellows of the Seminar are critical scholars. To be a critical scholar means to make empirical, factual evidence—evidence open to confirmation by independent, neutral observers—the controlling factor in historical judgments. . . . Critical scholars adopt the principle of methodological skepticism: accept only what passes the rigorous tests of the rules of evidence. . . ."

extent that discourse configures what it indicates, it is a fiction as much as a representation."[16]

As a scholarly discourse, Historical-Jesus research, I suggest, can be investigated as "the study of the construction of the subject, the extent to which and the mechanisms through which individuals are attached to identities," as well as an investigation of the role the process of identity construction "plays in the disruption or stabilization of political formations and the relation of all these processes to distinctions of gender, ethnicity, and class."[17] In other words, one must investigate Historical-Jesus research as a discursive practice that, like historiography on the whole, seeks to constitute the identity of Jesus and Christian identity in terms of scientific positivism[18] as well as cultural androcentrism or, better, kyriocentrism. However, rather than investigate Historical-Jesus discourses *tout court*, I want to focus here on one of them, specifically on the discourse about "Jesus and wo/man."

## "HISTORICAL-JESUS AND WOMEN" RESEARCH

Scholarship generally has come to distinguish four periods of Jesus research and three quests for the historical Jesus. Whereas three of the four Quests have doggedly pursued the Historical-Jesus in various ways and with differing methods in positivist terms, the period between the First and the Second Quest, which began with the work of Martin Kähler in 1896[19] and ended with Ernst Käsemann's revival of Historical-Jesus research in 1953,[20] was actually a declaration against liberal "life-of-Jesus scholarship"[21] that claimed to represent the "real" Historical-Jesus free from all dogmatic overlay. This interlude of the No Quest lasted for about sixty years, during which time the Quest for the Historical-Jesus was virtually abandoned.

---

[16] Mark Poster, *Cultural History + Postmodernity: Disciplinary Readings and Challenges* (New York: Columbia University Press, 1997), 9.

[17] Ibid., 10.

[18] See Patricia Hill Collins, *Fighting Words: Black Women and the Search for Justice* (Minneapolis: University of Minnesota Press, 1998), 92.

[19] Martin Kähler, *The So-Called Historical Jesus and the Historic, Biblical Christ,* trans. and ed. Carl Braaten (Philadelphia: Fortress, 1988).

[20] This paper was published by Ernst Käsemann, "The Problem of the Historical Jesus," in his *Essays on New Testament Themes,* trans. W. J. Montague (London: SCM Press, 1964).

[21] See Barry W. Henaut, " Is the 'Historical Jesus' a Christological Construct? " in *Whose Historical Jesus?* ed. Arnal and Desjardins, 241–68.

The Third Quest[22] has emerged primarily among North American scholars who have lost confidence in the criteria of authenticity of the Second Quest but still hold on to the criterion of "plausibility." The Third Quest is not kerygmatic but social-scientific in intent. It is characterized by its interest in social history, the integration of Jesus into Judaism, and equal attention to noncanonical sources.[23] It is split in two directions: those who advocate a noneschatological understanding of Jesus (B. Mack, D. Crossan, L. Vaage, et al. in the Jesus Seminar) and those who defend the eschatological millenarian Jesus who hoped for the restoration of Judaism (E. P. Sanders, G. Theissen and A. Merz, D. C. Allison, J. Meier, R. Horsley, et al.).

Studies about Jesus and wo/men[24] often subscribe to the methodological positivism of the Third Quest. They generally take the grammatically androcentric language of our sources at face value and thereby reinscribe the wo/men-marginalizing and wo/men-erasing tendencies of such language. Hence, the history that they tell about biblical wo/men, and about wo/men today,[25] cannot but represent wo/men as marginal or not mention them at all. They "erase" wo/men from historical and religious consciouness not only because of the marginalizing and silencing tendencies of our androcentric sources written in grammatically masculine languages, but also because of the marginalizing and silencing tendencies of hegemonic biblical scholarship, its kyriocentric frameworks of interpretation and models of historical reconstruction.

In my own work I have consistently argued that a feminist reconstruction of Christian beginnings must cease to conceptualize the field as study *about* wo/men, making wo/men the object of the scholarly gaze. Nevertheless, in the context of the Third Quest, articles and books about

[22] The coining of the term Third Quest is attributed to S. Neill and T. Wright, *The Interpretation of the New Testament 1861–1986* (Oxford: Oxford University Press, 1988), 379ff.

[23] See the very helpful chart in Gerd Theissen and Annette Merz, *The Historical Jesus: A Comprehensive Guide* (Minneapolis: Fortress Press, 1988), 12.

[24] For the problematic meaning of the term woman/women, see Denise Riley, *"Am I That Name?" Feminism and the Category of Women in History* (Minneapolis: University of Minnesota Press, 1988); Judith Butler, *Gender Trouble: Feminism and the Subversion of Identity* (New York: Routledge, 1990).

[25] See, e.g., *Women and Christian Origins,* ed. Ross Shepard Kraemer and Mary Rose D'Angelo (New York: Oxford University Press, 1999) for such an approach. They rework most of the materials in *In Memory of Her* in terms of the study of women, gender, and religion. Since they know the broad influence of the book, it is unfathomable how they can go on to state: "To date, no one has written a comprehensive treatment of wo/men and Christian origins appropriate for a wide audience ranging from undergraduate to general readers to scholars previously unacquainted with this literature" (p. 3).

"Wo/men in the Bible" or "Wo/men in the Gospels" have proliferated. Instead of reinscribing wo/men as peripheral, I have argued, a pragmatic rhetorical understanding of language and a radical egalitarian model of historical reconstruction are able not only to tell the story of Jesus as belonging to a Jewish emancipatory movement but also to place Jewish wo/men as agents at the center of its historiography. Hence, in *In Memory of Her* I was concerned to reconstruct the Jesus movement as an egalitarian Jewish movement of wo/men. I argued against topical studies on "wo/men and Jesus" which frame their research in terms of the cultural model of patriarchal romance[26] between the great man Jesus and his wo/men followers. Consequently, I sought to replace this Historical-Jesus research framework, which takes the study of Jesus and wo/men as its object, with a feminist framework that focuses on wo/men as subjects of Historical-Jesus reconstruction. Imaginatively adopting the perspective of biblical wo/men rather than just looking at them as fixed objects in texts in a fixed context yields a different world and set of possibilities. Looking as a wo/man (i.e., from a wo/man's social location) and looking from a feminist perspective (i.e., with a hermeneutics of suspicion rooted in a feminist social analytic) is quite different from looking at a wo/man as an objectified research object.

Since the first phase of life-of-Jesus research in the nineteenth century sought to write a biography of Jesus, the great individual and heroic man, topical studies on wo/men in the life of Jesus and Christian origins have adopted an "add-and-stir" approach, which adds wo/men to the subject Historical-Jesus and continues to make Jesus and wo/men the object of its research rather than kyriarchal (lord/slave master/father/husband-determined) structures of domination. This approach overlooks that the understanding of Jesus as a powerful religious genius who transgressed all normal boundaries is the product of an elite masculinist Eurocentric liberal imagination. Jesus the extraordinary and heroic man becomes the paradigm of true (Western male) humanity and individuality, which can be approximated only by those who are like him.

Many popular studies on the relationship of Jesus to wo/men remain in the framework of this first phase of life-of-Jesus research when they seek to write biographies of Jesus, stress his close relationship with wo/men, or argue that he developed psychologically in his interactions with wo/men.

---

[26] For the impact of such reading, see Janice A. Radway, *Reading the Romance: Women, Patriarchy, and Popular Literature* (Chapel Hill: University of North Carolina Press, 1991).

Whereas Jesus is seen as the great [male] individual and hero who suffers conflicts and survives suffering and death, the wo/men around him, especially Mary of Magdala, are pictured in typically feminine fashion as romantically involved with him or as his loving support staff. Historical-Jesus images and publications function to inculcate religiously feminine cultural values and roles. Insofar as Jesus' behavior is imagined as always generous, friendly, helpful, kind, and loving, he appears as a human being who successfully combines masculine and feminine qualities.

The second phase of Jesus research began after World War I and was dubbed by Marcus Borg the "No Quest" period.[27] This period distinguishes between the Historical-Jesus of modern scholarship and the resurrected Christ of kerygmatic theology. Kerygmatic theology insisted that it is no longer possible to distill a liberal historical Jesus freed from early Christian interpretation and apostolic tradition. The gospels are to be studied as documents of faith and theological arguments of the evangelists and the communities they address.

Whereas many studies of the First Quest on Jesus and wo/men see him in a gendered framework, many of the studies that follow in the footsteps of the No Quest utilize not only redaction criticism and literary criticism but also feminist analysis for investigating the evangelists' portrayal of wo/men and the traditions they incorporated. Exemplary here is the Jesus book of Elaine Wainwright, *Shall We Look for Another?*, which uses feminist theory to reread Matthew's story about Jesus.[28]

In general, feminist studies of the gospels seek to analyze the androcentric narrative constructions of the evangelists and to trace their gendered traditions and sources in order to show how androcentric texts and traditions restrict discipleship to the male characters and thereby marginalize wo/men and their traditions. To mention only a sampling of feminist authors: Luise Schottroff, Mary Rose D'Angelo, Amy-Jill Levine on Q; Hisako Kinukawa, Joanna Dewey, Mary Ann Tolbert, Ulrike Metternich, Irene Dannemann, and Monika Fander on Mark; Jane Schaberg, Linda Maloney, Turid Karlsen Seim, Ivone Richter Reimer, Sabine Bieberstein, and Clarice Martin on Luke-Acts; Elaine Wainwright and Antoinette Clark Wire on Matthew; Sandra Schneiders and Adele Reinhartz on John; Karen King and Anne McGuire on the *Gospel of Mary* and Gnostic literature. All

---

[27] Marcus J. Borg, *Jesus in Contemporary Scholarship* (Valley Forge, Pa.: Trinity Press International, 1994), 4.

[28] Elaine M. Wainwright, *Shall We Look for Another? A Feminist Rereading of the Matthean Jesus* (Maryknoll, N.Y.: Orbis Books, 1998).

these studies were written after the sixty-year interval in Historical-Jesus research but continue the No Quest approach in feminist terms.

It must also be noted, however, that most popularizing studies about Jesus and women in the gospels are not feminist. Often they uncritically assume linguistic determinism (i.e., that androcentric language cannot be changed), and hence cannot but "naturalize" the grammatically masculine language representation as well as the anti-Jewish tendencies of the gospels and their traditions. Such studies are especially prone to reinscribe the anti-Jewish polemic of the gospels into their own historical narrative, and they do so in terms of cultural gender stereotypes. For instance, they assume that wo/men were second-class citizens, as they are still today in Christian churches, and then go on to argue that this also must have been the case in Judaism.

The third period of Historical-Jesus research—or the Second Quest, which was dubbed the New Quest by James Robinson—owes its existence to the reaction against kerygmatic Jesus theology. It flourished in the 1950s and 1960s and insisted that it is possible to extract or distill the historical Jesus from the early Christian sources like a kernel from the husk. To that end, the New Quest articulated criteria of historical authenticity. In order to be regarded as authentic, words and deeds of Jesus must, first, be documented in more than one source (the criterion of multiple attestation). Second, they must not be found in the Jewish culture of the time or be explainable as stemming from the interests of the early church (the dissimilarity or exclusivity—not difference—criterion). And third, they must cohere with the material judged previously as authentic (the coherence criterion).[29] In other words: the New Quest adopts a reductionist historical method which does not take into account that historiography must evaluate and place texts and artifacts in a coherent frame of meaning or reconstructive model in order to tell a story about Jesus that makes sense. There is no history that is not reconstruction.

Moreover, this reductionist method assumes that Jesus is totally separable from both Judaism and from his followers, the early church. He is the totally Other.[30] In order to establish the historical singularity of Jesus and

---

[29] Norman Perrin (*Rediscovering the Teaching of Jesus* [New York: Harper & Row, 1967], 39f.) has labeled the criterion of exclusivity as the criterion of dissimilarity.

[30] In an editorial comment Lyn Miller elaborates this point: "You're trying to get at something with this totally Other Jesus that connects him with the Native, I know, but the multivalent implications of this link don't seem to me to be fully manifest. Is 'Jesus himself' oppressed by this isolation and fetishization? Is that what Christology does? What is gained

his ethics, the New Quest, like the Old, needed a negative depiction of Judaism as its foil. Jesus supposedly knew that his teaching undermined the fundamentals of Jewish belief. The Roman imperial authority executed him allegedly because of his conflict with a ritualistic and legalistic Judaism. This anti-Jewish framework has also determined many studies on Jesus and women.

It was a male[31] and not a female scholar who early on articulated the thesis that Jesus was a feminist because he allegedly broke the purity laws and, in distinction to Jewish rabbis, spoke to wo/men and admitted wo/men as his disciples. However, because of the challenge of Jewish feminists such as Judith Plaskow, Christian feminist scholarship much earlier than malestream Historical-Jesus scholarship has recognized and discussed the anti-Jewish prejudice resulting from attempts to depatriarchalize Jesus without challenging the scholarly construction and popular understanding of Judaism as patriarchal.[32] It must not be overlooked, moreover, that popular studies on Jesus and women have not invented but have taken over their interpretive prejudices and stereotypes from malestream Christian scholarship. They often do not intend to be anti-Jewish but seek to picture Jesus as a critic of his patriarchal religion and culture in order to indict their own church polity and hegemonic Christian practices.

Insofar as one of the most fertile grounds for Christian anti-Jewish articulations has been Historical-Jesus research, assertions of the uniqueness of Jesus, the feminist, and his atypical relations to women adopt the arguments of liberal Historical-Jesus scholarship, which is permeated by anti-Judaism. Since such feminist assertions about Jesus are formulated

---

by those who make Jesus totally Other? Do they want to colonize him/God for their own meaning systems? Make him a floating signifier that can be annexed to any cause? This seems implicit in all your arguments, but you rely a lot, it seems, on the expression itself to convey these dimensions and it doesn't say quite enough. I guess actually Jesus as Native becomes, like native women, the fixed object of the gaze, so that rather than, as Christians, to look out at the world through his eyes and try to see what he might have seen, he himself becomes a fetish that fascinates the eye and obliterates the context without which he is nothing (exactly an empty sign)."

[31] Leonard Swidler, "Jesus Was a Feminist," *Catholic World* 212 (1971): 177–83; idem, *Women in Judaism: The Status of Women in Formative Judaism* (Metuchen, N.J.: Scarecrow Press, 1976).

[32] Although our knowledge of Jewish wo/men has increased considerably since *In Memory of Her* appeared, unfortunately until today no *feminist* reconstruction of early Judaism has been written. One wonders whether this is the case because leading Jewish wo/men scholars like Ross Kraemer and Amy-Jill Levine favor the women's or gender studies approach.

within a historical and theological discourse produced by predominantly malestream scholarship and theology, it becomes necessary to examine what kind of Historical-Jesus discourses engender feminist collusion in the reproduction of Christian anti-Judaism.

This collusion also seems to be at work in the Third Quest of Historical-Jesus research. The beginning of the Third Quest is generally dated in the early 1980s, and its initiation is attributed to North American scholarship. In distinction to the Old and the New Quests, the Newest or Third Quest does not seek to reconstruct the historical Jesus over and against first-century Judaism but sees him as totally integrated into his time and culture. Even among the advocates of the Cynic hypothesis the debate is not about whether Jesus was a Jew but what kind of Jew Jesus was.

The Third Quest was facilitated through new studies of early Jewish writings, research on the Qumran scrolls, and archaeological discoveries. Whereas these studies have amply documented that Judaism in the first century C.E. was variegated and pluralistic, the arguments about Jesus' Jewishness seem often to presuppose a unitary patriarchal form of Judaism. If scholars use not a sociological-conflict model but an integrationist model for their reconstruction of Jesus, they cannot picture Jesus as a member of a variegated Jewish *basileia* movement that stood in conflict with the hegemonic kyriarchal structures of the Roman empire, of which hegemonic Judaism also was a part. In short, they are not able to articulate a reconstructive frame of reference that can conceptualize the emergent Jesus movement and its diverse articulations as participating in popular Jewish and Greco-Roman movements of cultural, political, and religious survival, resistance, and change.

One wonders whether it is a historical accident that the Third Quest for the Historical-Jesus exploded not only during the resurgence of the political right and the revival of religious fundamentalism but also in a time when the wo/men's movement in the churches and the academy gained ground and developed rhetorical power. Yet, whereas the Second Quest stressed the difference of the "feminist" Jesus over and against Judaism, the Third Quest argues for his integration into his patriarchal Jewish society and religion. Jesus was a devout Jewish man[33] who did not question the dominant structures of his society but fully subscribed to them. If the dissimilarity criterion is replaced with the criterion of plausibility within a kyriarchal frame of reference, one cannot but reconstruct Jesus' Jewishness

[33] See the new book by Paula Fredriksen, *Jesus of Nazareth, King of the Jews: A Jewish Life and the Emergence of Christianity* (New York: Alfred A. Knopf, 1999).

in terms of the dominant patriarchal ethos of the first century. At this point the entrapping character of this new criterion of Historical-Jesus research becomes obvious.

Some scholars in biblical wo/men's studies who seek to avoid Christian anti-Judaism in their research on Jesus and women, also use this criterion when they argue that it is not plausible that Jesus and his followers challenged the dominant patriarchal institutions of his time. To the contrary, they insist, he was completely in line with Jewish and Greco-Roman patriarchalism.[34] Such scholars, however, do not realize that they also fall prey to negative stereotypical assumptions about Judaism insofar as they cannot imagine that the Jesus movement, like other Jewish movements of the time, could possibly have questioned the second-class citizenship of wo/men and disenfranchised men and have done so on Jewish theological grounds.[35]

[34] See, e.g., the dissertation of Helga Melzer Keller, *Jesus und die Frauen: Eine Verhältnisbestimmung nach den synoptischen Evangelien* (Freiburg: Herder, 1997), 440f: "Auch sonst nahm Jesus in seinen Reden die patriarchale Gesellschaftsordnung als das Normale hin. . . . Die traditionellen Verhaltensmuster und Schablonen wurden von ihm in keiner Weise hinterfragt oder gar aufgesprengt. Für wenn Jesus sich vor allem einsetzte, waren die Notleidenden, die religiös Marginalisierten und die sozial Benachteiligten—auch wenn er kein Reformprogramm oder sozialrevolutionäre Aktionen verfolgte. . . . Wir müssen vielmehr das Fazit ziehen, dass er überhaupt kein Problembewusstsein hinsichtlich der in einem patriarchalen Gesellschaftssystem ungleichen Verteilung von Rechten und Möglichkeiten zwischen den Geschlechtern hatte, kein Gespür für eine sowohl rechtliche als auch lebenspraktische Benachteiligung von Frauen, kein Interesse an einer disbezüglichen Veränderung des Status quo." The ideological interests of this text are obvious. A Roman Catholic wo/man student who claims to be a feminist has to prove that she is a "good student" of her Doktorvater and that she is not interested in changing the status quo.

[35] See, e.g., Amy-Jill Levine, "Second Temple Judaism, Jesus, and Women: Yeast of Eden," *Biblical Interpretation* 2 (1994): 8–33, who concedes a "feminist impulse" in Judaism, but then in her argument against Luise Schottroff ("Itinerant Prophetesses: A Feminist Analysis of the Sayings Source Q," *Institute for Antiquity and Christianity, Claremont Graduate School Occasional Papers*, 21 [1991]; and eadem, "Wanderprophetinnen: Eine feministische Analyse der Logienquelle," *Evangelische Theologie* 51 [1991]: 332–44) retreats from it. Instead of researching the emancipatory tendencies in first-century Judaism, she ends up trivializing the textual information and justifying patriarchal religion: "To the outsider, the life of women in an ultra-orthodox Jewish community is restricted. To many insiders and especially to the convert, life in Williamsburg, just as life under Islamic Law or life in a Carmelite convent, is liberating. Such regulated societies provide all their members order, meaning and sanctification of daily existence; a distance from the outside (profane) world that distracts and detracts from the sanctified life; strong women-based groups (i.e. sisterhoods); and the developed traditions that overcome or at least counterbalance the patriarchalism involved in the communities' institutions and maintenance. Regulation of

## THE SOCIOPOLITICAL LOCATION
## OF HISTORICAL-JESUS DISCOURSES

Some have therefore argued that Historical-Jesus research must be abandoned because it is part of the problem rather than part of the solution. In my view, however, Historical-Jesus research cannot be simply abandoned but must be problematized and critiqued.[36] Moreover, it is necessary to engage in research of the Historical-Jesus traditions if one seeks to dislodge the exclusionist tendencies inscribed in the gospel portrait of Jesus that marginalize Christian wo/men and vilify Jewish wo/men.

In addition, Jesus research must be critically assessed because in Western societies it is a discourse that affects a larger public. Jesus discourses are intertwined with hegemonic cultural and societal ideologies. A politics of meaning contends that the Jesus of history is important not just for religious communities. Rather, as master narratives of Western cultures, Historical-Jesus discourses are always implicated in and collude with the production and maintenance of systems of knowledge that foster either exploitation and oppression or contribute to a praxis and vision of emancipation and liberation.

Hence, Historical-Jesus research as a rhetorical practice must critically explore and assess its own internalization of hegemonic knowledge about Jesus and discursive kyriocentric frameworks that make "sense" of the world and produce what counts as the "commonsense reality" of Jesus. Consequently, it must make visible the contesting interests and theoretical frameworks that determine the Historical-Jesus discourses of both malestream and feminist biblical studies.

In an article entitled "The Interest in Life of Jesus Theology as a Paradigm for the Social History of Biblical Criticism," Dieter Georgi has investigated the politics of Jesus discourses and constructed a trajectory of bourgeois Historical-Jesus theology throughout Christian history, beginning with the early Christian "divine man" theology and continuing to the New Quest for the historical Jesus.[37] According to Georgi, Historical-Jesus

---

clothing, action, relationships is even found by some to counteract the far too frequent abuse and violence against women" ("Second-Temple Judaism," 32).

[36] See Elisabeth Schüssler Fiorenza, "Jesus and the Politics of Interpretation," *Harvard Theological Review* 90, no. 4 (1997): 343–58, which is reworked in chapter 2.

[37] Dieter Georgi, "The Interest in Life of Jesus Theology as a Paradigm for the Social History of Biblical Criticism," *Harvard Theological Review* 85, no. 1 (1992): 51–83.

research understands Jesus as the great exceptional individual, genius, and hero.

> This view that Jesus had been a genius of some sort became the dominant view in the late eighteenth, nineteenth, and twentieth centuries, not only in Germany but also in Western Europe and North America, among both Protestants and Catholics.[38]

Georgi observes that the First Quest's interest in Jesus, the exceptional man, is continued and reformulated in the New Quest, which stressed Jesus as active subject of history and focused on individual consciousness, intention, and decision. Jesus' unique claim to extraordinary consciousness presupposes a peerless relationship to G*d in whose place he stood and acted. Jesus' essentially eschatological outlook and stress on G*d's sovereignty, according to Georgi, brought him into conflict not only with the Romans but also with his own people and leadership.

The emphasis of both the Old and New Quests on the exemplary or unique historical figure of Jesus and his radical ethics required a negative portrayal of Judaism as its foil. Since Jesus is said to have been conscious that his preaching radically undermined the fundamental beliefs of Judaism, he is understood as having gone to Jerusalem in the full awareness that he risked death. In this interpretation Jesus' conflict with the Roman authorities is the result of his basic conflict with ritualistic or legalistic Judaism.

Georgi concludes that the New Quest, like the quest for the Historical-Jesus on the whole, has its

> social location within the evolution of bourgeois consciousness, not just as an ideal but as an expression of a socioeconomic and political momentum. The contemporaneity of the New Quest with the end of the New Deal and the restoration of the bourgeoisie in the United States and Germany after World War II and within the confines of a burgeoning market-oriented Atlantic community is not accidental.[39]

Although Georgi does not point to the racist, Eurocentric identity formation of Historical-Jesus research, he concludes with the assertion that the modern quest for the Historical-Jesus is revived whenever a revolutionary situation abates. Historical-Jesus research therefore has always had a conservative, Eurocentric, kyriarchal (i.e., lord/father/master/husband-domination) function.

---

[38] Ibid., 76.
[39] Ibid., 83.

Moreover, the Chinese theologian Kwok Pui-Lan has pointed out that most surveys of biblical scholarship neglect to reflect on the fact that the quest for the historical Jesus flourished in nineteenth-century Europe at the height of Western colonization. She argues that there were in fact not one but two quests taking place at the same time:

> The quest for the historical Jesus was an obsession of the West. It first took place at a time when the power of Europe was at its zenith—the quest for Jesus went hand in hand with the quest for land and people to conquer. From a postcolonial perspective we must plot the quest for the *authentic* Jesus against the search for knowledge of *authentic* "natives" for the purpose of control and domination.[40]

The Eurocentrism of Historical-Jesus research is confirmed by a look at "two-thirds world" biblical scholarship. Just as critical feminist, so also "two-thirds world" scholars are not engaged in the (heroic) quests for the Jesus of history. Among others, Grant LeMarquand has pointed to the ignorance of the Western academy about African biblical scholarship.[41] Whereas African and postcolonial biblical scholars are well aware of the issues raised by Western Historical-Jesus scholarship, they frame and shape their own discourses on Jesus differently. Their major concern is to deconstruct colonialist readings of the Bible and to establish the common ground between their own cultures and the Bible. They focus on this issue not only because biblical cultures often come very close to their own but also because their own cultures were constructed as inferior and even "satanic" by missionaries with the help of the Bible.

In short, the Third Quest continues to produce Jesus, the Lord or kyrios, as a naturalized historical fact thereby asserting Western hegemonic identity formations as Christian and as elite male.[42] It does so in the face of a widespread liberal white male anxiety that feels threatened by feminists, immigrants, 2/3 World persons and everybody else who seeks to decenter academy and society in general and biblical studies in particular. Finally, I

---

[40] Kwok Pui-Lan, "Jesus/the Native: Biblical Studies from a Postcolonial Perspective," in *Teaching the Bible: The Discourses and Politics of Biblical Pedagogy,* ed. Fernando F. Segovia and Mary Ann Tolbert (Maryknoll, N.Y.: Orbis Books, 1998), 76.

[41] Grant LeMarquand, "The Historical Jesus and African New Testament Scholarship," in *Whose Historical Jesus?* ed. Arnal and Desjardins, 161–80.

[42] See the self-interview of Kwok Pui-Lan, "On Color-Coding Jesus: An Interview with Kwok Pui-Lan," in *The Postcolonial Bible,* ed. R. S. Sugirtharajah (Sheffield: Sheffield Academic Press, 1998), 176–89.

myself have pointed to the conservative political contextualizations of the Third Quest which emerged in the United States during the Reagan/Thatcher years and in a period when the United States had become the only superpower in the world after the demise of the Soviet Union and the failure of socialist state capitalism.[43]

The political context and rhetorical situation in which feminist as well as malestream Historical-Jesus research takes place is constituted by the resurgence of the religious Right around the world claiming the power to name and to define the true nature of religion.[44] Right-wing, well-financed think tanks are supported by reactionary political and financial institutions that seek to defend kyriarchal capitalism.[45] The interconnection between religious antidemocratic arguments and the debate with regard to wo/men's proper place and role is not accidental or just of intra-religious significance. In the past decade or so, right-wing movements around the globe have insisted on the figuration of emancipated wo/men as signifiers of Western decadence or of modern atheistic secularism, and have presented masculine power as the expression of divine power.[46]

In the article quoted in the beginning of this chapter Jane Schaberg details her experience of verbal and physical violence unleashed with the publication of her book *The Illegitimacy of Jesus* and of an article on Mary of Magdala in *Bible Review*.[47] The Associated Press and many newspapers picked up this article, informing the public that "Mary Magdalene was not

[43] See my *Jesus: Miriam's Child, Sophia's Prophet*, 5–12.

[44] See the varied contributions in *Fundamentalism as an Ecumenical Challenge*, ed. Hans Küng and Jürgen Moltmann (Concilium; London: SCM Press, 1992).

[45] See above, p. 4 n. 9.

[46] See especially the declaration of the Division for the Advancement of Women on "International Standards of Equality and Religious Freedom: Implications for the Status of Women, " in *Identity Politics & Women: Cultural Reassertions and Feminisms in International Perspective*, ed. Valentine M. Moghadam (Boulder, Colo.: Westview Press, 1994), 425–38; Rebecca E. Klatch, "Women of the New Right in the United States: Family, Feminism, and Politics," ibid., 367–88. Most of the contributions in *Identity Politics & Women* are on women and Islam in different parts of the world. However, see Sucheta Mazumdar, "Moving Away from a Secular Vision? Women, Nation, and the Cultural Construction of Hindu India" (pp. 243–73), and Radha Kumar, "Identity Politics and the Contemporary Indian Feminist Movement" (pp. 274–92); see also the three-part award-winning PBS series *God and Politics*, in which Bill Moyers explores the connections between state and church and its impact on U.S. foreign policy.

[47] Jane Schaberg, *The Illegitimacy of Jesus: A Feminist Theological Interpretation of the Infancy Narratives* (San Francisco: Harper & Row, 1987; reprint, New York: Crossroad, 1990).

a whore." Since Schaberg was at first pleased to receive the same publicity for her work as the Jesus Seminar,[48] she was not prepared for the vitriolic attacks that almost cost her her teaching position. A subsequent profile of Schaberg in the *Detroit Free Press* unleashed hundreds of letters to the administration threatening loss of financial support for the university and demanding that she be fired and even threatening her life. Schaberg sums up her personal experience as political:

> These letters . . . tell us what we already knew: that the general public is ignorant of the basics of historical criticism, and proud of it; that it serves the interest of the clergy and hierarchy to keep the general public in such ignorance and unable to think for themselves; . . . that fundamentalism is a powerful and often cruel force; that feminist concerns and perspectives are not studied, but reduced to slogans, and perceived by many as immoral; and that . . . [s]exism and misogyny are deeply rationalized, theologized, and spiritualized. . . .[49]

Whereas Jesus Seminar scholars boost the sale of their books when they are celebrated as "Jesus experts" on radio and television, feminist work that uses the same historical-critical methods but questions the status quo is vilified and leads to threats of violence. In this context of struggle, it becomes apparent that the publication and proliferation of Historical-Jesus books for popular consumption, on the one hand, and the trivializing or nonrecognition of feminist work by malestream biblical scholars, on the other hand, go together. Historical-Jesus books feed into literalist fundamentalism by reasserting disinterested scientific positivism in order to shore up the scholarly authority and universal truth of their research portrayal of Jesus.

The proliferation of "new" scientific Historical-Jesus books does not undermine but sustains the literalist desire of biblical fundamentalism for an "accurate," reliable biography of Jesus as firm foundation of Western culture and biblical religion. Hence, "scientific" Historical-Jesus scholarship that does not threaten the status quo seems to function politically as the reverse side of the fundamentalist literalist coin. Like Historical-Jesus research, fundamentalist interpretations seek to "fix" the pluriform expressions of Christian scriptures and traditions, the variegated texts and ambiguous metaphors of Jesus the Christ, and to filter them into a "commonsense," realistic narrative.

---

[48] See Powell, *Jesus*, 73.
[49] Jane Schaberg, in *Whose Historical Jesus?* ed. Arnal and Desjardins, 156.

Supposedly distinct from all forms of fundamentalist readings, "liberal" biblical scholarship insists on its scientific character, value-neutrality, methodological correctness, and detachment from theological and contemporary interests. If one asks why feminist, postcolonial, or other scholarship from the margins is not taken seriously but evokes violent public reactions, one is justified in suggesting that the reason is the insistence of such "liberal" scholarship on shrouding its work in the cloak of disinterestedness. Emancipatory scholarship, however, is not less objective and critical than hegemonic malestream scholarship. Rather, one could argue, it is more so because its bias is self-consciously and openly admitted in favor of an emancipatory reading and historical reconstruction.

In a very perceptive conclusion to *Whose Historical Jesus?* William Arnal points out that the reaction to feminist or postcolonial scholarship reveals

> what is ultimately at stake in the *desire* for objectivity: a desire to view the object of one's inquiry through the lens of things-as-they-are. The distinction between a fact and a value is itself not based on fact, but on a dichotomy between things as they are and things as one wishes them to be; the removal of so-called value from scholarship is really the removal of hope, something which is not central or necessary to the daily ideological work of the privileged.[50]

The refusal of the Third Quest to problematize its own methodological assumptions and ideological interests as well as its sophisticated advocacy of historical positivism corresponds to political conservatism. Its emphasis on the "realia" and "facts" of history and the reliability of its methods serves to promote scientific fundamentalism. Its universalizing discourses obfuscate that historians select and interpret archaeological artifacts and textual evidence as well as incorporate them into a scientific model and narrative framework of meaning. As long as the Third Quest, for instance, tacitly and often unknowingly assumes that Christian (male) identity remains bound up with a positivist "scientific" reconstruction of the historical "Jesus," the heroic patriarchal man, it cannot but produce the historical "fact" of Jesus' maleness as an objectified historical given that is said to be constitutive for hegemonic Christian Western (male) identity.

---

[50] William Arnal, "Making and Re-Making the Jesus-Sign: Contemporary Markings on the Body of Christ," in *Whose Historical Jesus?* ed. Arnal and Desjardins, 317.

## AN ALTERNATIVE MODEL OF HISTORICAL RECONSTRUCTION

It is not surprising, then, that feminist work on the Jesus movement and Christian beginnings has not had any palpable impact on the public discussion of the Third Quest. Since *In Memory of Her* appeared in the early 1980s, it belongs to the beginning stage of the fourth period and Third Quest of Historical-Jesus research. In discussion with social world studies and feminist historiography, the book sought to articulate a critical feminist theoretical model of the Jesus movement and early Christian history that is not pejorative of Jewish or Christian feminist identity. However, with the exception of a short discussion by Marcus Borg and its selective reception by Richard Horsley,[51] my methodological proposals and critical historiographical explorations[52] have been virtually overlooked in recent Historical-Jesus research. One wonders whether this is the case because my work makes its feminist interests explicit and thereby challenges the positivist and empiricist ethos of the discipline. Or is it the case because the nondiscussion of feminist work allows for its appropriation without citation?

When I set out to develop the reconstructive model shaping the narrative of *In Memory of Her,* I did not start with the goal of producing an objectivist, empiricist description of what actually happened in early Christian beginnings, nor did I want to prove that Jesus himself was totally egalitarian and without bias. Rather I wanted to show that the historiography of early Christian beginnings was one of the theoretical-historical discourses of domination that was imagined and produced by contemporary scholarship. Consequently, I set out to prove not that the hegemonic early Christian historiography was factually wrong but rather that it was *wrongheaded* and incomplete because of its kyriocentric frameworks and positivist empiricist rhetoric.

After I had become fully familiar with the feminist critique of language and historiography, I set out to show that the early Christian story could be told—and must be told—*otherwise.* My question was not "did it actually happen?" but do we still have sufficient information and source texts to tell the story of the movement carrying Jesus' name *otherwise,* envision-

---

[51] Marcus Borg, "Portraits of Jesus in Contemporary North American Scholarship," *Harvard Theological Review* 84, no. 1 (1991): 1–22; Richard A. Horsley, *Sociology and the Jesus Movement* (New York: Crossroad, 1989).

[52] See especially chapters 2 and 3 of *In Memory of Her.*

ing it as that of a "discipleship of equals"? The task, I argued, involves not so much discovering new sources as rereading the available sources in a different key.[53] Not only was there plenty of material that could be read in an egalitarian frame of interpretation, but such an egalitarian reading also could do more justice to our sources[54] that speak about wo/men's leadership, which traditional scholarship always felt compelled to explain away, to overlook, or to interpret in terms of cultural femininity. Notorious, for instance, is the interpretation of Phoebe in Romans 16 as serving tea at Paul's meetings or of Mary of Magdala and the other wo/men supporting Jesus and his itinerant male disciples by doing the necessary "housework" and helping them out financially.

Since *In Memory of Her* and its reconstruction of the Jesus movement is often read in terms of the liberal Protestant historiographical model of pristine egalitarian origins and rapid decline into patriarchy,[55] its underlying historical model of struggle between egalitarian vision and its realizations, on the one hand, and kyriarchal reality and its dehumanizing effects, on the other hand, is not understood.[56] To read early Christian history in terms of the model of rapid decline from the heights of radical equality to patriarchal institution is to overlook the struggles that are ongoing throughout Christian history between those who understand Christian identity as radically inclusive and egalitarian and those who advocate kyriarchal domination and submission.

[53] Ibid., xx.

[54] I thereby anticipated in a somewhat different form the criterion for the adjudication of Historical-Jesus research that Larry Hurtado has formulated in analogy to that used in textual criticism, "where the aim in weighing 'internal evidence' is to reconstruct the reading that best explains all the variants" (Hurtado, "Taxonomy," 294).

[55] See *In Memory of Her*, 92: "The sociological-theological model for the reconstruction of the early Christian movement suggested here should, therefore, not be misread as that of a search for true, pristine, orthodox beginnings which have been corrupted either by early Catholicism or by 'heresy,' nor should it be seen as an argument for an institutional patriarchalization absolutely necessary for the historical survival of Christianity. The model used here is that of social interaction and religious transformation, of Christian 'vision' and historical realization, of struggle for equality and against patriarchal domination."

[56] See, e.g., Mark A. Powell (*Jesus*, 2), who not only mistakes my hermeneutics of suspicion for "reading between the lines" but also misapprehends my reconstructive model of ongoing struggle: "By the second century the Christian church had become an extremely patriarchal institution, dominated by an all-male clergy." Although he perceives the paradigm shift which I advocate—("Nevertheless she has been extremely successful in sensitizing modern scholars to an awareness of the social and political contexts in which the Gospels were produced and to consideration of ways in which this might have influenced the stories they relate.")—he does not explore this paradigm shift further.

In short, when writing *In Memory of Her* I did not want to write another book about "women and Jesus" or wo/men in the Bible, but rather I wanted to see whether it was possible to write a feminist history of the Jesus movements in Palestine and in the Greco-Roman cities by placing wo/men at the center of attention. Since feminists are not concerned with conserving the world "as it is" but rather want to change it to fit their own experience of being in the world as wo/men, they are not interested so much in the Historical-Jesus as in the historical people—Jewish wo/men and men—who joined a socioreligious Jewish movement which they understood as an emancipatory *basileia*-movement. It was obvious to me that I was able to imagine the beginnings of early Christianity differently because I was fortunate to belong to a social movement for change today.

If one shifts from a kyriarchal preconstructed frame of reference to that of the "discipleship of equals," one no longer can hold, for example, that wo/men might or might not have been members of the communities that produced the hypothetical Sayings Source Q and the earliest Jesus traditions. If one cannot *prove* that wo/men were not members of this group and did not participate in shaping the earliest Jesus traditions, one needs to give the benefit of the doubt to the textual traces suggesting that they did. Rather than taking the androcentric text at face value, one must unravel its politics of meaning.

The objection that this is a circular argument applies to all hermeneutical and historiographical practices.[57] For instance, social-scientific studies that produce the preconstructed dualistic frame of the opposition between "honor and shame" as a given "fact" of Mediterranean cultures will read early Christian texts "about women" within this theoretically "constructed," kyriocentric frame of reference and thereby reproduce the cultural "common sense" that wo/men are marginal people. So-called social-scientific narratives, therefore, appear to be more "realistic" and "objective" than feminist ones because kyriocentric discourses function as ideologies that "naturalize" the structures of domination as "what is." That is, they mystify the "constructedness" of their account of historical reality in terms of their own understanding and experience of reality. Therefore malestream narratives of "how the world of Jesus really was" are easily accepted as "common sense," objective, scientific-historical accounts although they are as much a "construction" as feminist ones are.

---

[57] See the forthcoming book of Francis Schüssler Fiorenza, *Beyond Hermeneutics: Theology as Discourse* (New York: Continuum, 2001) for a critique of the method of correlation.

THE QUEST FOR THE HISTORICAL-JESUS

Egalitarian social movements striving to change unjust relations of domination are not just a product of modernity but are found throughout history. Ancient social movements and emancipatory struggles against kyriarchal relations of exploitation do not begin with the Jesus movements. Rather they have a long history in Greek, Roman, Asian, and Jewish cultures. The emancipatory struggles of biblical wo/men must be seen within this wider context of cultural-political-religious struggles. Such a historical model of emancipatory struggles sees the Jesus of history and the movement that has kept alive his memory not over and against Judaism but over and against kyriarchal structures of domination in antiquity and today. The history of these struggles in antiquity and throughout Western history still needs to be written today.

## PLAUSIBILITY OR POSSIBILITY?

Since the Third Quest justifiably rejects the Second Quest's reductionistic criteria of authenticity, it needs to develop new methods and criteria of evaluation. To that end the Jesus Seminar, whose members are mostly white, male, and Christian,[58] has adopted forms of opinion research and voting practices in order to stratify the traditions about Jesus. In addition, scholars have developed the plausibility criterion, which judges materials on the grounds of whether their content can be made plausible historically and be understood as fitting into the time and culture of Jesus.[59]

However, this criterion overlooks that what is regarded as "common sense" or plausible in a culture depends on the hegemonic ideological understandings of "how the world is." For instance, the assumption that wo/men were marginal or second-class citizens in all forms of first-century Judaism makes it impossible to assert plausibly that they were equal members in the Jesus movement if one understands it as a Jewish movement. The inability of such discourses to plausibly discuss the possibility of

[58] For the intent of the Jesus Seminar and the controversy surrounding it, see Powell, *Jesus*, 65–82.

[59] This hermeneutical circle between a preconstructed image of Jesus and evaluations of individual texts is recognized by Gerd Theissen and Dagmar Winter, *Die Kriterienfrage in der Jesusforschung: Vom Differenzkriterium zum Plausibilitätskriterium* (Novum Testamentum et Orbis Antiquus 34; Göttingen: Vandenhoeck & Ruprecht, 1997), 206: "Ein zutreffendes historisches Gesamtbild ist eine Idealvorstellung, ein Grenzwert, dem wir uns immer nur in Form von Plausibilität annähern können." However, they do not critically question the plausibility criterion on the basis of this insight.

understanding the Jesus movement as an alternative Jewish movement that sought to abolish kyriarchal domination and believed in the basic equality of all the children of G*d not only bespeaks antifeminist tendencies; it also bespeaks a lack of feminist self-affirmation on the part of wo/men scholars who subscribe to the positivist methods of the Third Quest, as Judith Plaskow has recognized:

> I read this book [*In Memory of Her*] excited and resisting every word. I made furious notes in the margins asking, "How do you know women participated? Isn't it a large assumption, indeed an *a priori* commitment?" Forced to sort out my feelings for an American Academy of Religion symposium on *In Memory of Her*, I realized that I found the book deeply disturbing because it thrusts women into an unaccustomed position of power. To take seriously the notion that religious history is the history of women and men imposes an enormous responsibility on women: It forces us to take on the intellectual task of rewriting all of history. . . . It does these things, moreover, without allowing us the luxury of nursing our anger and waiting for the patriarchs to create change, for it reminds us that we are part of a long line of women who were simultaneously victims of the tradition and historical agents struggling within and against it.[60]

If feminist self-affirmation is the *sine qua non* of writing history *otherwise*, it is not surprising that biblical women's studies have not always been able to resist the lure of malestream Historical-Jesus research and the reconstruction of early Christian origins in positivist terms. Hence, I suggest that the reductionist criterion of dissimilarity of the Second Quest or, better, exclusivity and the conservative criterion of plausibility of the Third Quest be replaced with the criterion of "possibility."

What is "thinkable " or "possible" historically must be adjudicated in terms of an emancipatory reconstructive model of early Christian beginnings and how it utilizes its source information and materials. Instead of asking if it is likely that wo/men shaped the Jesus traditions, one must ask if it is historically possible and thinkable that they did so. This shift requires scholars to prove that such a possibility did not exist at the time. Such an argument would presuppose that scholars have studied not only hegemonic historical formations but also the emancipatory elements in Greco-Roman and Jewish societies. In using the criterion of possibility,

---

[60] Judith Plaskow, "Critique and Transformation: A Jewish Feminist History," in *Lifecycles*, Vol. 2, ed. Deborah Orenstein and Jane Rachel Litman (Woodstock: Jewish Light Publishing House, 1997), 99.

one must, however, be careful not to answer it with reference to what is deemed "plausible" and "commonsense" truism.[61]

Such a change of theoretical framework from one that uncritically reinscribes "what is" to one that imagines "what is possible" makes it plausible to understand the Jesus traditions and early Christian beginnings as shaped by the agency and leadership of Jewish, Greco-Roman, Asian, African, free and enslaved, rich and poor, elite and marginal wo/men. Those who hold the opposite view—for instance, that slave wo/men or Jewish wo/men were not active shapers of early Christian life—would have to argue their point. A feminist reconstructive historical model of egalitarian possibility, I suggested with *In Memory of Her*, is able to place the beginnings of the Galilean prophetic-wisdom-*basileia* movement within a broader cultural-religious historical frame of reference that allows one to trace the tensions and struggles between emancipatory understandings and movements inspired by the radical democratic logic of equality, on the one hand, and the dominant kyriarchal structures of society and religion in antiquity, on the other.

A *possible* emancipatory reconstruction of early Christian beginnings as egalitarian does not mean that the extant early Christian sources do not also allow for a hegemonic kyriarchal reconstruction of the Jesus movements. The opposite is the case, since our sources are all written in grammatically androcentric/kyriocentric language that functions as generic language. It only means that one needs to show that a feminist egalitarian reconstruction is "possible," in terms of a critical reading of the extant sources with a hermeneutics of suspicion, and preferable in terms of the Christian identity construction that the writing of history engenders. In other words, scholars no longer can justify their reconstructive models in a positivist scientistic fashion but need to stand accountable for them and their political functions in light of the values and visions they promote for today.

As I noted in the introduction, Patricia Hill Collins has outlined three epistemological criteria for developing a critical self-reflexivity that could sustain emancipatory oppositional practices.[62] Adapting these criteria to Historical-Jesus study one would need to ask:

---

[61] This is the primary mode of arguing by Ekkehard and Wolfgang Stegemann, *The Jesus Movement: A Social History of Its First Century* (Minneapolis: Fortress Press, 1999), 361–409, when discussing wo/men's leadership in the Jesus movement.

[62] Hill Collins, *Fighting Words*, 398–99.

1. Does a reconstruction of the Historical-Jesus "speak truth to people about the reality of their lives" and the lives of wo/men in the first century? Who are the experts, what are the standards they used, and what counts as knowledge? Who decides and why do we accept or reject what the Jesus experts say?

2. What is the "stance toward freedom" in a particular source text as well as in a particular rendition of the Historical-Jesus? What are its visions of emancipation and the strategies of change it suggests? Does it encourage people to resist relations of domination, and can it engender social and religious change?

3. Does a particular Historical-Jesus reconstruction move people to struggle, or does it advocate the status quo? Does it provide an ethical foundation and framework for struggle that is grounded in notions of justice and authority? How effectively does it provide moral authority to the struggles for self-determination?

Obviously, such criteria are contrary to the scholarly ethos that comes to the fore in the dialogue between Crossan and Jesus with which he introduces his "little" Jesus book.

> "I have read your book, Dominic, and it is quite good. So now you are ready to live by my vision and to join me in my program?"
> "I don't think I have the courage, Jesus, but I did describe it quite well, didn't I, and the method was especially good, wasn't it?"
> "Thank you, Dominic, for not falsifying the message to suit your own incapacity. That at least is something."
> "Is it enough, Jesus?"
> "No, Dominic, it is not."[63]

This dialogue is at one and the same time self-congratulatory authorization and apologetic defense of "scholarly objectivity." Its rhetoric subtly assures readers that they will encounter in Crossan's work the "real" Jesus and at the same time may not draw any practical consequences from this encounter for their lives. Placed in a context of struggle, Crossan's revolutionary Historical-Jesus remains an idealized figure one cannot follow. As such an ideal projection, the Historical-Jesus does not disturb our contemporary status-quo assumptions. Scholarship remains safe.

---

[63] John Dominic Crossan, *Jesus: A Revolutionary Biography* (San Francisco: Harper-Collins, 1994), xiv.

A different understanding of the task of critical social theory as well as of Historical-Jesus studies comes to the fore in Patricia Hill Collins's statement of what she learned in writing her book which sums up her discussion of the critical criteria for evaluating scholarly discourses:

> In other words, the difference lies in distinguishing between theory as a dogma or closed system of ideas to be verified and tested, and theory as a story or narrative operating as an open system of ideas that can be retold and reformulated. How Bible stories are used illustrates this process: Everyone knows and shares the same story. However, the changing collectivity constructing such stories—new interpretations, listeners, tellers, and the context itself—changes the meaning of the story with each retelling. Moreover, congregations are moved to struggle by their moral, ethical principles. ... Writing *Fighting Words* has given me a better sense of not only how the wo/men of my block kept going but why they were able to do so. Certainly, their visionary pragmatism was shaped by a commitment to truth, a belief in freedom, a concern for justice, and other ethical ideals.[64]

There is no question that Hill Collins's theoretical work takes "revolutionary" praxis as its touchstone and ethical vision as its goal. Emancipatory Historical-Jesus scholarship cannot but follow her in striving for the contemporary significance of its theoretical and historical work. Such significance is negotiated not only historically but also theologically, as I will show in the next chapter.

[64] Hill Collins, *Fighting Words*, 200.

# 2

# JESUS MATTERS
## Historical and Theological Approaches

I N 1970 I HAD JUST FINISHED DOCTORAL STUDIES AND HAD BEGUN
teaching at Notre Dame University. One of the first lessons I received from
a senior colleague was this: Elisabeth, remember you are teaching here not
as a theologian but as a critical exegete and historian. Consequently, never
allow your students to ask what is the religious or theological significance
of biblical texts and interpretations for today. If you allow this question,
scholarship will founder on the slippery slope of relevance. I was puzzled
and disturbed by such counsel—to say the least—because as a student in
Germany I had not encountered such antitheological scientific positivism[1]
but rather had been reared in a hermeneutical-theological tradition. What
had been exciting for me in biblical studies was the experience that epistemological, hermeneutical, and theological questions were also cutting-
edge issues in biblical scholarship.

Most importantly, my teachers—who only recently had been freed from
the fetters of doctrinal censure—insisted on the significance of critical
scholarship for contemporary theology and theological education. Such a
hermeneutical approach is articulated by Helmut Koester in the first two
of the five theses regarding the theological importance of biblical research
for today with which he concludes his article entitled "The Structure of

---

[1] With the African-American feminist sociologist Patricia Hill Collins, whom I just cited
at the end of the last chapter, I understand scientific positivism as a discourse that is constituted by the assumption that "the tools of science," scientific methods, and logical rea-
soning are able "to represent reality and to discover universal truth." See Patricia Hill
Collins, *Fighting Words: Black Women and the Search for Justice* (Minneapolis: University of
Minnesota Press, 1998), 279.

Early Christian Beliefs." Whereas his first thesis insists that "it is our task to clarify the various positions of our time in order to be relevant to our contemporaries," his second thesis concludes: "it is the Jesus of history—and by no means an inaccessible object of speculation—which must be the center of our concern."[2]

By choosing the title "Jesus Matters," coined in analogy to my colleague Cornel West's book *Race Matters*, I want to signal that I have not heeded the advice given to me at the beginning of my scholarly career because, on the one hand, "Jesus matters," that is, is of importance (verb), and, on the other hand, "Jesus matters" (noun) must be a subject and substance of critical scholarly reflection. The scholarly discourse on Jesus must be critically investigated as rhetorical discourse because Jesus research—whether it understands itself in theological or purely cultural scientific terms—still shapes the self-understanding not only of Christians but also of most people in Western cultures.

For that reason, feminist scholars cannot busy themselves to produce the objectified historical data of Jesus knowledge. Rather they must investigate the scholarly discourses on Jesus and their rhetorical and sociopolitical function. For Western wo/men in general and Christian wo/men in particular—and I use the term here as I always do as inclusive of subordinated men[3]—have internalized very diverse images of Jesus. They often do not realize, however, that their understandings of Jesus have been produced by elite men's scholarly or devotional interpretations and reconstructions of Jesus.

Our understanding of Jesus and our view of the world generally correlate. In the early 1970s Francis Schüssler Fiorenza[4] and I team-taught an

[2] James M. Robinson and Helmut Koester, *Trajectories through Early Christianity* (Philadelphia: Fortress Press, 1971), 230.

[3] As already noted, since the term "woman/women" is often read as referring to white women only, my unorthodox writing of the term seeks to draw to the attention of readers that those kyriarchal structures that determine women's lives and status also impact the lives and status of men of subordinated races, classes, countries, and religions, albeit in different ways. Hence the spelling wo/men seeks to communicate that whenever I speak of wo/men I mean to include not only all women but also oppressed and marginalized men. The expression wo/men must therefore be understood as inclusive rather than as an exclusive, universalized gender term.

[4] For his work on christology, see his *Foundational Theology: Jesus and the Church* (New York: Crossroad, 1984); "Redemption Between Colonialism and Pluralism," in *Reconstructing Theology*, ed. Rebecca Chopp and Mark K. Taylor (Minneapolis: Fortress Press, 1994); and "The Jesus of Piety and the Historical Jesus," *Catholic Theological Society of America* 49 (1994) 90–99.

undergraduate course entitled "Images of Jesus."[5] In this course we discussed not only images of Jesus in scripture, spirituality, and theology but also in literature, art, and film. Not only religious but also Western cultural productions are permeated with images of Jesus. The Jesus rhetoric that wo/men have assimilated through sermons, Bible study, hymns, literature, pictures, and movies correlates the image of Jesus with hegemonic cultural and religious values of gender, race, class, and ethnicity. In other words, how wo/men see Jesus bespeaks the values both they and hegemonic culture consider important. What Marcus Borg observes for the theological also applies to the cultural ethos of wo/men:

> My point is the correlation between images of Jesus and images of the Christian life. Given this correlation, the question is not so much *whether* images of Jesus *ought* to have theological significance at the very practical immediate level of Christian understanding, devotion and piety. Our choice is to let that significance be largely unrecognized, unconscious, and unchallenged or to be conscious and intentional about that relationship. In short, because historical scholarship about Jesus affects our image of Jesus and thus our image of the Christian life, it matters.[6]

If Jesus discourses produced by biblical scholarship still affect people's religious and cultural life, critical feminist research cannot restrict itself to exegetical investigation and historical reconstruction. Rather it must also engage in a critical investigation of the Jesus discourses produced by scientific research and ask what they "do" to promote justice or what functions they have in situations of domination. It must seriously explore the contemporary presuppositions and frameworks of exegetical-historical and theological work and critically engage the "politics of interpretation" —to invoke a much used but little understood phrase—that governs Historical-Jesus research. Such a scrutiny of the politics of interpretation seeks to make visible the contesting interests and theoretical frameworks that determine the reconstructions of the Historical-Jesus and their implications for contemporary communities of faith as well as for the wider public of Western societies.

An ethics of interpretation contends that Bible, history, and theology are not just important for religious communities. Rather, as master narra-

---

[5] "Images of Jesus." In *Teaching Religion to Undergraduates: Some Approaches and Ideas from Teacher to Teacher*, ed. L. T. Johnson (New Haven: SHRE, 1973), 65–69.

[6] Marcus J. Borg, *Jesus in Contemporary Scholarship* (Valley Forge, Pa.: Trinity Press International, 1994), 194–95.

tives of Western cultures they are always already implicated in and collude with the production and maintenance of systems of knowledge that either foster exploitation and oppression or contribute to a praxis and vision of emancipation and justice. In short, an ethics of interpretation seeks to analyze the nexus between reconstructions of the Historical-Jesus and those theoretical, historical, cultural, and political conceptual frameworks that determine Jesus research. Hence biblical scholarship, I have argued elsewhere,[7] must learn to understand itself as a critical rhetorical practice which carefully explores and assesses its own impregnation with hegemonic knowledges and discursive frameworks that make "sense" of the world and produce what counts as "reality" or as "common sense."

A politics and ethics of meaning requires that any presentation of Jesus, scientific or otherwise, must own that it is a "reconstruction"[8]—and for various reasons I still prefer the category of reconstruction over the Derridean category of rewriting. It must do so in order to open up its historical models or reconstructive patterns to public reflection and critical inquiry. Such reconstructive models are to be scrutinized not only for how much they can account for our present textual and archaeological information on the historical Jesus and his sociopolitical contexts, but also for whether they are able to expose the rhetorical interests and theological functions of historical knowledge productions.

Even a truncated account of the politics and ethics of interpretation, as I have attempted to give here, indicates that such a critical inquiry into the politics of meaning that determines Historical-Jesus research would have to pay special attention to four areas:

1. It would need to explore whether and how Historical-Jesus research reinscribes in and through contemporary Jesus discourses the anti-Judaism inscribed in the gospels, and thereby perpetuates the language of

[7] See my books *But She Said: Feminist Practices of Biblical Interpretation* (Boston: Beacon Press, 1992); *Jesus: Miriam's Child, Sophia's Prophet: Critical Issues in Feminist Christology* (New York: Continuum, 1994); and *Rhetoric and Ethic: The Politics of Biblical Studies* (Minneapolis: Fortress Press, 1999).

[8] A lively discussion ensued after my presentation of the theses of this paper at a symposium honoring my colleague Helmut Koester as to the adequacy of the notion of reconstruction. Helmut Koester objected that in archaeological work the term communicates more the sense of restoration than construction. The following suggestions were made to replace the term: refigure, refashion, rewrite, recuperate, revision, rebuild, and remodel. However, I am not convinced that any of these suggestions expresses more adequately the intended meaning of historical reconstruction.

hate that has caused so much suffering for Jewish people, the people of Jesus, throughout the centuries.

2. It must pay attention to how much historical reconstructions of Jesus function either to undo or to continue the marginalization and erasure of women and other nonpersons from historical records and consciousness.

3. Since Historical-Jesus research has served the interests of Western colonization and hegemony, it must problematize the theologies or ideologies that have fostered colonization and domination and which are reinscribed through biblical texts and interpretive discourses on Jesus the Native.

4. In a situation of ever-increasing globalization of communication and concomitant impoverishment of peoples, an ethics of interpretation must scrutinize all reconstructive Jesus models as to how much they promote or undermine the politics of exclusivity, inferiority, prejudice, and dehumanization that determine cultural or religious identity formations.

In the following I will review and critically discuss two such Jesus discourses,[9] their sociopolitical locations, and their implications and rele-

[9] For a review and discussion of Jesus research, see, e.g., William M. Thompson, *The Jesus Debate: A Survey & Synthesis* (New York: Paulist Press, 1985); Marcus J. Borg, "Portraits of Jesus in Contemporary North American Scholarship," *Harvard Theological Review* 84, no. 1 (1991): 1–22; idem, *Jesus in Contemporary Scholarship* (Valley Forge, Pa.: Trinity Press International, 1994); James H. Charlesworth, "Annotated Bibliography," in *Jesus' Jewishness: Exploring the Place of Jesus within Early Judaism,* ed. Marcus J. Borg (New York: Crossroad/The American Interfaith Institute, 1991); John F. O'Grady, "The Present State of Christology," *Chicago Studies* 32, no. 1 (April 1993): 77–91; Werner G. Kümmel, "Jesusforschung seit 1981," *Theologische Rundschau N.F.* 53 (1988): 229–49; 54 (1989): 1–53; E. P. Sanders, "Jesus: His Religious 'Type,'" *Reflections* 87 (1992): 4–12; idem, *The Historical Figure of Jesus* (London: Allen Lane, 1993); Daniel Kosch, "Neue Jesusliteratur," *Bibel und Kirche* 48 (1993): 40–44; Ferdinand Hahn, "Umstrittenes Jesusbild?" *Münchener Theologische Zeitschrift* 44 (1993): 95–107; John T. Pawlikowski, "Reflections on the Brown-Crossan Debate," *Explorations* 10 (1996): 2-3; Seán Freyne, "The Historical Jesus and Archeology," and Geza Vermes, "Jesus, the Jew and His Religion," *Explorations* 10 (1996): 6–8; Horst Robert Balz, *Methodische Probleme der neutestamentlichen Christologie* (Wissenschaftliche Monographien zum Alten und Neuen Testament 25; Neukirchen-Vluyn: Neukirchener Verlag, 1967); Roy A. Eckhardt, *Reclaiming the Jesus of History: Christology Today* (Minneapolis: Fortress Press, 1992); Marinus de Jonge, *Christology in Context: The Earliest Christian Responses to Jesus* (Philadelphia: Westminster Press, 1988); Paula Fredriksen, *From Jesus to Christ: The Origins of the New Testament Images of Jesus* (New Haven: Yale University Press, 1988); Richard A. Horsley, *Jesus and the Spiral of Violence* (San Francisco: Harper & Row, 1989); John P. Meier, *A Marginal Jew: Rethinking the Historical Jesus,* 3 vols. (New York: Doubleday, 1991); Eugene M. Boring, *The Continuing Voice of Jesus: Christian Prophecy and the Gospel Tradition* (Louisville: Westminster/John Knox Press, 1991).

vance for Christian self-understanding and theology. Since it seems that Historical-Jesus research presently is stuck with the choice between either historical or theological positivism, I will sketch out crucial elements of an alternative reconstructive paradigm that understands history not so much in terms of "scientific proof" as in terms of memory. Throughout I will use feminist research, including my own, as a "telltale sign" for the politics of interpretation at work in historical Jesus discourses.

## THE POLITICS OF HISTORICAL-SCIENTIFIC
## JESUS RESEARCH

As we have seen in the last chapter, scientific historical liberal Jesus research understands Jesus as the exceptional individual, charismatic genius, and great hero. As Dieter Georgi has observed:

> This view that Jesus had been a genius of some sort became the dominant view in the late eighteenth, nineteenth, and twentieth centuries, not only in Germany but also in Western Europe and North America, among both Protestants and Catholics.[10]

Therefore it does not come as a surprise that despite its intention to the contrary, the Third Quest continues the reifying politics of meaning and methodological positivism of the First Quest.[11] In order to illustrate this point I will focus on Dominic Crossan, one of the most successful and sophisticated scholars of the Third Quest.[12] I focus on him partly because I agree with and admire much of his work. For instance, I could not agree more with the following statement:

> The Kingdom of G*d is in opposition to systemic injustice. The radical egalitarianism or ethical radicalism of Jesus was a profound rejection of the systemic evil and *structural* violence of his social situation, one of both patriarchal and imperial oppression.[13]

---

[10] Dieter Georgi, "The Interest in Life of Jesus Theology as a Paradigm for the Social History of Biblical Criticism," *Harvard Theological Review* 85, no. 1 (1992): 76.

[11] For a review and discussion of this "newest quest," see Marcus J. Borg, *Jesus in Contemporary Scholarship* (Valley Forge, Pa.: Trinity Press International, 1994).

[12] John Dominic Crossan, *The Historical Jesus: The Life of a Mediterranean Jewish Peasant* (New York: HarperCollins, 1991).

[13] John Dominic Crossan, "Responses and Reflections," in *Jesus and Faith: A Conversa-*

I equally concur with Crossan that the basic problem for Western Jesus scholarship to explore is the question of how a Jewish peasant revolutionary became the imperial Lord (*kyrios*), and all the historical and ethical implications that this change entails.

I also focus on Crossan because he has addressed most clearly the problem of method and of the relationship between historiography and theology in Jesus research. In considering his work I will focus on two issues: (1) the politics of scholarly discourses; and (2) the significance of Historical-Jesus studies for Christian faith and theology, which I will discuss in the next section.

At a conference hosted by DePaul University entitled "Jesus and Faith: Theologians in Conversation with the Work of John Dominic Crossan,"[14] Catherine Keller raised three important problems with respect to Crossan's work:

*First,* she queries why Crossan does not engage feminist scholarship. According to her one can find "virtually no engagement [and] virtually no dialogue with feminist sources" although "his text overflows with quotations."[15] Keller also observes that, although Crossan's work intersects with my own, "especially concerning the criteria of inclusive, communal and commensal mutuality" understood as radical equality, he does not engage it.

*Second,* Keller points out that, compared with the feminist work of Rita Nakashima Brock, Crossan's "Historical-Jesus" still remains caught up in the scientist liberal framework of the Old Quest, envisioning Jesus as the extraordinary heroic individual despite Crossan's expressed interest to the contrary. She argues that the

> events upon which Crossan focuses our attention seem to flow unilaterally from "Jesus' own extraordinary, if not ontologically unique, set of talents and projects. He is the one who models and generates mutuality" whereas according to Nakashima Brock "Jesus *learns from* and is *empowered by*" the women who risk relationship with him. . . . Hence she is able to "redeem" christology, wide rather than high or low, by relocating the christic reality in the relationships themselves.[16]

---

tion on the Work of John Dominic Crossan, Author of the Historical Jesus, ed. Jeffrey Carlson and Robert A. Ludwig (Maryknoll, N.Y.: Orbis Books, 1994), 154.

[14] For the conference proceedings, see *Jesus and Faith,* ed. Carlson and Ludwig.

[15] Catherine Keller, "The Jesus of History and the Feminism of Theology," in *Jesus and Faith,* ed. Carlson and Ludwig, 75.

[16] Ibid., 77.

*Third,* Keller directs attention to the importance of sociopolitical contextualization by sharing her experience of wo/men's struggles in El Sal-
vador. She also points out that, like most scholars, Crossan does not
critically reflect on how his own social location affects his scientific work
and determines his historical and theological reconstruction of Jesus.

In his response to Keller, Crossan openly confirms her first contention
that he did (and does) not take notice of feminist scholarship. He agrees
that in his work "there is virtually no dialogue with feminist sources." This
is not a neglect of feminist work, he contends, but it is the result of his
interests. His main concern is "programmatically to initiate a Third quest
for the Historical Jesus by ignoring the Second ('new' hermeneutical)
quest 'as an almost total failure.'" Crossan points out that he even ignored
Bultmann—an omission he promises to rectify, however.[17] Yet he seems to
feel that it is not necessary to correct his neglect of feminist scholarship.
Neither does his response to Keller or his popular book that appeared a
year after Keller's intervention engage the question of how much he has
learned from feminist historical and theological scholarship. Nor does he
refer to *In Memory of Her* although he ends his "big Jesus" book as well as
his "little" one with the headline "In Remembrance of Her,"[18] which seems
an unmistakable allusion to it. Instead he goes on to ask a string of rhetorical questions that divert blame from himself and direct it to his feminist
colleagues:

> But there is a special problem with "feminist sources" on the historical Jesus.
> Where are they? Why are so few women interested in that area of research?
> . . . Why are so few Christian feminists focusing on the historical Jesus or on
> questions of inventory, stratigraphy, and attestation, on, that is, the precise
> cartography of Christianity's *earliest* re-oppression of women?[19]

With these rhetorical questions Crossan not only seeks to absolve himself from studying feminist works but also in a sweeping gesture declares
all critical feminist Jesus scholarship as nonexistent because it has not
adopted Crossan's method. Despite his protestations to the contrary,
Crossan still seems to operate out of the liberal scientific paradigm of
Historical-Jesus research in which method is paramount. As a result, he is
not able to explore the differences and affinities between his own model of
historical reconstruction and my own feminist one. If he had done so he

---

[17] Crossan, "Responses and Reflections," 142–64, especially 151.
[18] John Dominic Crossan, *Jesus: A Revolutionary Biography* (San Francisco: Harper-
Collins, 1994), 190.
[19] Crossan, "Responses and Reflections," 151.

could have reflected on why his reconstructive model is so similar to mine although my work did not engage his rigorous method of stratigraphy and dating. He could have reflected on the striking parallels between his historical Jesus and the reconstructive model underlying *In Memory of Her*, or he could have reasoned why in other key points he disagrees with it.

Moreover, Crossan could have pointed to the methodological difference between his reconstruction of the historical Jesus and my own. For instance, whereas *In Memory of Her* focuses on the reconstruction of the Jesus movement in only one chapter belonging to a much broader reconstructive enterprise of Christian beginnings, his book is focused on distilling the historical individual, Jesus. Having done so, however, he seems to have come to realize that Jesus cannot be had without the Jesus movement, since his follow-up book addresses the earliest beginnings of Christianity.[20] Yet he thereby reinscribes the Lukan periodization of "Jesus" followed by the "early church." Such a periodization does not recognize that epistemologically Jesus can only be found in and through the memory and words of those who, like him, were part of the emancipatory *basileia* movement. This periodization scheme of first Jesus and then the church is reinscribed as a "fact" by modern Historical-Jesus studies.

It is not surprising therefore that Crossan seems unable or unwilling to grasp Keller's second question as to whether he avoided "the trap of heroic individualism." For Crossan it is Jesus who "models and generates mutuality," whereas for Rita Nakashima Brock, as Keller notes, it is "Jesus who *learns from and is empowered* by the women who risk relationship with him. He is, thus, dependent upon—and only thus truly part of—the mutuality he seeks."[21] Even after the conference, in his written response, Crossan replied glibly to this intervention that he had not read Nakashima Brock's book *Journeys by Heart*[22] but conjectured which texts she may have used to make her point. His response avoids a critical engagement with her understanding of mutuality and simply states his own by pointing to the mutuality of healing and eating which makes present the *basileia*

> on earth here and now in Lower Galilee. Anyone could do it, any time, any place. It was not present in Jesus alone, nor even in the interstices between

---

[20] John Dominic Crossan, *The Birth of Christianity: Discovering What Happened in the Years Immediately after the Execution of Jesus* (New York: HarperCollins, 1998).

[21] Keller, "Jesus of History," 77.

[22] Rita Nakashima Brock, *Journeys by Heart: A Christology of Erotic Power* (New York: Crossroad, 1988).

Jesus and his first followers, but in the interstices between the process of free healing and shared eating.[23]

Crossan's pragmatic understanding of mutuality comes close to my own, and I would agree that it is as profound as that of Nakashima Brock but it is conceptually quite different from hers. However, his response does not explore this difference in conceptualizing the Historical-Jesus either as the great individual or in terms of Christa-community. Nor does he address the problem raised: Given his own thesis of mutuality, why does he write a "biography" of Jesus and thereby still subscribe to a modern liberal understanding of Jesus, the great man and charismatic leader? Why does he write a biography rather than a profile of the social movement(s) of which Jesus was a part and which gathered and continued in his name?

It is obvious that Crossan cannot enter into any serious hermeneutical conversation with feminist work on this question because the persisting liberal understanding of Jesus the great man still determines his "third quest." If he had engaged with feminist work, he would be aware that feminist scholars, more than malestream scholars, have extensively problematized the liberal Quest's reinscription of anti-Judaism in the process of elaborating Jesus the exceptional man, charismatic leader, and superhuman hero. As I attempt to show in this book, such a reconstruction of Jesus the exceptional man and sole charismatic leader is not only an anti-Jewish but also an antidemocratic[24] and antifeminist construct.

To Keller's third challenge Crossan responds defensively and asks rhetorically:

> Catherine Keller notes that I never "perform any ritual of social location."
> ... But what exactly would an inaugural or even repeated admission of being a live, white, middle class, European, heterosexual male, scholar, etc., actually accomplish?[25]

He observes that "the more one multiplies such admissions, the more one trivializes any consensual ethical possibilities."[26] He bristles that to do justice to Keller's request would have meant to spend his time writing his autobiography rather than having written a "biography of Jesus." And he

---

[23] Crossan, "Responses and Reflections," 152.

[24] As a German living after the Holocaust I am suspicious of any personality cult that extols the charismatic "*Führer.*"

[25] Crossan, "Responses and Reflections," 149.

[26] Ibid., 150.

concludes with a common scholarly misunderstanding of the epistemo-logical demand for critical articulation of one's social location: "Confession replaces criticism and the public display of internal organs obviates the need for the public scrutiny of ethical decision."[27]

Thus Crossan's ironic rhetoric makes clear that he misunderstands the liberationist theological epistemological imperative to critically reflect on one's social location as a demand for autobiographical statement. Like many of my students, he reads in an individualistic confessional fashion and consequently is unable to investigate how his academic, "ekklesial," gender, race, and class location shape his scholarly investigations and rhetoric.

For instance, if Crossan would critically reflect on his privileged gender location, he could not so cavalierly dismiss the feminist challenge of Keller nor feminist work in biblical studies generally. If he would analyze his privileged gender, race, academic, and national location he would realize that it is part and parcel of the regime of domination and kyriarchal discourses of the academy either to dismiss *tout court* feminist or other subaltern work, or to appropriate and co-opt it while at the same time trivializing it. If Crossan would seriously reflect on his social location, he would recognize his collusion in producing and maintaining the silencing discourses and historical forgetfulness that make wo/men historically invisible and eradicate from memory feminist historical work. It is precisely this kind of inquiry that would open up the way to what he calls "consensual ethical possibilities."

## HISTORICAL-JESUS STUDIES AND CHRISTIAN THEOLOGY

I submit, however, that positivist Historical-Jesus studies cannot engage in such a critical inquiry because of their long-standing antagonistic relationship to theology. By theology I do not mean systematic or dogmatic theology, but the whole universe of religious thought, institutions, and disciplines. In the narrow sense theology means for me the systematic theoretical exploration of how we speak about G*d. Consequently, theology is the disciplined study of G*d discourses. In contrast to such an understanding of theology, biblical scholars tend to understand theology as normative and therefore restrict their work to historical investigation. Hence,

[27] Ibid., 151.

Jesus scholarship has sought to separate itself from an explicitly theological agenda. Whereas the rhetoric of the First Quest understood Jesus over and against the church, the No Quest period placed the kerygmatic Christ in the center, and the Second Quest sought to reintroduce the centrality of the historical Jesus into theology, the Third Quest seems to subscribe to a hermeneutical model of scientific description and theological application. First one reconstructs Jesus historically with scientific methods and without any theological agenda, and only then can one raise the question of theological significance. Marcus Borg summarizes his own and Crossan's position:

> To deny a theological agenda is not to claim a positivistic objectivity for either myself or Crossan; we are both aware of the subjectivity of the historian, the relativity and particularity of all vantage points, and the fact that unconscious factors (including theological ones) may shape our perception. But it is to say that the generative questions addressed to the texts have not been posed by the doctrinal claims of Christian theology.[28]

Borg argues, therefore, that one should abandon the expressions "Jesus of history" and "Christ of faith" and replace them with "pre-Easter" and "post-Easter" Jesus. This not only would establish a continuity between them but also would make clear that both must be subjected to historical inquiry. Moreover, he wants to replace the sharp dichotomy between the pre-Easter and the post-Easter Jesus with a "both and" "dialogical and dialectical relationship of the two rather than . . . a binary choice between two opposites."[29]

Crossan also seeks to overcome this dichotomy between historical Jesus and Christ of faith through a dialectical method. He states, on the one hand, that "Christian belief is (1) an act of faith (2) in the historical Jesus (3) as the manifestation of God."[30] On the other hand, he claims:

> I presume that there will always be divergent historical Jesuses, that there will always be divergent Christs built upon them, but I argue, above all, that the structure of Christianity will always be: *this is how we see Jesus*-then as Christ-now. Christianity must repeatedly, generation after generation, make its best historical judgment who Jesus was then, and on that basis, decide what that reconstruction means as Christ now.[31]

---

[28] Borg, *Jesus in Contemporary Scholarship,* 198 n. 13.
[29] Ibid., 195.
[30] Crossan, *Jesus: A Revolutionary Biography,* 200.
[31] Crossan, *Historical Jesus,* 423; idem, *Jesus: A Revolutionary Biography,* 200.

Crossan resolutely insists on the priority of the Historical-Jesus, although he acknowledges that this Jesus is a scholarly construct. However, if there are a multitude of historical Jesuses, how is one to make that "best historical judgment"? How is one to navigate between postmodern relativism and modern historical positivism? In which historical Jesus is one to believe? Although Crossan claims to be motivated neither by a present-day theological agenda nor by the nineteenth-century agenda of "dispassionate, objective historical study," his aim "to reconstruct the historical Jesus as accurately and honestly as possible,"[32] and to make him the object of faith, seems to be fueled by both agendas.

Unlike Crossan, John Meier does not think that faith should be built on the Historical-Jesus. He agrees with Martin Kähler and Rudolf Bultmann that the Historical-Jesus cannot be the object of faith. Since he is aware how context shapes scholarly understandings, he forthrightly states that his Catholic faith context will tempt him to read back into the past "the expanded universe of later church teachings." To avoid such a temptation he promises that he will "bracket" what he "holds by faith" and present only "what can be shown to be certain or probable by historical research and logical argumentation." He points to Thomas Aquinas for this distinction "between what we know by reason and what we affirm by faith."[33]

Meier states that the Historical-Jesus has no usefulness to people of faith since he cannot be the object and essence of faith.[34] He argues, however, that the Historical-Jesus is "an integral part of modern theology" because he "eludes all our neat theological programs" in at least four ways:

1. The Quest for the Historical-Jesus prevents a reduction of faith in Christ to a contentless cipher or timeless symbol and archetype.
2. It prevents the real humanity of Jesus from being swallowed up by docetism, mysticism, or orthodox exclusive stress on the divinity of Jesus.
3. It prevents the domestication of Jesus and his co-optation for bourgeois respectable Christianity.
4. It prevents a co-optation of the Historical-Jesus for programs of political revolution.

---

[32] Crossan, *Jesus: A Revolutionary Biography,* xiv; see also Crossan, "Responses and Reflections," 159.

[33] Meier, *Marginal Jew,* 1:6.

[34] Ibid., 198.

Meier concludes that,

> like good sociology, the historical Jesus subverts not just some ideologies but all ideologies. . . . Properly understood the historical Jesus is a bulwark against the reduction of Christian faith in general and Christology in particular to "relevant" ideology of any stripe. . . . hence, the historical Jesus remains a constant stimulus to theological renewal.[35]

But, again, *how* can the Historical-Jesus function as such an anti-ideological antidote if, as Meier himself observes, there are many different historical Jesuses: Is it "Jesus the violent revolutionary or Jesus the gay magician? Jesus the apocalyptic seer or Jesus the wisdom teacher unconcerned with eschatology?"[36] One could add here: Is it Jesus the marginal Jew or Jesus the revolutionary peasant, Jesus the Mediterranean Cynic or Jesus the millenarian prophet, and so on? How can the scholarly construct of the Historical-Jesus, which depends on theoretical frameworks and many individual judgments in light of them, subvert all ideologies if it is itself an ideological construct?

Despite protestations to the contrary, the Third Quest seems to remain caught up in scientific positivism insofar as it insists that scientific methods and tools can produce the reality and universal truth of the historical Jesus. While the scientific ethos of absolute objectivity and historical facticity is questioned by Crossan, Borg, Meier, and other scholars of the Third Quest, it is not critically investigated as to its rhetorical function in the discourses of the Third Quest to maintain the critical priority of Historical-Jesus research over canonical theology. Hence, both the priority of the historical approach in Jesus research and its corroborating scientific methodology are in question.

### JESUS RESEARCH: THEOLOGY WITHOUT HISTORY?

The most publicized challenge to the Historical-Jesus of the Third Quest has come from Luke Timothy Johnson, who, like Meier and Crossan, is a Roman Catholic. Hence he may serve here as the representative of the second major approach in Jesus research. In my view this approach seeks to replace historical scientific with theological fideist positivism. As the title

---

[35] Ibid., 200.
[36] Ibid., 198.

of Johnson's book *The Real Jesus: The Misguided Quest for the Historical Jesus and the Truth of the Traditional Gospels*[37] announces, he sets out to challenge the presuppositions that govern Jesus research and to argue that the "real" Jesus is the Jesus of the canonical gospels and the Christian creed.

Although he comes from a more conservative theological perspective, Johnson seems to agree with Georgi's negative assessment of the modern scholarly quest for the Historical-Jesus, albeit on different grounds. His polemic is directed not so much against the bourgeois character of Jesus scholarship as against the methods and practices of the Newest Quest for the Historical-Jesus, which emerged in the early 1980s. Johnson focuses in particular on the practices of the well-publicized Jesus Seminar under the leadership of Robert Funk and Dominic Crossan, which has resorted to polling practices derived from consumer research and political campaigns in order to distill the authentic sayings of the Historical-Jesus from the canonical and noncanonical gospel texts.[38]

However, Johnson does not point out that this Newest Quest for the Jesus of history has exploded during the resurgence of the political right and the revival of religious fundamentalism. Not only the Jesus Seminar but also its more conservative counterpart, the American Interfaith Institute under the leadership of James Charlesworth,[39] has contributed to the restoration of historical positivism that corresponds to political conservatism. Their emphasis on the *realia* of history serves to promote scientific fundamentalism since they generally do not acknowledge that historians select and interpret archaeological artifacts and textual evidence as well as incorporate them into a scientific model and narrative framework of meaning.

Johnson recognizes this when he points out again and again that the reconstructive attempts of modern Jesus research, in particular those of Borg, Crossan, and Mack—whose politics of meaning is more progressive —replace the theological frameworks of the gospels with modern frames of meaning and models of historical reconstruction. He therefore maintains that historical research has only a very limited function in the formation of Christian identity and community because it can achieve only probable but not definitive knowledge. Instead of utilizing a reductionis-

---

[37] Luke T. Johnson, *The Real Jesus: The Misguided Quest for the Historical Jesus and the Truth of the Traditional Gospels* (San Francisco: Harper & Row, 1996).

[38] For a defense of the Jesus Seminar, see Robert W. Funk, *Honest to Jesus: Jesus for a New Millennium* (San Francisco: HarperCollins 1996).

[39] See my discussion of its practices in *Jesus: Miriam's Child, Sophia's Prophet*, 67–70.

tic method for distilling the figure of the Historical-Jesus from his narrative context, Johnson argues, biblical scholars should engage the accounts of the canonical gospels that together with other canonical writings have a high degree of historical probability.

The "real" Jesus is not the reconstructed Jesus of critical scholarship, Johnson insists, but the resurrected Lord who confronts persons in the pages of the Christian Testament.[40] The four gospels together with Paul's letters and other Christian Testament writings yield some historical information, but this is neither their purpose nor their power. Rather, they display as a pattern of meaning the pattern of his existence, which can find expression in new narratives and in the life of others. This pattern is one of "obedience and service": "It expresses the meaning of Jesus' ministry in terms of its ending: Jesus is the suffering servant whose death is a radical act of obedience toward God and an expression of loving care for his followers."[41] It is obvious that the articulation of this "pattern" is as much determined by the modern neo-orthodox stress on radical obedience[42] as by a reading of Christian Testament writings. While Johnson criticizes other Jesus scholars for substituting a modern frame of meaning for that of the gospels, he himself does the same by reducing the narrative elaborations and contradictions of the gospels to an essentialist pattern that he formulates on neo-orthodox grounds.

Nevertheless, to deny the normativity of historical reconstructions does not mean abandoning the critical function of biblical scholarship, because, as Johnson observes, "the texts of the NT are open to criticism on other than historical fronts. They can be challenged morally, religiously, and theologically for their adequacy, consistency, and cogency."[43] For instance, if texts support a society in which wo/men are oppressed, these texts should be criticized on theological grounds, not on grounds of an alternative historical reconstruction because such a historical reconstruction achieves only probability but not normativity.

While I agree with Johnson's point that critical scholarship must engage in ideological, ethical, and theological criticism, I would not advocate aban-

---

[40] I use Christian Testament rather than New Testament and Hebrew Bible rather than Old Testament in order to avoid Christian supersessionism. Both Hebrew Bible and Christian Testament (CT) constitute the Christian Bible or Christian scriptures.

[41] Johnson, *Real Jesus,* 165–66.

[42] See, e.g., Cynthia Kittredge, *Community and Authority: The Rhetoric of Obedience in the Pauline Tradition* (Harvard Theological Studies 45; Harrisburg, Pa.: Trinity Press International, 1998).

[43] Johnson, *Real Jesus,* 175.

doning historical criticism as constitutive for Christian self-understanding. Contemporary theology, ethics, and culture are always already shaped by understandings of the past. Moreover, it must not be overlooked that Johnson's essentialist normative pattern of meaning is equally a historical reconstructive account that cannot simply be termed canonical. This method of distilling an underlying pattern or deep structure from four very different literary accounts, which I am describing as essentialist, follows the logic of identity with its drive to a unity that abolishes difference. Although Johnson tries to distance himself from the method of Tatian's *Diatessaron* or Augustine's *Gospel Harmony*, he nevertheless does not escape this essentialist drive to uniformity.

The neoconservative interests of Johnson's work and frame of meaning come to the fore not only in his rejection of the noncanonical gospels as equal sources but also in statements such as the following which permeate the rhetoric of the book:

> Most of all we need to understand the primary task of theology not to be the reform of the world's social structures, nor the ideological critique of the church as institution, nor the discovery of what is false or distorting in religious behavior, but the discernment and articulation of the work of the living God.[44]

While one cannot quibble with such a statement at first glance, at second glance one needs to point out that to speak about G*d as living and life-giving, theology cannot but engage in social, ideological, ecclesiastical, and religious critique. It cannot simply adopt the theological frameworks of the canonical gospels, because to do so would reinscribe not only their anti-Jewish reframing of the memory of Jesus but also their kyriocentric perspective, which focuses both on Jesus the divine man, who is seen no longer as a member of an egalitarian community but as "G*d striding over the earth" (Käsemann), and on Jesus the charismatic leader, who as an integrated member of his Mediterranean society gathered around him a fellowship of male itinerants. To acknowledge this kyriocentric perspective of the gospels as normative would mean to endorse Christian anti-Judaism and the marginalization of Christian wo/men.

*To sum up my argument:* Present Jesus research appears to founder either on the Scylla of liberal-bourgeois Jesus research focused on Jesus the charismatic leader, or on the Charybdis of canonical-orthodox Jesus the-

---

[44] Ibid., 170.

ology reinscribing the kyriocentric discourses of empire. The proliferation of Jesus books for popular consumption by malestream scholarship seems to have the same cultural and religious function as literalist Jesus fundamentalism. Fundamentalist as well as neo-orthodox doctrinal readings seek to "fix" the pluriform expressions of Christian scriptures and traditions, the variegated texts and ambiguous metaphors of Jesus in order either to consolidate them into a discourse of definite, one-to-one meaning or to reduce them into one, essentialist pattern of meaning. Jesus books by Christian Historical-Jesus scholars in turn tend to reassert the importance of historical-critical work rather than of theology and often do so in the guise of scientific positivism.

Thus, the proliferation of "new" scholarly and popular Jesus books does not undermine and undo the fundamentalist desire for a reliable account of the historical Jesus or for religious certainty about the meaning of one's life—a desire engulfed by a sea of ever-changing cultural relativity. Rather than corroborate this desire for certain truth and charismatic authority, historical and theological Jesus scholarship must redirect it into a desire for justice and the well-being of all. Hence, critical feminist scholarship cannot abandon the task of historical and theological meaning-making about Jesus. Rather, it insists that any presentation of Jesus—scientific or otherwise—must own that it is a "re-construction" and discursive formation. Hence, it must open up both its historical and theological models or patterns of Jesus research to critical inquiry and public reflection.

From a critical feminist liberationist perspective, neither the "liberal quest for the historical Jesus" nor the neo-orthodox advocacy of canonical essentialism provides a satisfactory frame of interpretation. I have argued therefore that a feminist historical and theological reconstruction of Jesus must adopt neither the liberal reconstructive framework of Jesus the heroic individual, which isolates him from his people or his followers. Nor may it adopt the neo-orthodox apologetic politics of canonical normativity. Rather, such a feminist reconstruction must adopt both a sociopolitical frame of conflict and struggle and a theological-inclusive frame of radical equality and well-being as its reconstructive framework of interpretation. This requires a shift in research paradigms.

### JESUS RESEARCH AS A CRITICAL RHETORICAL PRACTICE

Rather than understand itself either as a scientific-historical or a normative-theological practice, I argue, Jesus research must be reconceptualized as a critical rhetorical practice and process that encompass both historical reconstruction and ethical or theological assessment and evaluation. Rhetorical inquiry always asks, Who is telling the (his)story, why and for what purposes is the (his)story told, and to whom is it addressed? What kind of experiences, emotions, values, and visions imbue a rhetorical reinscription of the Jesus story? Does this scientific telling of the Jesus story reinforce relations of domination or does it subvert them?

To approach an answer to these questions one needs to foster a critical reflexivity that would enable the discipline of biblical studies to intervene in and to contribute to the readings and use of the Jesus story in the public discourses of society and church.[45] For instance, as a public discourse Jesus studies would have to

- explicitly reflect on the sociopolitical religious locations and ideological functions of Jesus discourses
- understand Jesus discourses as inscriptions of struggle and reconstruct them as public debates of the *ekklēsia*
- mark the languages of hate and the death-dealing ideologies inscribed in canonical, extracanonical, and postcanonical Jesus interpretations
- identify the visions and values ascribed to Jesus that would contribute to a radical democratic understanding of society and religion
- explore cultural practices such as film, music, or art and their use of the Bible which produce the public image of Jesus[46]
- foster an understanding of biblical authority that allows for the questioning of Jesus discourses and Jesus images in a critical practice of the discernment of the Spirit
- create public discourses and debates that could intervene in the Jesus discourses of the religious Right and other antidemocratic groups
- refashion Jesus research and its communicative practices such as education, preaching, or cultural mediations in such a way that it engenders Jesus scholars who are critical public intellectuals

Such a change in the ethos and praxis of Jesus research also would engender a change in the self-understanding of the Jesus scholar. In order to become a critical transformative intellectual[47] rather than just a profes-

---

[45] Ronald F. Thiemann, *Religion in Public Life: A Dilemma for Democracy* (Washington, D.C.: Georgetown University Press, 1996).

[46] For the use of the Bible in film, see the fascinating work of Adele Reinhartz, Alice Bach, and Cheryl Exum.

[47] Stanley Aronowitz and Henry Giroux argue that critical pedagogies require and con-

sionalized one,[48] I contend, s/he must reclaim the public space of the *ekklēsia* as the arena of historical, theological, and cultural Jesus studies. Since *ekklēsia* is not primarily a religious but a political term,[49] such a change would socially locate Jesus scholarship neither in the academy nor in the church but in the public sphere of the *polis* (the political community) and would transform it into a critical discourse that seeks to further the well-being of all the inhabitants of the *cosmopolis* today.

Such a redefinition of the rhetoric and ethos of Jesus studies has as its goal a critical cosmopolitan culture of equality. It can build rhetorically on the ancient Greek democratic notions of *polis* (city-state) and *ekklēsia* (democratic assembly) but would need to change them from signifying exclusion and privilege[50] to signifying radical democratic equality. If biblical studies were positioned in the space of the *ekklēsia*, redefined in egalitarian inclusive terms, they could speak both to the publics of the church, synagogue, or mosque and to the civic publics of society at large. Feminist theory and theology are an indispensable resource, I submit, for achieving such a transformation of biblical studies.

To understand Jesus research as a critical practice of *re-membering*,[51] as I have suggested, rather than as a quest for certainties, engenders a shift from a rhetoric of scientific or theological positivism that seeks to produce scientific certainty and theological normativity to one that aims at critical retrieval and articulation of *memory*. Memory and *re-membering* as a reconstructive frame of meaning do not require one to construe a dualistic opposition between history and theology, objectivity and interestedness, Jesus and Judaism, Jesus the exceptional individual and Jesus shaped by his community; between the pre-Easter and the post-Easter Jesus, the historical Jesus and the kerygmatic Christ. If the memory of Jesus' suffering and resurrection, understood as an instance of unjust human suffering

---

struct "transformative intellectuals" who "can emerge from and work with any number of groups, other than and including the working class, that advance emancipatory traditions and cultures within and without alternative public spheres" (*Education under Siege* [South Hadley, Mass.: Bergin, 1985], 45).

[48] William Dean argues that scholars in religion must become public intellectuals (*The Religious Critic in American Culture* [Albany: State University of New York Press, 1994], xiv). He understands the religious critic as analogous to the social critic and the culture critic.

[49] K. L. Schmidt, "*ekklēsia*," in *Theological Dictionary of the New Testament*, ed. Gerhard Kittel (Grand Rapids: Eerdmans, 1964), 3:514–16.

[50] See Page duBois, *Torture and Truth* (New York: Routledge, 1990).

[51] I owe this expression and its conceptualization to the work of Mary Daly.

and survival, is at the heart and center of Christian memory, then the critical ethical and theological line must be drawn between injustice and justice, between the world of domination and a world of freedom and well-being.

One might object that historical and theological reconstructions of Jesus that are conceptualized as rhetorical practices of memory and remembering function as "myth," that is, as stories of "pristine" beginnings for contemporary subaltern wo/men, which again place Jesus the great individual at the center of attention. However, such an objection overlooks the different power relations that determine hegemonic and critical feminist interests in Jesus research. It also neglects that the expressed interest of a model of historical and theological reconstruction understood in terms of memory is not the same as neo-orthodox canonical apologetic interpretation or the liberal quest for the historical Jesus, the "great heroic individual." It is not the same because its rhetoric is not that of scientific positivism.

If history always serves to foster cultural or religious identity formation, then any *historical* reconstruction—be it positivist or ideology-critical—participates in "myth-making." In an article entitled "History and Rhetoric," Paul Ricoeur has underscored this aspect of historical understanding. He argues that historical interpretation is a "historical activity" which has a "complex relation to the people of the past who themselves 'made history.'" History, according to Ricoeur, is a mode of knowledge "in which the subject and object belong together"[52] in a temporal and practical field. Historical interpretation and historiography are possible not only because of a single "tempo-spatial framework" but also because of

a single field of praxis, evidenced by the historian's dependence on the "making of real historical actors" for his [sic] own "history making." Before presenting themselves as master craftsmen [sic] of stories made out of the past, historians must first stand as heirs of the past. . . . Before even forming the idea of re-presenting the past, we are in debt to the men and women of the past who contributed to making us what we are. Before we can represent the past we must live as beings affected by the past.[53]

[52] Paul Ricoeur, "History and Rhetoric," *Diogenes* 168 (1994): 22. This is overlooked if one creates a dichotomy between those who construe "a Jesus who is just like one of us" and a Jesus "who does not fit our categories." Any historical knowledge is attained in and through our socially conditioned categories and lenses; for example, eschatology is a modern concept. The question is not whether but which categories one privileges.

[53] Ibid., 23.

To my mind the question is not whether critical feminists or cultural critics should participate in such a rhetorical "history making" but rather how they do it and to what ends. Awareness of the politics of interpretation must not lead either to a reassertion of historical and theological positivism or to theological dogmatism.

In his response to John Kloppenborg's review article on Q and Historical-Jesus research,[54] Helmut Koester also has taken up the category of memory but in a quite different vein. He asks:

> How did Jesus' followers preserve the memory of this proclamation? It is useful to return to the insights of Johann Gottfried Herder, which have been so deplorably neglected in two centuries of life-of-Jesus scholarship. The most immediate memory of history, Herder claimed, has nothing to do with accurately recording what happened; rather, memory is immediately recast (or "inscribed," or transformed) into hymn, song, story, myth, legend, and celebration.[55]

Yet whereas Koester seeks to explicate his conceptualization of memory with reference to Herder, my own understanding of memory is indebted to critical social theory and political theology. The feminist sociologist Patricia Hill Collins defines such a critical social theory as:

> [t]heorizing about the social in defense of economic and social [religious] justice. Stated differently, critical social theory encompasses bodies of knowledge and sets of institutional practices that actively grapple with the central questions facing groups of people differently placed in specific political, social, and [religious-cultural] historic contexts characterized by injustice. What makes critical social theory "critical" is its commitment to justice, for one's own group and/or for other groups.[56]

Consequently, I have tended to place critical practices, systemic structures, and the agency of wo/men rather than religious rituals and church assemblies in the center of historical imagination, whereas in line with form criticism and kerygmatic theology, Koester's work underscores the "word," that is, the sayings and proclamation of Jesus. He conceptualizes memory and its transmission in ritualistic religious terms rather than as rhetorical practices of re-membering. Such differences in theoretical

---

[54] John S. Kloppenborg, "The Sayings Gospel of Q and the Quest for the Historical Jesus," *Harvard Theological Review* 89, no. 4 (1996): 307–44.

[55] Ibid., 248.

[56] Patricia Hill Collins, *Fighting Words: Black Women and the Search for Justice* (Minneapolis: University of Minnesota Press, 1998), 276.

framework must be negotiated, therefore, on the level of reconstructive model rather than adjudicated in terms of "truth" or "data," because "sources" and "data" will receive a different meaning if one's reconstructive model is inspired by bourgeois liberalism rather than canonical essentialism, by Benjamin rather than Herder.

Such a change of theoretical framework or hermeneutical "binoculars" makes it possible to understand Jesus and early Christian beginnings as rhetorically shaped and re-membered by Jewish, Greco-Roman, Asian, African, free and enslaved, rich and poor, elite and marginal wo/men. Those who hold the opposite view that, for instance, slave women were not active shapers of early Christian life, would have to argue their point. If one shifts from the frame of reference that centers on Jesus as exceptional charismatic man and hero or as "G*d striding over the earth" to that of memory in a movement of equals, one no longer can hold that the Jesus traditions were not shaped by wo/men's work of re-membering. Rather than take rhetorical texts and sources at face value, one must unravel their politics of meaning.

In addition, a rhetorical reconstructive model of emancipatory struggle understands the historical Jesus and the movement that has kept alive his memory not over and against Judaism but over and against kyriarchal structures of domination in antiquity. It is able to place the beginnings of the Galilean prophetic-wisdom-*basileia* movement named after Jesus within a broader universalizing historical frame of reference. This frame allows one to trace the tensions and struggles between emancipatory understandings and movements inspired by the democratic logic of equality, on the one hand, and the dominant kyriarchal structures of society and religion in antiquity, on the other. Ancient movements of emancipatory struggles against kyriarchal relations of exploitation do not begin with the Jesus movement. Rather they have a long history in Greek, Roman, Asian, and Jewish cultures.

Nonetheless, it is important to see that such a rhetorical reconstructive model in the horizon of memory that does not subscribe to historical or theological positivism requires a different understanding of method and criteria. Underlying such a model of rhetorical reconstruction as memory, which I have elaborated elsewhere in more detail,[57] are two primary theoretical assumptions.

*First*, a rhetorical-political model of historical reconstructive memory

---

[57] See my book *Rhetoric and Ethic.*

understands its *methodological approach* as different from either liberal or neo-orthodox Jesus research in the following points:

1. It does not place Jesus the great individual charismatic leader at the center of attention, nor does it understand language and text either as window to the world or as reflective of reality. Instead it conceives of them as rhetorical-constructive. It does not take sources, be they textual or material, as "data" but understands them as perspectival interpretations and retellings. What we see depends on where we stand. Historical objectivity can be approximated only in and through a careful rhetorical analysis of our own social location as well as that of the ancient authors.

2. Historical-Jesus reconstructions can claim only probability and possibility but not normativity and plausibility. Jesus scholars must reason out why their own reconstructive proposals are more adequate to the sources and more probable than alternative scholarly discourses. However, they may not adopt the criterion of plausibility because what is considered plausible depends on what is considered "common sense," which in kyriarchal societies is always shaped by relations of domination. Hence, what is considered probable in light of other Jesus research must be complemented by the criterion of possibility.

3. An ethics of interpretation must carefully spell out the criteria with which it adjudicates different texts, sources, and interpretations. Such criteria are rules or norms that are applied to Jesus discourses in order to arrive at a judgment. I concur with Meier and Johnson that Jesus-research can never claim normativity on historical grounds but only on strictly theo-ethical grounds.

4. However, I also agree with Crossan that such theo-ethical normativity must always be historically located and adjudicated in terms of an ethics of interpretation. If—as Christians believe—G*d has become present and visible in Jesus of Nazareth, if Jesus' human life and death are a manifestation of the Divine, then it is important not only to reconstruct the historical Jesus but to do so in many different possible ways in order to assess what kind of G*d has been revealed in and through Jesus.

*Second,* a critical rhetorical-political model of historical reconstruction is not interested in proving the facticity or normativity of Jesus and his popular and scholarly reinscriptions but in arguing the historical possibility of the reconstructions such a model engenders. To that end it identifies scholarly agreements regarding central historical information in order to use them as touchstones for the probability of its reconstruction. I want to single out four topoi as crucial for my own critical reconstructive proposal. Whether these four historical touchstones, which modify the criteria of authenticity, are accepted or not depends on the politics of interpretation that governs Historical-Jesus research:

1. Early Christian writings, non-Christian contemporary references, and modern scholarship all agree that Jesus was a Galilean Jew. Hence he must be seen not in contrast to but as a part of the variegated Judaism of his time. The criterion of dissimilarity needs to be replaced with that of *contextuality*. The question becomes then not whether but what kind of Judaism Jesus belonged to or what kind of Mediterranean prophet he was.

2. The criterion of contextuality must be supplemented by that of *distinctiveness*. If asked what, then, is distinctive about Jesus which can be used as a historical point that differentiates him from his contemporaries, I would argue that Jesus is historically distinct from many of his companions in the movement and from his Jewish compatriots because of his execution. In that aspect he is different but not unique, since many people suffered the excruciating death by crucifixion at the hand of the Romans. This historical event of the brutal violent fate of Jesus and his crucifixion as "king of the Jews"[58] is to be seen as the most important generative rhetorical problem that called forth interpretation.

3. Hence, our source materials must be explored as to whether they try to make sense out of this historical "fact" or whether they espouse a pre-crucifixion perspective. Texts that displace this conflict engendered by Jesus' execution from Rome onto Judaism must have been articulated after Jesus' violent death. Such a criterion of *conflict* modifies the criterion of multiple attestation. Scholars generally agree that Jesus preached the *basileia tou theou*, a proclamation that was sociopolitical rather than individualistic-spiritual. We generally are no longer able to appreciate the critical-political impact of this central proclamation, although Jesus hearers could not but think of the Roman empire when they encountered the expression *basileia*.

The *basileia* that is the *commonweal* of G*d was a *tensive* religious sym-

---

[58] See also Paula Fredriksen, *Jesus of Nazareth, King of the Jews: A Jewish Life and the Emergence of Christianity* (New York: Alfred A. Knopf, 1999), 8f. However, she understands the crucifixion of Jesus as "the single most solid fact" rather than as the most difficult problem faced by early Christian meaning-making.

bol[59] of ancestral range proclaiming G*d's power of creation and salvation. It lived from the tension between its already incipient reality in the miracles and inclusive discipleship community and its alternative utopian vision. It was also a political symbol that appealed to the oppositional imagination of people victimized by the imperial system.[60] Texts and sources must therefore be read and adjudicated in terms of *this religious-political vision of G*d's different world.*

4. Scholars generally agree that poor and despised, ill and possessed people, the outcasts and prostitutes, the tax collectors and sinners—that is, all those marginal in his society—gathered around Jesus. Hence, the criterion of dissimilarity should be replaced with that of *inclusivity and equality*. Jesus was shaped by the radical egalitarian vision and commensality of the *basileia* movement as much as he shaped it.

*In conclusion:* I have argued here that Historical-Jesus research is best understood as a critical practice and process of memory which attempts again and again to re-vision on historical-critical grounds our knowledge about Jesus and the discipleship community that carries Jesus Christ's name. It does so in order to be able on theological grounds to critically judge Christian historical-political-religious identity formations and their rhetorical-theological legitimizations. The hermeneutical interest in theological inclusivity, pluriformity, and ecclesiality is helpful for an emancipatory historical-theological re-vision of Jesus and early Christian beginnings because it critically indicts sociopolitical, cultural, and religious structures of alienation and domination. As I will argue in the next chapter, Historical-Jesus discourses that claim to be scientific must therefore adopt a critical social theory and hermeneutics of interpretation.

[59] Norman Perrin, *Jesus and the Language of the Kingdom: Symbol and Metaphor in New Testament Interpretation* (Philadelphia: Fortress Press, 1976).

[60] For such an emphasis, see also Helmut Koester, "Jesus the Victim," *Journal of Biblical Literature* 111, no. 1 (1992): 14–15, although his polemical emphasis on eschatology seems to depoliticize the *basileia* proclamation. Hence his n. 15, where he reduces my overall proposal to one key element, the understanding of Jesus as prophet and messenger of Sophia.

# IN SEARCH OF THE "REAL" JESUS

## The Social-Scientific Quest

IN THIS CHAPTER I AM AGAIN NOT SO MUCH INTERESTED IN SKETCH-ing out a feminist social-scientific reconstruction of the Historical-Jesus; nor am I interested in discussing here the social situation of "Jesus and wo/men." Rather, as in previous chapters I am concerned with the "politics of meaning" that governs social-scientific Historical-Jesus research. I focus here on a politics of meaning in order to investigate the social-scientific narratives about the Historical-Jesus as discourse and the theoretical, social, cultural, and political frameworks that determine both malestream and feminist Jesus interpretations. I do so again by confronting malestream social-scientific reconstructions of the social world of the Historical-Jesus with feminist social-scientific theoretical concerns regarding such knowledge production.

### FEMINIST AND SOCIAL-SCIENTIFIC JESUS RESEARCH

Feminist and social-scientific biblical scholarship have several things in common: They are interested in the social world, not in dogmatic state-ments; they are both interdisciplinary in their conception, and they both are still considered by many to be marginal. Hence, one would expect that both areas of study would work closely together since neither seeks to understand Jesus in confessional theological terms but rather to compre-hend the social worlds and cultures of antiquity in which Jesus and the early Christian movements lived. However, such a collaboration between social-scientific and critical-feminist studies has for the most part not taken place. While feminist scholars use social-scientific research, social-scientific Jesus research for the most part does not bother to study critical feminist or postcolonialist works. This noncollaboration and the neglect of feminist scholarship by social-scientific studies, I suggest, are due not so much to their different methods as to their different scientific ethos and hermeneutical goals.

It is generally assumed that "woman" or "gender" is not only the research object but also the socioanalytic category of feminist studies. However, in contrast to wo/men's studies or gender studies, critical feminist studies do not simply take "woman" or "gender" as their object of inquiry. Rather they utilize a social-scientific method of analysis and critical social theory, which can investigate and comprehend the sociopolitical structures of domination and oppression that have determined wo/men's lives in antiquity and still do so today. Both social-scientific and feminist Historical-Jesus studies therefore are in need of a critical social analytic, which is crucial for social-scientific Historical-Jesus studies.

Whereas feminist biblical research utilizes as a key analytic method ideological criticism,[1] social-scientific biblical research insists on its "scientific socio-rational"[2] descriptive character. Hence it distances itself from "feminism, deconstruction, fundamentalism, and hermeneutic" as "romantic."[3] However, whereas deconstruction and hermeneutics have made considerable inroads into biblical studies, feminist scholarship is still widely seen as "unscientific" or it is not noticed at all, although it has greatly contributed to the knowledge about and the reconstruction of the social worlds of early Christianity. If feminist research is mentioned at all, it is suspected of being ideological. Either it is maintained that feminist scholarship is not "scientific," that is, value-neutral and objective, or it is argued that it does not say anything new that has not been said better already by malestream scholarship.

Since in the first chapters I have critically investigated malestream Historical-Jesus discourses about "Jesus and women,"[4] I want to take the

---

[1] For a succinct introduction to ideological biblical criticism, see The Bible and Culture Collective, *The Postmodern Bible* (New Haven: Yale University Press, 1995).

[2] Bruce Malina, "Rhetorical Criticism and Social-Scientific Criticism: Why Won't Romanticism Leave Us Alone?" in *Rhetoric, Scripture & Theology: Essays from the 1994 Pretoria Conference,* ed. Stanley E. Porter and Thomas H. Olbricht (Sheffield: Sheffield University Press, 1996), 72.

[3] Ibid., 96.

[4] See also my book *Jesus: Miriam's Child, Sophia's Prophet: Critical Issues in Feminist Christology* (New York: Continuum, 1994).

opportunity here to raise and place at the center of attention critical feminist questions with regard to the methodology and epistemology of social-scientific Jesus research. Insofar as feminist studies utilize a "hermeneutics of suspicion" as an ideology-critical tool of investigation, they insist on a critical methodological discussion and scrutiny of the presuppositions, frameworks, and functions of social-scientific Jesus research. All critical inquiry that deserves to be called scientific has to start with a critical discussion of methodology before it is able to turn to a social-historical reconstruction of the Jesus movement.

One must first clarify, for instance, which scientific concepts, frameworks of thought, or social models are reified as "facts" and "data" in historical social-scientific Jesus studies. One also must ask whether and how historical and social-scientific Jesus research consciously or unwittingly perpetuates ideologies of domination and thereby reifies structures of oppression. Only after such an ideology-critical metareflection and hermeneutic conscientization has taken place is Jesus research able to turn to the reconstruction of the Jesus movement from the perspective of multiply oppressed wo/men in the first century C.E.

In short, critical feminist studies insist that as critical theoretical and historical practices Historical-Jesus studies must become conscious of their permeation with hegemonic knowledges and interests of domination. If they want to be scientific they must critically analyze the discursive frameworks and heuristic models they use to explain the world and thereby produce what comes to be known as "reality" or "common sense." They must make visible the competing ideological and economic interests and theological frameworks that determine the development and the results of their research.

Since social-scientific Historical-Jesus studies pride themselves on being more scientific than other approaches because they engage in interdisciplinary work and use not only historiographical methods but also the approaches and theories of the social sciences such as anthropology, ethnography, or cultural sociology, it is important for them to look carefully at the genealogy of these disciplines as well as the social-cultural-political contexts that have shaped them.

It has long been recognized that the discipline of cultural anthropology and ethnology has been developed in the interest of Western colonialism. For instance, A. R. Radcliffe-Brown, one of the founding fathers of functionalist social anthropology, which stresses stability, unity, integration, and equilibrium as most important for the functioning of a society, states this link between anthropology and colonialism quite openly:

Now I think this is where social anthropology can be of immense and almost immediate service. The study of the beliefs and customs of the native peoples, with the aim not of merely reconstructing their history but of discovering their meaning, their function, that is, the place they occupy in the mental, moral and social life, can afford great help to the missionary or the public servant who is engaged in dealing with practical problems of the adjustment of the native civilization to the new conditions that have resulted from our occupation of the country. . . .[5]

However, what is less often recognized is the function of social anthropology not only in service of colonial administrations in the last century but also in the service of contemporary U.S. economic and political hegemony. As the world's only remaining superpower, U.S. military institutions and governmental agencies use social scientists in the interest of American imperialism for controlling so-called third-world developing nations. For instance, social scientists were invited to undertake studies for the notorious Camelot Project that make

> it possible to predict and influence politically significant aspects of social change in the developing nations of the world. . . . The U.S. Army has an important mission in the positive and constructive aspects of nation-building in less developed countries as well as a responsibility to assist friendly governments dealing with active insurgency problems. (From the recruiting letter for Project Camelot).[6]

While not every research project and social theory has such immediate political affiliation and relevance, cultural anthropology still provides the theories and materials for managing the world today. Insofar as Western social scientists study those peoples who are either poor or living under neocolonialism but not the elites of their own society and culture, they always produce knowledge that can be used against the oppressed and exploited who are studied.

> But how could the data not be relevant to imperialism? Anthropological research is research on the people of the world subject to imperialism, but these are people who have always fought back in their ways, off and on, now passively, and now fiercely, in one area at one time in another area at another time, rebelling against forces which oppress them. . . . Imperialism, to sur-

<hr>

[5] A. R. Radcliffe-Brown, "The Methods of Ethnology and Social Anthropology," *South African Journal of Science* 20 (1923): 124–47, 142f..

[6] Irving L. Horowitz, *The Rise and Fall of Project Camelot* (Boston: MIT Press, 1969), 47–49.

vive, must counterattack with ever more sophisticated weapons, hard and "soft." It must understand the people it domineers, so as to understand how to prevent them from overthrowing that domination.[7]

Recognizing the permeation of anthropological theories and frameworks with imperialist interests, Historical-Jesus research must investigate the models and theories adopted from the social sciences as to their worldview and normalizing function rather than simply taking over anthropological theories in order to prove biblical studies to be scientific.

Moreover, not only cultural anthropology but also history as a discipline was shaped in the nineteenth century in the interest of imperial domination. If it is correct that historiography in general serves to form identity, and Historical-Jesus research in particular has promoted and continues to reinscribe the Christian Eurocentrism, anti-Judaism and kyriarchal gender relations of elite Western educated propertied men, then the discussion of and the controversy around the Historical-Jesus must be conducted much more self-critically on the level of theory formation and methodology than has been the case until now.

Methodology (Greek *meta* = after; *hodos* = way; *logos* = word/teaching) usually refers to the critical scientific level of reflection at which basic decisions are made. It asks not only how Historical-Jesus research deals with the fact that its societal and institutional context belongs to its area of research, and thus always already determines studies about Jesus;[8] it also asks why Historical-Jesus studies are not able to acknowledge this. Hence, a critical feminist theory challenges Historical-Jesus studies to reflect on the preconstructed[9] ideological frameworks that are tacitly mediated through scientific methods.

As a critical metareflection, feminist methodology focuses especially on those factors in Historical-Jesus research which govern and determine the use of its scientific methods. Among them are, for instance, the social formation of the "soft" disciplines—anthropology, sociology, political science, history, and biblical studies—in the service of colonialism; the sub-

---

[7] Jack Stauder, "The 'Relevance' of Anthropology to Colonialism and Imperialism," in *The "Racial" Economy of Science: Toward a Democratic Future*, ed. Sandra Harding (Bloomington: Indiana University Press, 1993), 425f.

[8] Annette Noller, *Feministische Hermeneutik: Wege einer neuen Schriftauslegung* (Neukirchen-Vluyn: Neukirchener Verlag, 1995), 70–75.

[9] For this expression, see Rosemary Hennessy, *Materialist Feminism and the Politics of Discourse* (New York: Routledge, 1993).

ject of interpretation and its social location; the area of research; the goal to be achieved, the basic questions and concepts of analysis; the addressees who need to be persuaded; the models and frameworks of historical reconstruction; or the presuppositions that determine the application of the scientific tools of investigation and the selection of topics to be researched.

Not only are the subjects, basic concepts, reconstructive models, presuppositions, and audiences of feminist studies different from malestream social-scientific biblical studies, but also its goals. With Jürgen Habermas feminist studies insist over and against a scientific-positivist, sociorational, and hermeneutic program that questions of power are central not only for the understanding of language, tradition, and canon, but also for Historical-Jesus research itself. Habermas distinguishes three basic forms of knowledge: the empirical-analytical, the hermeneutic-historical, and the critical-emancipatory. We search for knowledge in order to control social situations and the facts of nature (empirical-analytic), to understand and appreciate historical realities (hermeneutic-historical), and to change our individual and collective knowledge of reality (the critical-emancipatory form) so that human potential and possibilities for freedom and equality can be maximized.

Whereas social-scientific Historical-Jesus research claims to be interested primarily in the first and maybe in the second form of knowledge production, a critical feminist hermeneutics of liberation is concerned especially with the third form of knowledge about the world. It seeks not just understanding but argues for a change of the status quo. Hence, in and through the process of a hermeneutics of suspicion, it problematizes and questions the functions and claims of social-scientific Historical-Jesus studies. Before one can turn to a reconstruction of the Historical-Jesus in a feminist perspective, one must ask how much social-scientific Jesus research would contribute to change and transformation or how much it seeks to maintain the status quo. In short, one must ask by whom, why, and in whose interests social-scientific Historical-Jesus knowledge is produced.

## THE SUBJECTS OF SOCIAL-SCIENTIFIC JESUS RESEARCH

Critical feminist analyses of malestream Historical-Jesus discourses and their history have pointed to the social context and ideological functions of Historical-Jesus research. Jesus scholars are historically formed people with certain personal experiences and cultural horizons. The majority are European and American, educated white men who not only pursue certain goals and interests but also bring unconscious assumptions and often unreflected presuppositions to the task when they try to understand the texts about Jesus and to reconstruct his history.

A critical feminist or emancipatory politics of interpretation therefore insists that the critical reflection on the social contextualization, theoretical perspective, and rhetorical situation of scholars must become an integral part of research. A clear-cut reconstitution of the world of Jesus and his historical influence that is not affected by the person of the interpreter and her/his social-political situation is impossible and outdated from a scientific-epistemological point of view. Considering the race, gender, and national-social location of most biblical scholars, it is not surprising that the center of interest is the historical man Jesus whom christology understands as *kyrios*, a title that means lord, slave master, patriarch. Consequently, the social and "ekklesial" location of Historical-Jesus studies must belong to its very own area of investigation since it always already determines research itself.

Students of culture and sociology such as Pierre Bourdieu therefore have demanded that the subjects of research, the intellectuals, must become first ethnologists of their own discipline and analysts of their own status in society if they want to work scientifically. Those who intend to work sociologically must always first engage in a "sociology of sociology," in order to become conscious of their own social location, of the notions and pre-constructions which they use and of their interests or dependencies as well in order to arrive at a theory of scientific praxis.

> When reading many sociological works, I find it regretful that people whose profession it is to objectify the social world are so little able to objectify themselves and that they do not see that what comes to the fore in their allegedly scientific discourses is precisely not the object but much more their relation to the object, *ressentiment*, envy, social desire, unconscious strivings, a whole lot of unanalyzed things.[10]

A critical feminist hermeneutic, however, must interrogate not only the masculinity and gender constructions of malestream social-scientific Historical-Jesus research but especially also its theoretical horizon of positivism. Both strategies, the analysis of the ideological undergirding of positivist biblical scholarship and the problematization and deconstruction of

<hr>

[10] Pierre Bourdieu, *Homo Academicus* (Frankfurt/Main: Suhrkamp, 1989), 12.

Jesus' masculinity as an objectively given fact of history, are necessary in order to recognize its functions in the service of domination which historical-social scientific Jesus research often unwittingly performs. The refusal of Historical-Jesus scholarship to critically reflect on its own ideological and theological interests, together with the restoration of historical positivism, corresponds to political conservatism. As the feminist sociologist Dorothy Smith has argued, objectified forms of knowledge structure the relationship of the knower to the known object.[11] The emphasis on the scientific "facts" of history serves to foster a scholarly fundamentalism that usually does not acknowledge that in the process of understanding, historians and social scientists select, evaluate, underscore, or reject social models and at the same time reformulate them by placing them in a scientific scenario or a narrative frame of meaning.

As we have seen, Dieter Georgi has pointed out that Historical-Jesus research originated in the time of the bourgeois European Enlightenment,[12] and Gerd Theissen and Annette Merz have observed that Historical-Jesus research flourished in Germany during the imperial era of Wilhelm II. Jesus as the paradigm of true humanity and individuality, according to Georgi, becomes the ideal of the brilliant and heroic man, an ideal that can be achieved through education and imitation. Jesus as the great hero and leader serves to foster the identity discovery and formation of the European male citizen.

Georgi's sociotheological contextualization of Historical-Jesus research in the European bourgeoisie is expanded and focused by the Chinese theologian Kwok Pui-Lan. She underscores that Historical-Jesus research is occasioned by the colonial territorial expansion of Europe, which was legitimated through racist ideologies of the highly developed European and his uncivilized savage counterpart.

> In the nineteenth century, Europe underwent tremendous cultural and political changes as the colonizers were confronted by the colonized in many parts of the world. The first quest could not have taken place without the new knowledge brought to the metropolitan centers about the myths, cultures, and religions of the colonized people. . . . The search for Jesus must be read against the search for "natives" to conquer and to subdue. The encounter with the "natives" created anxiety and necessitated the quest for

---

[11] Dorothy E. Smith, *The Conceptual Practices of Power: A Feminist Sociology of Knowledge* (Boston: Beacon Press, 1990), 63.

[12] Dieter Georgi, "Leben Jesu Theologie/Leben Jesu Forschung," in *Theologische Realenzyklopädie* 20 (1990): 566–75.

self-identity. The epistemological framework of the first quest was constructed out of a combination of Orientalist philology, racist ideology, and Eurocentric study of other people's mythology and religions.[13]

Kwok argues that in the encounter with the indigenous peoples in the Americas or Australia the European colonizers developed the strategy of "noble savaging." This strategy constructed and functionalized indigenous peoples as "uncivilized nature," as "noble savages," as the totally other of European culture in order to criticize the social evils of their own society. In a similar way, European biblical scholars constructed biblical people as the primitive[14] others, who are separated from people today by an unbridgeable historical chasm. In such a Eurocentric, "enlightened" frame of interpretation, Jesus becomes the "noble savage" par excellence.[15] The hero and leader figure of Jesus the "noble savage" served not only to foster the Eurocentric colonial identity construction of whites but also to shape the anti-Jewish identity formation of Christians since Christian discourses have cast Judaism as the "other."

The image of Jesus, the extraordinary (white) man or "noble savage" who as an especially gifted and powerful individual transcends all normal boundaries, corresponds to the liberal ethos of elite Western men. Hence, malestream historical and social-scientific Jesus discourses must be critically analyzed as European-American discourses in the service of Western domination that nonetheless claim universal validity. They continue to produce not only the self-understanding and religious horizon of Christians but also that of Western culture if they do not critically question the ideological functions of their own methods and theoretical lenses.

Since science and religion are primary educational institutions that shape subjects and their identity, colonialist Historical-Jesus discourses inculcate and perpetuate the hegemony of elite white men and the inferiority of wo/men. Hence, as we have seen, one must critically investigate whether and how much Jesus research contributes to the fashioning of well-adapted consumers who are easily manipulated and exploited in a global service economy. In light of the function of anthropological research and theories in support of neoliberal capitalism, it seems no acci-

---

[13] Kwok Pui-Lan, "On Color-Coding Jesus: An Interview with Kwok Pui-Lan," in *The Postcolonial Bible,* ed. R. S. Sugirtharajah (Sheffield: Academic Press, 1998), 178.

[14] The German word *Urchristentum* is still translated as "primitive" Christianity.

[15] Kwok Pui-Lan, "Jesus/the Native: Biblical Studies from a Postcolonial Perspective," in *Teaching the Bible: The Discourses and Politics of Biblical Pedagogy,* ed. Fernando F. Segovia and Mary Ann Tolbert (Maryknoll, N.Y.: Orbis Books, 1998), 83.

dent that the importance of anthropology in Historical-Jesus research is increasing. The explosion of popular and scientific Jesus books must be understood in this political context and seen as a part of the global politics of meaning that works with the accumulation of information and simultaneous reification of its intellectual frameworks, and thus produces what is considered "common sense." In short, social-scientific Historical-Jesus discourses must be critically interrogated as to their structural functions in maintaining the domination of elite men and the subordination of wo/men.

## FEMINIST CRITIQUE OF POSITIVIST UNDERSTANDING
## OF SCIENCE AND LANGUAGE

Feminist discussions of social-scientific Jesus research have critically pointed out that such research often does not do justice to its scientific claims, insofar as it tends to uncritically reinscribe the positivistic understanding of science not only of historical biblical studies but also of sociology and anthropology. Although the history of Jesus research documents that scholars always reconstruct Jesus in their own image and likeness, many scholars still claim that they can produce the true correct meaning of a biblical text, the facts of history, or social-scientific data with scientifically controlled methods.

However, such a universal, objectively given and detectable Historical-Jesus cannot be distilled once and for all from our sources and texts since texts are multivalent and allow for a multiplicity of valid readings. Biblical texts and sources must be understood as rhetorical communications, that is, as linguistic practices that are shaped by their originating situations and interests. Only with regard to context is it possible to limit the pluriform textual meanings and linguistic symbols for Jesus and to characterize the possible or probable range of textual meanings.

A foundational methodological contribution of critical feminist studies to social theory and scientific understanding consists in the recognition of the rhetoricity and kyriocentric function of grammatically masculine, so-called generic language. As a postmodern literary theory, so also a critical feminist theory questions and renders problematic the understanding of language presupposed by social-scientific and social-historical Jesus research. Both social-scientific and social-historical Jesus research tend to understand androcentric—or, better, kyriocentric—language as a window to the world of the Historical-Jesus and to presuppose that texts reflect and represent reality objectively. However, kyriocentric language does not describe and reflect reality but constructs and prescribes it. It creates the symbolic worlds that it pretends simply to depict. Language is not just descriptive-reflective-pragmatic but also prescriptive-performative-political. Kyriocentric language serves kyriarchal interests; conversely, kyriarchal interests determine the meanings of kyriocentric language.

Grammatically masculine languages such as Hebrew, Greek, or Latin claim to be generic inclusive languages that always include wo/men without explicitly mentioning them. They mention wo/men explicitly only if they are exceptions, pose a problem, or if individuals need to be marked by gender identification. Thereby kyriocentric language inscribes and prescribes not only gender but also other hierarchies of domination. Since, for instance, slave wo/men are subsumed under slaves and Jewish wo/men under Jews, they are effectively made invisible in our historical source "data." How grammatically masculine generic languages are to be understood can only be decided with reference to the social reality which in turn is linguistically produced. For example, if one sees a reference to biblical scholars, one is able to decide whether wo/men and/or men are referred to and to understand this reference only if one places it in a historical context. If the text refers to the reality of the nineteenth century, then one knows from other sources that wo/men were not biblical scholars, but if it is a twentieth-century text, one needs to assume that wo/men scholars are meant unless one has proof to the contrary.

Although I questioned the topical approach that focuses on "Jesus and wo/men" more than twenty years ago in *In Memory of Her*,[16] books on Jesus and wo/men seem to proliferate again. Such publications thereby reinscribe the androcentric language pattern that defines wo/men in relation to men. Moreover "woman" or "women" is often still "segregated" and treated in a special chapter as though wo/men did not belong to the disciples of Jesus or to the members of other Jewish movements of the time. For instance, Gerd Theissen and Annette Merz, after discussing the Jesus movement in general, have a special section on wo/men; or Ekkehard Stegemann and Wolfgang Stegemann in turn headline their two special sections on wo/men with "women among the followers of Jesus," assuming the generic masculine for followers of Jesus.[17] Such an "add-and-stir"

---

[16] Elisabeth Schüssler Fiorenza, *In Memory of Her: A Feminist Theological Reconstruction of Christian Origins* (New York: Crossroad, 1984; 10th Anniversary Edition With a New Introduction, 1994).

[17] Gerd Theissen and Annette Merz, *The Historical Jesus: A Comprehensive Guide* (Minneapolis: Fortress Press, 1998); Ekkehard W. Stegemann and Wolfganng Stegemann, *The Jesus Movement: A Social History of the First Century* (Minneapolis: Fortress Press, 1999).

approach is well intended but continues to marginalize wo/men by reinscribing the ideological tendencies of kyriocentric language. If one points
to this failure of social-scientific method, it is often asserted that it is already
progress if wo/men are mentioned at all in a scientific study.

Social-scientific Jesus research still seems not to have quite recognized
that sex/gender, patriarchy/androcentrism, or kyriarchy/kyriocentrism are
central socioanalytic categories and instruments of analysis without which
one cannot adequately comprehend andro-kyriocentric language and
sociohistorical reality. It continues to neglect the methodological problem
posed by the recognition of androcentric language because it does not recognize and adapt a feminist social analysis that can lay open the structures
of domination in antiquity and today. Nevertheless, Historical-Jesus books
that do not critically question the androcentric language model are still
considered to be scientific, although they work with an outdated notion of
language.

Moreover, following Max Weber, social-scientific Historical-Jesus
research understands language as transparent, and it does not recognize
the possible gap between subjective meanings and objective social practices. The androcentric text becomes script in a positivistic posture of
Historical-Jesus research that pretends to describe the "real" Jesus or "what
actually happened." The gaps, omissions, breaks, and partial truths of the
andro-kyriocentric text are filled in with reference to the conventions,
knowledges, and practices of a kyriarchal society, which are understood as
common sense and universal insight. The literary critic Catherine Belsey
has identified such a scientific-positivist reading as "expressive realism."

> The strategies of the classic realist text divert the reader from what is con-
> tradictory within it to the renewed recognition (misrecognition) of what he
> or she already "knows," knows because the myth and signifying systems of
> the classic realist text re-present experience in the ways in which it is con-
> ventionally articulated in our society.[18]

According to Belsey, such "expressive realism" is at home in the period of
industrial capitalism. Itumeleng Mosala in turn has argued that such
"expressive realism" is also operative in social-scientific biblical research
and works hand in glove with neocapitalist tendencies of reification.[19]

In short, social-scientific Jesus research must recognize that andro-

---

[18] Catherine Belsey, *Critical Practice* (New York: Methuen, 1980), 128.
[19] Itumeleng Mosala, "Social Scientific Approaches to the Bible: One Step Forward, Two
Steps Backward," *Journal of Theology for Southern Africa* 55 (1986): 15–30.

centric language and kyriocentric knowledge are rhetorical and perspectival. That is, they are articulated by certain people for a certain audience and readership, and they operate grammatically with certain articulated or unacknowledged kyriarchal interests. Hence, an intra- and intertextual analysis of language and text does not suffice. It must be bolstered by a critical-systemic analysis of religious-political structures of domination.

## A FEMINIST SOCIAL THEORY AND ANALYTIC

In light of such an ideology-critical feminist analysis of language and symbolic worlds that normalize and legitimate sociopolitical and religious systems of domination as "common sense," social-scientific Historical-Jesus research can no longer claim to tell us "what really happened"—as the subtitle "Discovering What Happened . . ." of Crossan's *Birth of Christianity* promises. It can no longer assert that it describes the reality of the Historical-Jesus as objectively and scientifically as possible. Instead, social-scientific Historical-Jesus studies must critically reflect on the social theory that shapes their work in order to make good on their claim to scientific objectivity.

From its beginnings social-scientific research has worked with the category of patriarchy, particularly Ernst Troeltsch's notion of love-patriarchalism, but has never developed it theoretically. For instance, the macrosociological societal model of Gerhard Lenski is widely used in biblical studies, but this model does not deal with patriarchal relations of domination. It rather, according to Crossan, seeks to model as to how to

> balance the twin warring emphases of functional and conflictual analysis within the social sciences. Functionalists emphasize common interests, common advantages, consensus and cooperation; conflictualists emphasize dividing interests, domination, exploitation, and coercion. Lenski synthesizes both approaches, and surely both together are more accurate than either one alone.[20]

Whereas Stegemann and Stegemann acknowledge B. Mayer-Schärtel's contention that the introduction of gender would change Lenski's model,[21]

---

[20] John Dominic Crossan, *The Birth of Christianity: Discovering What Happened Immediately after the Execution of Jesus* (New York: HarperCollins, 1998), 153.

[21] They refer to her dissertation (Barbara Mayer-Schärtel, "'Die Frau ist in jeder Hinsicht schwächer als der Mann': Eine sozialgeschichtliche und kuturanthropologische

they do not make such changes.[22] Crossan also recognizes that Lenski's model does not structure gender into his typology, but he argues that it does not do so because it is a model of social class.[23] He seeks to remedy this by integrating Lenski's model with an anthropological model of gender roles that was developed in the late 1970s. This model is therefore not able to take into account the extensive feminist discussions on the sex/gender system that have taken place in the last decade.

Whereas in the 1970s feminist theorists used as key analytic categories androcentrism/gender (= male-female dualism) and patriarchy (= the domination of the father/male over women) and distinguished between sex and gender roles, such a dualistic gender approach has been seriously questioned by other feminist theorists who are pointing to the multiplicative structures of domination determining most wo/men's lives. In order to theorize structures of domination in antiquity and the multiplicative intersection of gender, race, class, and ethnicity in modernity I have sought to articulate a social feminist heuristic model that replaces the notion of patriarchy/patriarchalism with the neologism of kyriarchy as a key analytic category. While at first glance this model seems to be similar to Lenski's, it is not a simple class model. This can be seen if one compares Lenksi's class stratification model as developed by Stegemann and Stegemann with my kyriarchal stratification model.

"Kyriarchy" means the domination of the lord, slave master, husband, the elite freeborn educated and propertied man over all wo/men and subaltern men. It is to be distinguished from kyriocentrism, which has the ideological function of naturalizing and legitimating not just gender but all forms of domination. Kyriarchal relations of domination are built on elite male property rights over wo/men, who are marked by the intersection of gender, race, class, and imperial domination as well as wo/men's dependency, subordination, and obedience—or wo/men's second-class citizenship.

Such kyriocentric ideology and systemic kyriarchy are characteristic not only of modern Western societies. Already Aristotle had argued that the freeborn, propertied, educated Greek man was the highest of moral beings and that all other members of the human race were defined by their functions in his service. Kyriarchal relations of domination and subordination

---

Untersuchung zum Frauenbild des Josephus" [Neuendettelsau, 1994]) but not to her published work.

[22] Stegemann and Stegemann, *Jesus Movement*, 65–67.

[23] Ibid., 151.

are explicitly articulated in Western political philosophy in the context of Greek democracy and Roman imperialism. They have been mediated by Christian scriptural-theological traditions and have decisively determined modern kyriarchal forms and ideologies of democracy.

Modern political philosophy continues to assume that propertied, educated elite Western man is defined by reason, self-determination, and full citizenship, whereas wo/men and other subordinated peoples are characterized by emotion, service, and dependence. They are seen not as rational and responsible adult subjects but as emotional, helpless, and childlike. In short, kyriarchal societies and cultures need for their functioning a "servant class," a "servant race," or a "servant people," be they slaves, serfs, house servants, coolies, or mammies. The existence of such a "servant class" is maintained through law, education, socialization, and brute violence. It is sustained by the belief that members of a "servant class" of people are by nature or by divine decree inferior to those whom they are destined to serve.

This kyriarchal system is structured in modernity by race, gender, class, ethnicity, heterosexuality and imperialism. In such a kyriarchal social system and kyriocentric worldview, Jesus is understood not only as the divine son and extraordinary man but also as the lord and master over the world. Genevieve Lloyd, among others, has documented that modern [and postmodern] understandings of rationality and of the world have been articulated by white European American elite educated man, the Man of Reason. He has not only defined white women as "others," but also all the "others" as nonpersons who lack human, that is, masculine, qualities.

Nineteenth-century scientists in one way or another constructed the socalled lower races, women, the sexually deviant, the criminal, the urban poor, and the insane as biological "races apart." Their differences from the white male, and their likeness to each other, "explained" their different and lower position in the social hierarchy. In this scheme the lower races represent the feminine aspect of the human species, and women the "lower race" of gender.

Feminist theorists have elaborated that gender, like race, is not a natural given but a societal construct, a sociocultural principle of classification that imposes psychological, social, cultural, religious, and political meaning upon biological sexual identity. The category "gender" questions seemingly universal beliefs about women and men and unmasks their cultural-societal roots. According to Simone de Beauvoir "wo/men are not born but made." However, whereas at first women's studies distinguished social gender roles from biological sex, in the mid-1980s gender studies emerged as a distinct field of inquiry within feminist criticism. In the last decade feminist theory, which in my understanding is a political discourse, has elaborated that both sex and gender are sociocultural constructs that together constitute the Western sex/gender system.

If one does not distinguish between sex and gender as a biological given and a cultural construct but sees both sex and gender together with race, ethnicity, or class as sociocultural constructions, one can analyze the Western kyriocentric ideological system as a cultural symbolic structure of representation that has become naturalized and "common sense." As an ideological structure, gender, like race, class, and ethnicity, is active through grammar, language, biology, and culture to naturalize and make its construction of difference "common sense."

However, gender is not just an ideological representation but also a social institution, not just kyriocentric but kyriarchal. According to Judith Lorber, kyriarchal gender (race, class, ethnicity) encompasses social and individual gender status. *Gender as a social status* has the following components: Generally *accepted kyriarchally defined gender norms* and expectations define the socially recognized genders in a given society.

The *gendered division of labor* assigns work according to gender, *whereas gendered kinship* spells out family rights and responsibilities for each gender. Gender scripts prescribe behavior and grant prerogatives to the members of the dominant gender, whereas subordinate genders may be exploited. *Gendered social controls,* the rewards for conforming behavior and the stigmatization and isolation of aberrant conduct, produce *gendered personalities* that conform to hegemonic gender roles. Finally, *gender ideology and gender imagery,* the cultural representations of *kyriarchal gender* in symbolic language and artistic production, as we have seen above, legitimate and support dominant gender statuses.

However, gender as a social institution must not be isolated from other structures of domination. *Gender as a sociopolitical and psychological practice of domination and subordination* is only one of several social ascriptions that promote the exploitation of wo/men. If one realizes that gender is always inflected by race, class, age, religion, sexual preference, or ethnicity, one is able to demystify naturalized gender oppositions. One can see that actual wo/men and men are not just gendered. Gender as a sociopolitical-religious discursive practice produces not only sex differences but also those of race, class, sexual preference, culture, religion, age, and nationality.

Like those of race, class, or ethnicity, the social relations which give rise to gender differences are socioculturally constructed as relations of domination and are not simply biological givens. In other words, the world is determined by relations of domination. Sex/gender is a part of such relations of ruling, which also ground other divisions such as class or race. The definition of other races and peoples as the "feminine Other," for instance, has enabled colonial Western powers to exploit and utilize religion in the expansive capitalist quest for identity and property.

Thus, the social formation of gender can be theorized in terms of power relations. If one conceptualizes the reality of wo/men not in terms of gender dualism, but rather in terms of a socially constructed web of interactive systems of power structured as pyramids of domination and subordination, then one is able to understand societal oppression as engendered by variegated social, interactive, and multiplicative structures of exploitation and dehumanization. Hence, the modern kyriarchal system must be scrutinized not only for its economic-cultural heterosexist biases; it must also be analyzed with respect to its classist, racist, and colonialist underpinnings.

Hence, it is important to see gender as one among several systems of domination and to conceptualize the formation of gender in terms of power relations. Gender is structured and constructed as it is because it serves to sustain the hegemonic sexual/economic, racial/cultural/national/religious unequal distribution of power and wealth. If social-scientific Historical-Jesus research would recognize and work with the analytic concept of kyriarchy, it would be able not only to analyze their own imbrication with colonialist and Christian Western elite male interests but also to reconstruct their key analytic concept of Mediterranean society and culture differently.

For instance, it is often maintained that the reconstructive model of Mediterranean society that works with the dualism "honor-shame" adequately describes the reality of the ancient world. In using it, researchers are supposedly protected from projecting their own modern ideas and presuppositions unto the past. However, this maneuver obscures that Mediterranean society in antiquity would be more adequately comprehended with the patriarchy/kyriarchy social model since the dualism "honor-shame" is only one, though an important, feature of the kyriarchal ethos of antiquity.

Mediterranean-area studies that stress "honor-and-shame" culture not only do not adequately describe the ancient world; they also prevent contemporary interpreters from engaging in "cross-cultural" dialogue because they project the "honor-shame" system unto "other" cultures but do not explore it for their own cultural context. Such studies identify Mediterranean culture with the distant and alien culture of the Bible. This culture allegedly favors being over doing, cultural dyadic relations over individualism, the present or past over the future, subordination over mastery, a view of human nature as a mixture of good and bad elements over a view of human nature as exclusively good or bad.[24] For instance, John J. Pilch and Bruce J. Malina argue:

> Thus in the United States, males generally are *expected* [emphasis added] to achieve (doing) and only secondarily permit themselves to be spontaneous (being), women in general are primarily expected to be spontaneous, and only secondarily to be dedicated to achieving.
>
> In Mediterranean society relative to this same area of concern, men are primarily socialized to spontaneity, while women are primarily socialized to achievement, doing, "work."[25]

The authors seem not to realize (or to care), however, that by constructing their dualistic oppositions they effectively reinscribe gender dualism as a social reality and as a fact rather than problematizing it as an ideological expectation.

Halvor Moxnes concedes that those cultural anthropologists who have initiated Mediterranean studies have more recently distanced themselves from the understanding of the Mediterranean as a "fixed cultural area." They have recognized that the "Mediterranean" is a monolithic scientific construct and have pointed out that "honor and shame" as well as other concepts are found in many different cultures. They are valued not only in the South and East but also in the North and the West. Systems of prestige and precedence are not restricted to the Mediterranean but are common to many social groups and geographical areas. Yet, despite recognizing the constructedness of the Mediterranean, Moxnes nevertheless insists:

> But it is the specific relationship between the honor-and-shame code and male and female roles, that has been put forward as distinctive for the Mediterranean region. It is this theory that is at the center of the current discussion. Both linguistically and conceptually languages in the Mediterranean divide the world into masculine and feminine domains, and "male" and "female" thus become metaphors for other types of divisions. The outcome of this discussion appears to be that the one aspect that qualifies for a

[24] John J. Pilch and Bruce J. Malina, eds., *Biblical Social Values and Their Meaning* (Peabody, Mass.: Hendrickson, 1993), xxii.
[25] Ibid., xxiii–xxiv.

separate treatment of the Mediterranean region remains the relationship of honor and shame to masculinity, sexuality, and gender distinctions.[26]

It is curious that Moxnes does not reflect on the fact that not just Mediterranean languages but all Western languages are gendered and as such "divide the world up into masculine and feminine." Hence, such a relationship is not distinct to Mediterranean cultures but is a characteristic of kyriarchal Western cultures. Moreover, Moxnes does not discuss that such binary dualism is a construct of scholars intent on producing "Mediterranean biblical culture" as totally different from our own. Rather than problematize this reconstructive model of the Mediterranean, the social-scientific context group insists that one can engage in intercultural dialogue and avoid ethnocentrism only if one constructs the Mediterranean biblical world as totally different from our own. Thus they juxtapose biblical and U.S. culture as exclusive opposites, without recognizing that within the United States, for instance, the South, both white and black, operates by honor/shame as do Native tribal, Hispanic, and Asian communities.

If one were to use not a contrast but an equivalence analogical model of reconstruction, one could see that "honor and shame" as well as its concomitant gender dualism are not peculiar to Mediterranean biblical culture. Most of the characteristics listed by Pilch and Malina as pertaining to Mediterranean culture could also be found in U.S. culture if one looked at both cultures in terms of kyriarchal relations of domination. Moreover, one cannot simply compare cultures without taking the intersection of race, class, gender, ethnicity, and social location into account.

Rather than construct the dualistic binaries Mediterranean and U.S. culture, past and present culture, one needs to look at kyriarchal domination and democratic equality in both the Mediterranean biblical and our own contemporary cultures. If one were to pay attention to changing relationships of kyriarchal domination, one could trace their change throughout Western history, albeit in ever varying forms. Gender dualism is not something peculiar to Mediterranean culture but is produced by all sociocultural systems of domination, which is transcultural.

Like historical-critical studies, so also social-scientific studies presuppose almost as a dogma that a deep chasm exists between people of the past and people today.[27] The interpretive model presupposed by historical-

[26] Halvor Moxnes, "Honor and Shame," in *The Social Sciences and New Testament Interpretation,* ed. Richard L. Rohrbaugh (Peabody, Mass.: Hendrickson, 1996), 33.

[27] Pieter F. Craffert, "Relationships between Social-Scientific, Literary, and Rhetorical Interpretation of Texts," *Biblical Theology Bulletin* 26 (1996): 45–55.

critical and social-scientific studies is not that of the neighbor or the ancestor but that of the foreigner. According to this hegemonic hermeneutical model, the people of the first century are not just foreigners but aliens who come from a different world. This distancing move, however, obscures on the one hand that we can comprehend historical worlds and societies only by means of contemporary languages, perceptions, theories, or analogies, and on the other hand that history is written by and for people today about people of the past.

To think of the past in terms of neighbor would prevent us from turning the other into the same and also would allow us to appreciate and respect the other as neighbor. To replace the model of the "other" with that of the "neighbor" would enable scholars to highlight both the differences and the similarities of past and present cultures and peoples. For instance, the social-cultural forms of kyriarchy in antiquity differ from those in modernity but at the same time they are similar as structures of domination.

Insisting on the total otherness of ancient peoples and their cultures obscures that we cannot understand the past if we do not stand in a relationship and continuity with it. Heuristic models of the past are always articulated in the present. Whether they are acknowledged as scientific depends not only on their scientific power of persuasion but also on the communicative relations of power in which they are embedded. Hence, social-scientific historiography, like any other historiography, serves ideological interests and must be accounted for in terms of an ethics of interpretation.

Consequently, a precritical social-scientific historiography is not able to recognize and problematize that the dualistic opposition of ancient Mediterranean society and modern society is not a descriptive account but a scholarly construction. Such a dualistic opposition of ancient kyriarchal and modern democratic society assumes, on the one hand, that in antiquity no democratic structures existed and, on the other, that in modern Western societies such as the United States democratic values and rights are already realized. Both assumption are patently wrong.

## MODELS AND METHODS OF
## SOCIAL-SCIENTIFIC JESUS RESEARCH

Social-scientific Historical-Jesus research often misunderstands and mystifies the linguistically constructed and prescriptive character not only of its androcentric language and source materials but also of its interpretive heuristic models. Through their choice of sources, reconstructive models, and chosen methods, as I have pointed out, scholars do not simply describe reality but at the same time produce and construct it in language.

The reality of the first century looks different if, for instance, one uses a sociological model of integration or if one employs a crisis model with respect to Roman imperialism and hegemonic Greco-Roman culture. It looks different if one describes the relationship of the Jesus movement to its mother culture, Judaism, in terms of an integrative reconstructive model or in terms of a conflictive crisis model. Both assumptions are possible, but result in quite different reconstructions of the Historical-Jesus and in quite different historical scenarios. Equally, the groups affiliated with Jesus look different if they are understood as social movements that are in conflict with the dominant society they seek to transform or if they are understood as sectarian splinter groups in conflict with Judaism.

Moreover, Mary Ann Tolbert has pointed out that social-scientific Christian Testament studies stand the social-scientific method on its head:

> . . . most sociological and anthropological studies of the New Testament tend to *invert* the social-science method: rather than making the theory the conjectural topic of investigation and the social data the arena of proof, New Testament explorations have often made the textual data the topic of investigation, and the theory or model the vehicle of proof. Social science models, however, are not designed to function in this manner.[28]

Tolbert points out that such a procedure contradicts the examination process of scientific method. She suggests that three major difficulties exist with the social-scientific paradigm's reliance on cultural anthropology as it is used in biblical interpretation. *First,* since the biblical texts and sources are frozen and fixed in time, scholars cannot ask them any additional questions to gain further information. *Second,* the rhetorical overall direction of biblical texts is not geared toward giving anthropological and sociological information but has as its goal to persuade its readers regarding its religious visions and understandings. *Third,* many texts do not have a generalized, typical point of view, but an individual one as, for instance, in the case of the Pauline letters. Hence, their information is inadequate for characterizing a community. Social-scientific research uses, for example, the construct of Mediterranean society to illuminate and to make sense out of

---

[28] Mary Ann Tolbert, "Social, Sociological, and Anthropological Methods," in *Searching the Scriptures,* vol. 1, *A Feminist Introduction,* ed. Elisabeth Schüssler Fiorenza (New York: Crossroad, 1993), 266f.

textual materials rather than testing out this theory in a critical process of interpretation.

According to Malina, the method and examination process of social-scientific inquiry recognizes three steps: postulating, testing, and changing the explanatory model.[29] If one applies these steps to a critical analysis of social-scientific Jesus research, one can see its faulty assumptions. Malina's first step consists in postulating a model (theory, or paradigm). Contrarily, social-scientific Jesus research understands the reconstructive model of, for example, Mediterranean society not as hypothesis and theory but as preconstructed fact. Hence, sociological models, interpretive frameworks, or linguistic patterns are often simply taken over and adopted but not critically questioned and problematized.

At this point a critical scrutiny not only of the construction of models and their selection but also of the scholars who articulate and select such models, along with their motivating interests, becomes necessary. For instance, it is maintained not only that the integrative functionalist and the conflictive crisis models are adequate and appropriate because they are sociological scientific models. It is also argued that with the help of these models, which are imagined to function as eyeglasses or lenses, the source texts can be better read and that thereby the complex reality of the Jesus movement emerges.

The second step requires the testing of the model with respect to actual experience in the "real" world, to which the model refers. Here it is often assumed that models or hypotheses can be proven right or wrong with reference to texts. However, this overlooks that texts do not represent the objective experience of reality. How can a model be tested if it cannot be measured against the experience of the first century, since such "pure" experience is no longer available to us? We have only androcentric texts that in turn are ideological constructions. True, the ideological functions of androcentric language and kyriocentric knowledges can be counteracted in and through a critical analysis of language. However, such a critical analysis is not forthcoming because of the social-scientific positivist assumption that language is reflective of reality. Since social-scientific models cannot be tested out with reference to actual experience in the first century C.E., they must be tested out with respect to contemporary experience. Such a critical test generally does not take place, however, because of the antiquarian ethos of social-scientific biblical studies.

---

[29] Bruce Malina, *The New Testament World: Insights from Cultural Anthropology* (Louisville: Westminster John Knox Press, 1993).

The third step in the process of critical examination consists in changing the model according to one's test results in order to correct its deficiencies. Since social-scientific Jesus research cannot provide proof of its heuristic models and hypotheses with reference to the experience of the Historical-Jesus and his compatriots in the first century C.E., Bruce Malina has advocated a retrodictive method that utilizes the results of historical development. That is, he argues with reference to our knowledge and "commonsense" understanding of the world today. Hence, the criterion of plausibility or probability[30] is introduced. However, such a methodological move does not sufficiently take into account that what seems plausible depends on one's overall understanding of the world because our "commonsense" understandings have ideological and naturalizing functions. The plausibility or probability criterion is always already implicated in discourses of domination that have become "common sense."

As Tolbert points out, such reliance on retrodictive clues can be disastrous "because it could be [and has been] argued that since women are not in positions of authority in the present, social relations must have kept them from these positions in the past."[31] Since retrodictive argument assumes a causal meaning connection between later social structures and earlier ones, it cannot but read later history into the past. The insistence of social-scientific scholarship on the gulf between the present and the past turns out to have ideological mystifying functions. It prevents a change of the productive paradigms and models chosen to interpret texts if they should turn out to be less than adequate.

To illustrate my point I want to apply the three methodological procedures outlined by Malina to a critical investigation of one social-scientific model and its deployment in Historical-Jesus research: millennialism.

### Establishing a Model or Paradigm

The millenarian or millennial cross-cultural model is widely utilized in Jesus research.[32] Dennis Duling defines it as follows:

[30] Gerd Theissen and Dagmar Winter, *Die Kriterienfrage in der Jesusforschung: Vom Differenzkriterium zum Plausibilitätskriterium* (Novum Testamentum et Orbis Antiquus 34; Göttingen: Vandenhoeck & Ruprecht, 1997).
[31] Tolbert, "Social, Sociological, and Anthropological Methods," 267.
[32] Dennis C. Duling ("Millennialism," in *Social Sciences and New Testament Interpretation,* ed. Rohrbaugh, 198-201) mentions among others the work of S. Isenberg, J. Gager, R.

Millennialism describes a social movement of people whose central belief is that the present oppressive world is in crisis and will soon end, usually by some cataclysmic event, and that this world will be replaced by a new, perfect, blissful and trouble free world, often believed to be a restoration of some perfect time and place of old. So intense is this hope that those who accept it engage in preparing for the coming new age, or even try to bring it about, especially by some political activity.[33]

Cultural anthropologists have synthesized this cross-cultural model of millenarianism from different times and places by isolating "common themes" emerging in diverse social movements. Their social-scientific explanation of these movements is either political, military, economic, heroic (the great man theory), cultural, or psychological, or all of these. Duling isolates the following elements as constitutive of the millenarian model.

- Social anthropologists assume that most people accept the social order as it is (functionalism) and that their political situation is relatively nonoppressive.
- A crisis must occur that disturbs this calm social order. The crisis can be military, cultural, economic, political, or psychological.
- This crisis situation compels groups of people to see the discrepancy between what they need and want and their everyday reality. They feel relatively deprived and become increasingly frustrated with the prevailing unjust situation.
- While some persons may engage in regressive behavior such as alcoholism, resignation, and passivity, others get together in groups and form a movement. *Such millennial movements have the following features in common:*

1. They are "religious" or "ideological" movements that expect imminent, ultimate, total, collective, this-worldly or otherworldly liberation and salvation and aim to bring about a more satisfactory society and culture which they seek to embody in their own group life. Many think that the new order will be established by divine

---

Horsley, W. A. Meeks, R. Jewett, G. Theissen, and J. Kloppenborg for the final version of Q. See also Paul W. Hollenbach, "Recent Historical-Jesus Studies and the Social Sciences," in *Society of Biblical Literature 1983 Seminar Papers* (Atlanta: Scholars Press, 1983), 61–78; and Bengt Holmberg, *Sociology and the New Testament: An Appraisal* (Minneapolis: Fortress Press, 1990).

[33] Duling, "Millennialism," 183.

intervention; others go about preparing for it. Such attempts in turn provoke hostility from the dominating powers.

2. This new world order and better world—be it immanent or transcendent—will be established for oppressed groups (the elect) and not just for individuals. Only a few millenarian social movements are organized in a hierarchical-kyriarchal fashion, and most of them are loosely organized and egalitarian.

3. Such movements have prophetic, messianic, or charismatic leaders who broker and mediate between this and the "other world." Such leaders gather around them followers, converts, and disciples.

4. Typical for such movements are an altered state of consciousness and strong emotions (trance, hysteria, paranoia, possession, and sexual asceticism or excess). However, if the majority of society and of the population accepts their vision of renewal, then social, cultural, and religious change can take place. A new social-cultural system emerges that is stable and functional.

## *Testing the Model*

It is obvious from Duling's summary of the typical features of millenarian social movements that our source texts lend themselves to the reconstruction of the variegated Jesus movement as such a millenarian social movement. However, a strong contingent of scholars insists that the original Jesus movement was noneschatological. Moreover, the advocates of using the millenarian model for understanding Jesus seem to be caught in a (vicious) methodological circle. The expression "millenarian" or "millennial" is derived from the Bible, more specifically, from the vision of Christ's thousand-year reign in the book of Revelation. Hence, it is not surprising that the millenarian social-scientific model encompasses all the features that in biblical studies are generally discussed under the heading "apocalyptic/apocalypticism."

Scholars who since W. Wrede and A. Schweitzer have generally understood Jesus in terms of apocalypticism and have used imminent, thoroughgoing eschatology as the organizing category for the extant materials now appeal to the social-scientific model of millenarianism, which in turn seems to be influenced by Jewish and Christian apocalyptic thought patterns. While it is correct that not all millennial movements have been influenced by Christianity, it is also true that the social-scientific "discipline" of millenarian studies has borrowed its nomenclature from a Jewish and Christian apocalyptic language arsenal, a language that is now imported back into Jesus studies under the label "social-scientific."

Since Jesus scholars are not able to test out their theoretical reconstructive models with reference to the Historical-Jesus and his experience, they have developed criteria that would enable them to get back as much as possible to the "authentic" historical figure of Jesus. While the Jesus-Seminar has resorted to the consumer evaluation model of polling in order to sort out the "authentic" materials about Jesus, Dominic Crossan, one of its leaders, has perfected the archaeological method of stratigraphy as a scientifically controlled means to reconstruct Jesus as a peasant leader who announced the brokerless kingdom. Crossan develops this scientific method rhetorically over and against other Jesus research which has "become something of a bad joke" that conveys "the impression of acute scholarly subjectivity" and is often taken as an excuse "to do theology and call it history, to do autobiography and call it biography."[34]

The scientific method advocated by Crossan proceeds in a threefold manner: It insists that Jesus reconstructions be placed into context by way of Greco-Roman history and cross-cultural anthropology. Crossan discusses the millenarian paradigm as such a cross-cultural model. Then, Crossan argues, one must make a scientific inventory of the Jesus materials, and he does so by first dating the sources and then stratifying them into time periods: (1) 30–60 C.E.; (2) 60–80 C.E.; (3) 80–120 C.E.; and (4) 120–150 C.E.). Finally, Crossan sorts out and groups the extant materials into one of four categories: those attested only once, those that are independently attested twice or three times, and those independently attested more than three times.

In so doing Crossan hopes to determine what materials precisely go back to the Historical-Jesus. It is appropriate, he argues, to begin with the first stratum but to bracket materials that are attested only once in one source. Moreover, in the first stratum "everything is original" until it is argued otherwise.[35] Those materials that go back to Jesus and are deemed to be "authentic" are marked with a plus (+) sign; those that do not are marked with a minus (-) sign; and those that do not lend themselves to such "positivistic simplifications"[36] are marked with both signs.

---

[34] John Dominic Crossan, *The Historical-Jesus: The Life of a Mediterranean Jewish Peasant* (San Francisco: HarperCollins, 1991), xxvii–xxviii.
[35] Ibid., xxxii.
[36] Ibid., xxxiv.

Dale Allison discusses Crossan's scientific method extensively and deconstructs its procedures point by point. He questions not only the very unstable and inconclusive method of dating but also the chronological delineation of the four stratigraphic layers. For instance, if one were to extend the period of the first stratum to 70 rather than 60 and the second to 100 rather than 80 C.E. the extant sources would need to be evaluated quite differently and hence a different "authentic" Historical-Jesus would emerge. Allison observes:

> The conclusion would seem to be that the Historical-Jesus cannot be caught if we are left only to our own historical-critical devices. As in the fairy tale, if the birds have eaten too many of the crumbs, the trail cannot be found. Indeed one might go so far as to argue that, if the sayings in the earliest Jesus tradition, taken in their entirety, are not roughly congruent with the sorts of things Jesus tended to say, then our task is hopeless. Even if we were to come to such a conservative conclusion, it must immediately be added that we can never demonstrate that our sources do in fact contain enough authentic material—however much that might be—to make questing a promising activity.[37]

Allison nevertheless does not want to give up the quest for the Historical-Jesus, although he is less sure of its scientific character. He asserts:

> The point is rather that as historians we do something different from mathematicians, who since Thales have eschewed intuition and demanded proofs. Unlike them we cannot formulate proofs for our theorems. We are also unlike scientists, if by that is meant people who fashion experimental trials which allow predictions to be concretely falsified . . . there is no foreseeable victory about uncertainty and no way around subjectivity.[38]

Despite this sober judgment, Allison goes on to propose his own reconstruction of Jesus as a thoroughly eschatological figure who is best understood in social-scientific terms as a millenarian prophet. Over and against those who reconstruct a noneschatological Jesus, as, for instance, Burton Mack, Marcus Borg, and Dominic Crossan, Allison, following the lead of Wrede, Schweitzer, and E. P. Sanders, paints a picture of a thoroughgoing eschatological Jesus.

In order to corroborate this reconstruction Allison points to the social-

---

[37] Dale C. Allison, *Jesus of Nazareth: Millenarian Prophet* (Minneapolis: Fortress Press, 1998), 35.

[38] Ibid., 35; see also D. G. A. Calvert, "An Examination of the Criteria Distinguishing the Authentic Words of Jesus," *New Testament Studies* 18 (1972): 219.

scientific parallel of millenarian movements. In so doing he stands social-scientific method on its head. Since he cannot test out the social-scientific millenarian model in light of the "authentic" materials about Jesus (we supposedly never can find with certainty), he seeks to prove his reconstruction of a thoroughgoing eschatological Jesus by parallelizing and "proof-texting" it with reference to the cross-cultural model of millennialism.

Although I agree with Allison's rigorous critique of the stratigraphic method and his assertion that interpretation and reconstruction of the Historical-Jesus must adopt an organizing theoretical framework, I do not think it is methodologically correct to use the social-scientific reconstructive model of millenarian movements to prove one's own reconstruction of an eschatological Jesus as he does. Rather, what becomes necessary is a critical debate on the rhetorical construction and function of theoretical frameworks and models or paradigms.

## Modifying the Model

Allison lists the following nineteen features that the pre-Easter Jesus movement has in common with millenarian movements:

1. Millenarian movements appeal first of all to the disaffected, the disenfranchised, and the unfortunate in periods of social change.
2. They interpret the present and near future as unprecedented suffering, catastrophe, and oppression.
3. They envision a divinely wrought change, a righting of the wrong that will turn the world "upside down."
4. Such change and reversal of fortunes will come soon. They are imminent.
5. Millenarian movements generate unusually intense commitments and fervor and break down local barriers.
6. Millenarian movements are egalitarian and envision a community where all things are held in common.
7. They often have a strong antitraditional rhetoric that challenges established authority.
8. They tend to think dualistically and to divide humanity into two opposing camps, the "sons of darkness" and the "sons of light."
9. They place emphasis on an indigenous cultural heritage that is threatened by the influx of foreign cultures.

10. In breaking down traditional customs they often replace traditional family and other social ties with a new "imagined" or "virtual" kinship community.

11. Traditional rituals and cultic personnel are deemed unnnecessary because G*d's grace and Spirit are unmediated, direct, and personal. Sometimes leaders mediate the sacred through new channels and experiences.

12. Central to millenarian movements are charismatic figures and prophetic leaders who expect intense commitment and unconditional loyalty.

13. Most often millenarian movements coalesce around a charismatic leader who is essential for their coming into being.

14. Their central beliefs are understood as "new" revelations authenticated by miracles and magic.

15. Millenarian movements take a pacifist political stance because they expect the imminent intervention of G*d.

16. They often believe in a restored world and paradise with the return of the ancestors.

17. They sometimes insist on experiencing the future utopia as a present reality.

18. They often grow out of precursor movements and reactivate previous charismatic experiences.

19. Any millenarian movement that survives historically has to come to terms with the fact that its imminent expectations and dreams have not been realized but have been postponed.[39]

Like other Historical-Jesus scholars, Allison stresses the aspects of imminent eschatological expectations and of charismatic leadership as central to millenarian movements. Both aspects therefore are also used to determine the Jesus movement. This stress on imminent eschatology, however, is not shared by all Jesus scholars. Marcus Borg, for instance, has argued that the scholarly consensus around the eschatological Jesus is in the process of breaking down.[40] Allison in turn seeks to utilize the model of millenarian movements in order to halt the breakdown of imminent eschatological Jesus interpretation and to reassert the Wrede-Schweitzer-Sanders imminent eschatology tradition.

---

[39] Allison, *Jesus*, 81–94.
[40] Marcus Borg, *Jesus in Contemporary Scholarship* (Valley Forge, Pa.: Trinity Press International, 1994) 18–43.

To adjudicate this debate, I suggest, one cannot simply marshal textual evidence in one or the other direction. Instead one must question the theoretical millenarian model that is formulated to favor one over the other. Although this millenarian research model has been formulated by anthropologists and ethnologists and not primarily by biblical scholars, it still has been formulated by Western scholars thinking within a Jewish and Christian symbolic universe, though they may have long rejected Christianity or Judaism. It is noteworthy that Christopher Columbus and other discoverers of the "New World" were influenced by millenarian ideas. As Josephine Massyngberde Ford points out: "Adherents of this eschatological tradition anticipated a new age which would be ushered in by spiritual persons, thus supplying a powerful incentive to colonize the 'New World.'"[41] In light of the discussion on the political function of social anthropology as an academic discipline serving colonialist ends, such a conclusion is inescapable.

It is curious that scholars resort to the language and paradigm of millenarianism among the "natives" when reconstructing the Jesus movement rather than looking critically at the new social movements of their own time and society such as the workers' movement, the civil rights movement, the feminist movement, or the ecological movement, among others. While apocalyptic hopes, dreams, and expectations of justice and restoration are central to social movements for change, I have suggested that they have a rhetorical rather than a predictive function.[42] They envision a different world in the interest of mobilizing resistance and revolt against unjust situations and oppressive structures here in the present. To understand social movements and their hopes and dreams in the way millenarianism does is to misunderstand their pathos for bringing about justice.

In contrast to the construct of millenarian movements, social movements for change are not always inaugurated by a charismatic leader nor do they expect that change will benefit only their own group, the "elect." For instance, the civil rights movement was not initiated by Dr. Martin Luther King Jr., nor was it considered to be "his" movement. Rather, he was a part of the civil rights movement and provided the rhetorical leadership that galvanized the movement. In a similar fashion, grass-roots women's movements are not organized around a single charismatic leader but around a vision for changing situations of injustice and dehumanization. Hence, I suggest that the reconstructive social-scientific model of millen-

---

[41] Josephine Massyngberde Ford, "Millennium," in *Anchor Bible Dictionary,* ed. D. N. Freedman (New York: Doubleday, 1992), 4:834.
[42] See my book *Revelation: Vision of a Just World* (Minneapolis: Fortress Press, 1991).

nialism, if it should serve as an appropriate paradigm for Jesus research, is best modified with a social-scientific model that focuses on social political movements for change.

How a millenarian imminent eschatological model depoliticizes interpretation can be seen in the way scholars understand the key notion in Jesus' preaching, the *basileia tou theou.* If one looks at the debate on the eschatological or noneschatological Jesus, one is struck by the fact that the leading antagonists E. P. Sanders and Burton Mack[43] agree on one point: Jesus was apolitical and not concerned with changing his social-religious worlds.[44] In such an apolitical reading the *basileia tou theou* becomes a purely religious eschatological or a noneschatological ethical notion. For instance, Gerd Theissen und Annette Merz argue that

> God's kingdom is the establishment of his ethical will, the kingdom is to be understood dynamically as rule. But the "kingdom of God" is not an end in itself. God's power serves to realize his goodness. God is "father" by nature. His "kingdom" is his instrument. Therefore this "kingdom" can be spoken of as a realm differentiated by God in which a person can enter. . . . If the "kingdom of God" is an image for the establishment of God's ethical will, there is even more of a demand on the human ethical will.[45]

Since the "kingdom" extends into the realm of death because the dead ancestors are envisioned as sharing its eschatological table community, Theissen and Merz conclude that it is certainly not a "political kingdom" but a "religious expectation with political relevance."[46] Hence, over and against Norman Perrin[47] they argue that the *"basileia* of G*d" is not a symbol and does not refer to any well-defined myth. It is not a symbol but a "living metaphor." While an apolitical reading of the *"basileia"* of G*d as metaphor or religious symbol is possible if the question is articulated as the problem of whether Jesus' preaching was eschatological or noneschatological, it is not possible if one foregrounds the aspect of social movement, since social movements emerge only if there is an actual or perceived

---

[43] E. P. Sanders, *Jesus and Judaism* (Philadelphia: Fortress Press, 1985); Burton L Mack, *A Myth of Innocence: Mark and Christian Origins* (Philadelphia: Fortress Press, 1988).

[44] Borg, *Jesus in Contemporary Scholarship,* 21.

[45] Theissen and Merz, *Historical-Jesus,* 275.

[46] Ibid., 276.

[47] I make this inference since their text does not refer to Norman Perrin, *Jesus and the Language of the Kingdom* (Philadelphia: Fortress Press, 1976), who adopted the symbol theory of P. Wheelwright and argued that the "kingdom of G*d" was a tensive symbol of ancestral range.

crisis and a need for sociopolitical change. However, one must be careful not to apply such a crisis model primarily to Judaism but to its domination by Roman imperialism. Depoliticizing the millenarian model unavoidably leads to Christian anti-Jewish reconstructions of the Jesus movements.

While most scholars agree that *basileia tou theou* is central to the message of Jesus and hence represents the "authentic" Jesus, they disagree on the translation of the term and its meaning context. With Theissen and Merz the majority of scholars understand *basileia* to mean "kingly rule and reign," although we have clear instances where Jesus speaks of it in a spatial sense as "entering the *basileia*." Such an emphasis on G*d's kingly rule is often explicated in terms of domination. In this reading G*d becomes the king and sovereign whose will is law and must be obeyed.

In contrast, a translation of *basileia* in a spatial sense as "royal realm," or a collective sense as "kingdom" focuses on the people who constitute the *basileia* because according to ancestral tradition Israel was a covenant partner, a "kingdom of priests" (Exod. 19:6; Isa. 61:6; etc.).[48] That is, this tradition speaks in monarchical symbols about a radical egalitarian democratic polity. Still, such a political translation of *basileia* further depends on its meaning context. If *basileia* is contextualized in terms of millenarianism's imminent or thoroughgoing eschatology it becomes a vision of the "other world," a vision of "pie in the sky" that perpetually must be disappointed by historical developments.

However, it has been convincingly argued that none of the early *basileia* sayings attributed to Jesus bespeaks such an otherworldly expectation.[49] Hence, the meaning of *basiliea* must be contextualized differently. If contextualized in the sociopolitical paradigm of social and religious movements for justice, *basileia* becomes a critical political term. Its meaning context is the Roman imperial system, which also was termed *basileia,* and Israelite liberation movements. *Basileia* becomes the hallmark of the movement around Jesus as an anti-imperialist egalitarian movement that seeks change for all those living on the bottom of the kyriarchal pyramid of domination—the poor, the dehumanized, the powerless, and the outsiders.

---

[48] See my dissertation *Priester für Gott: Zum Herrschafts- und Priestermotiv in der Apokalypse* (Münster: Aschendorff Verlag, 1972), as well as Sheldon R. Isenberg, "Millenarianism in Greco-Roman Palestine," *Religion* 4 (1974): 26–46; idem, "Power through Temple and Torah in Greco-Roman Palestine," in *Christianity, Judaism, and Other Greco-Roman Cults,* ed. Jacob Neusner (Leiden: Brill, 1975), 3:24–52; and Jacob Neusner's extensive work, especially his *First Century Judaism in Crisis* (Nashville: Abingdon, 1975).

[49] Borg, *Jesus in Contemporary Scholarship,* 69–97.

The crucial question in this contextual model of social movement is not whether Jesus and the movements gathered in his name did or did not expect the imminent end of the world. Rather, the crucial research question is whether they were compelled by the vision of a "different *basileia*" that radically changed the oppressive situation in which they found themselves and that abolished all status privileges among themselves.

## CONCLUSION

I have suggested here that a modification of the reconstructive social-scientific model of millennialism in terms of social movements for change allows one to reconstruct a movement gathered in Jesus' name that inspires political-religious change rather than spiritualizing and depoliticizing it. Social-scientific Historical-Jesus study would become more rather than less scientific and objective if it would engage critical feminist questions and methodologies. Critical feminist Jesus studies bring to the conversation their insistence on a hermeneutics of suspicion that scrutinizes the ideological frameworks and political functions of research in the discourses of domination. I have proposed such a collaboration of feminist and social-scientific Historical-Jesus studies in the interest of emancipation and liberation to which both are committed and dedicated.

# 4

# OF SPECKS, BEAMS, AND METHODS

## Anti-Judaism and Antifeminism*

WHILE IN THE PRECEDING CHAPTERS I HAVE FOCUSED ON THE ACA-
demic discourses of malestream Historical-Jesus research, in this chapter I
want to shift focus and critically investigate the anti-Judaism debate in
feminist Jesus biblical studies as an academic discourse. Despite intensive
discussions (and recriminations) on anti-Judaism in Christian feminist
exegesis and theology, the noxious virus of structural anti-Judaism seems
to continue to breed in Christian academic and popular writings. Although
such anti-Judaism in feminist writings is rightly branded as "unforgivable
sin" against the Spirit, it nevertheless seems to persist. In the following I
want to pursue the reasons for our inability to root out anti-Jewish prejudices. As with other issues in the previous chapters, I will interrogate the
feminist discourse on anti-Judaism and analyze its power inscriptions. In
so doing I am not interested in going once more over the pros and cons of
the debate. Rather I am interested in investigating this debate as a discourse
and in asking which interests this discourse serves and what functions it
has in sustaining or changing relations of domination and prejudice.

It is my contention that the politics of the anti-Judaism accusation in
feminist discourses often serves antifeminist ends. It functions either to
keep in line Christian feminists who deviate from hegemonic dogmatics,
or it serves to advocate a conservative social-cultural and theological

---

* I am very grateful to my colleagues Professors Adele Reinhartz, of McMasters University, and Tal Ilan, of Hebrew University, for carefully reading this chapter and for giving me
their expert feedback. I have especially appreciated their candid warning that this chapter
will be misunderstood and will get me in trouble. Nevertheless, I do hope that the theoretical issues that I attempted to raise rather than personal acrimony will shape the discussion.

agenda, or to show that Jewish wo/men played only a minimal role in the Jesus movement. Again, I am not as much interested here in critiquing the anti-Jewish blind spots in individual works as in laying open for critical reflection the mechanisms and assumptions that reinscribe both anti-Jewish prejudice and antifeminist arguments.

## THE FEMINIST ANTI-JUDAISM DEBATE[1]

Christian feminist discourses have not invented but have taken over and reinscribed the anti-Jewish theoretical frameworks of malestream biblical scholarship which work with the assumption that Jesus and Christianity correspond to feminism whereas Torah and Judaism stand for patriarchy and misogyny. Jesus was a "feminist." He liberated wo/men from their degraded status in antiquity and especially in patriarchal Jewish religion, so the argument goes. Although Jewish feminists have again and again pointed to the anti-Jewish character and historical falsity of this argument, popular and scientific works on Jesus continue to stress the positive attitude of Jesus toward wo/men and his negative stance toward Jews, as though Jews were not wo/men and wo/men were not Jews. Even though Jewish and feminist scholars have consistently pointed to the anti-Jewish tendencies in the texts about Jesus, even women scholars go on to repro-

---

[1] For this debate see, for instance, Judith Plaskow, "Christian Feminism and Anti-Judaism, *Cross Currents* 33 (1978): 306–9; eadem, "Feministischer Antijudaismus und der christliche Gott," *Kirche und Israel* 5 (1990): 9–25; eadem, "Anti-Judaism in Feminist Christian Interpretation," in *Searching the Scriptures*, vol.1, *A Feminist Introduction*, ed. Elisabeth Schüssler Fiorenza (New York: Crossroad, 1993), 117–29; Annette Daum and Deborah McCauley, "Jewish Christian Feminist Dialogue: A Wholistic Vision," *Union Seminary Quarterly Review* 38 (1983): 147–218; Susannah Heschel, "Anti-Judaism in Christian Feminist Theology," *Tikkun* 5, no. 3 (1990): 26–28; David Tracy and Elisabeth Schüssler Fiorenza, eds., *The Holocaust as Interruption* (Concilium 175; Edinburgh: T & T Clark, 1984); Marie Theres Wacker, "Feminist Theology and Anti-Judaism: The Status of the Discussion and the Context of the Problem in the Federal Republic of Germany," *Journal of Feminist Studies in Religion* 7, no. 2 (1991): 109–16; and *Verdrängte Vergangenheit, die uns bedrängt: Feministische Theologie in der Verantwortung für die Geschichte*, ed. Leonore Siegele-Wenschkewitz (Munich: Kaiser, 1988); *Weil wir nicht vergessen wollen: Zu einer feministischen Theologie im deutschen Kontext*, ed. Christine Schaumberger (Anfragen 1; Münster: Morgana Frauenbuchverlag, 1987); Susannah Heschel, " Jüdisch-feministische Theologie und Antijudaismus in christlich-feministischer Theologie," in *Verdrängte Vergangenheit, die uns bedrängt*, ed. Siegele-Wenschkewitz, 54–103; Katharina von Kellenbach, *Anti-Judaism in Feminist Religious Writings* (Atlanta: Scholars Press, 1990).

duce such anti-Jewish stereotypes, albeit often unwittingly. The persistent evil of open or hidden anti-Judaism in popular and scholarly Christian arguments for the liberating uniqueness of Jesus seems to be inextricably intertwined with Historical-Jesus research and christological belief systems.

In the context of the feminist anti-Judaism discussion in the late 1970s and the early 1980s that was initiated by Judith Plaskow, I was the first to articulate the implications of this discussion for biblical scholarship, especially scholarship on Jesus and Christian origins. Over and against the "Jesus the feminist" interpretive model and its numerous variations in the studies about "Jesus and women," I insisted that this model must be replaced by a different historical framework that could place Jewish wo/men in the center of any reconstruction of the Jesus movement(s). Hence, I attempted to develop such a feminist reconstructive model of early Christian beginnings that could retrieve the memory of Jewish wo/men and make them historically visible. Moreover, I argued that any feminist impulse detectable in the Jesus movement must be derived from Judaism, since Jesus and his first wo/men disciples were Jews. Hence I began the chapter about the Jesus movement with this assertion:

> To speak about the Jesus movement is to speak about a Jewish movement that is part of Jewish history in the first century C.E. It is therefore misleading to speak about "Jesus and his Jewish background" as though Jesus' Judaism was not integral to his life and ministry, or to describe the behavior of Jesus' disciples over and against Jewish practice as though the first followers of Jesus were not Jews themselves.[2]

The following methodological principles that inform the chapter on the Jesus movement, I argued, should also govern the reconstructions of Christian beginnings. To reconstruct the history of the Jesus movement(s) means to reconstruct Jewish wo/men's history and vice versa:[3]

1. Greco-Roman, Jewish, and Christian texts and historical sources must be read as androcentric texts that marginalize or completely leave out wo/men. Texts are therefore best understood as rhetorical rather than as reflective of reality.

---

[2] Elisabeth Schüssler Fiorenza, *In Memory of Her: A Feminist Theological Reconstruction of Christian Origins* (New York: Crossroad, 1983; 10th Anniversary Edition With a New Introduction, 1994), 105.

[3] Naturally, these methodological rules apply to *all* historical source texts for the first century C.E. be they Greek, Roman, Syriac, or Coptic.

2. The glorification as well as the vilification or marginalization of wo/men is to be understood as a social construction of reality in kyriarchal terms or as elite male projection. Hence, texts are not descriptive of reality and do not necessarily reflect the actual situation of wo/men.

3. The formal canons of codified law are generally more restrictive than the social reality which they govern and the actual interaction and relationship of wo/men and men.

4. Wo/men's actual social-religious status must be determined according to the degree of their economic autonomy and social status rather than according to ideological prescriptive statements of elite men. While wo/men's social status is always dependent on their status in the household, it is also determined by their economic resources.

5. Jewish and Christian scholars are prone to reconstruct early Judaism and early Christianism not only in terms of what has survived as "normative" in their own respective traditions but also as two oppositional religious formations. Since "rabbinic" Judaism and "patristic" Christianity were the historical winners among the diverse inner-Jewish movements, such reconstructions insinuate that normative Judaism and normative Christianity adequately represent pre-70 Judaism in general and the Jesus movement in particular.

6. If our general picture of pre-70 Judaism is blurred and that of Christian beginnings is equally vague, the picture of the position and function of wo/men in the multifaceted Jewish movements at the beginning of the common era, among which the Jesus movement is to be counted, must remain even more historically elusive. Although the available materials still give us some clues to the historical situation of wo/men,[4] our knowledge about wo/men's history in antiquity depends greatly on the reconstructive methods and theoretical frameworks scholars use.

I still believe that these or similar feminist methodological and hermeneutical propositions would further a feminist historical reconstruction of early Jewish and early Christian history as the history of wo/men. However, whereas these methodological theses have not received

[4] Schüssler Fiorenza, In Memory of Her, 106–10.

much attention in the feminist discussion of anti-Judaism, one reviewer's false claim that *In Memory of Her* declares the Jesus movement to have been the *only Jewish* reform movement at the time has been widely quoted and repeated with approval. Although I have consistently rejected such a misconstrual of my work and have tried to set the record straight in the introduction to the tenth anniversary edition of *In Memory of Her* as well as in *Jesus: Miriam's Child, Sophia's Prophet,* numerous articles continue to ascribe such an anti-Jewish position to me, although I continue to reject it.

However, I have tried to heed such criticism when justified. For instance, although Jacob Neusner does not direct at my work his criticism of Christian Jesus scholarship (which argues that the notion of "renewal" movement still could be understood in supersessionist terms, suggesting that Christianity is a better form of Judaism), I have nevertheless corrected my use of this nomenclature.[5] Since I did not want to suggest such an interpretation in any way, I changed the designation of the Jesus movement as "renewal or reform movement" in my subsequent work and replaced it with the notion of "emancipatory" or *"basileia"* movement, clearly indicating that the reference point of such emancipation was not Judaism but Roman imperial domination.

Such a correction notwithstanding, the accusation of anti-Judaism persists among some Christian feminists. Although my critics acknowledge such self-corrective attempts, they seem to be bent on reading my text against my clearly expressed intentions. Hence one must ask, what is the motivation that compels them to insist on adopting anti-Jewish lenses and reading anti-Judaism into a work whose expressed intent is to combat anti-Judaism? If, as I have often said, what one sees depends on the lens through which one looks, one must scrutinize the lenses used in the feminist anti-Judaism discussion.

Christian interlocutors must acknowledge what Susan Brooks Thistlethwaite pointed out some time ago: Racism is a chronic disease and every one of us is like a recovering alcoholic who never can come completely clean. Since we all live in a racist culture and have been raised on a diet of structural theological anti-Judaism, we constantly have to examine our work for the persistence of such prejudices. None of us, despite consistent effort, can ever quite consider ourselves to be cured of the disease of internalized anti-Judaism.

I recall vividly a Group Project discussion several years after *In Memory*

---

[5] See Elisabeth Schüssler Fiorenza, *Jesus: Miriam's Child, Sophia's Prophet: Issues in Feminist Christology* (New York: Continuum, 1994), 91.

*of Her* had appeared. The students had re-presented the story of the hemorrhaging wo/man in Mark 5 and repeated its malestream interpretation that understands the text in light of the purity regulations of Leviticus. There was stunned silence when I criticized the group for not paying attention to the fact that according to Mark the problem is medical and economic rather than one of cultic purity. Finally, a student mustered the courage to object: "But we just followed what you said in *In Memory of Her.*" I checked and she was right: Without noticing it I had not quite managed to avoid the anti-Jewish stereotype against cultic purity. In view of the rampant anti-Jewish prejudice in malestream biblical studies, it would be surprising if no traces of anti-Judaism could be found in feminist works.

Hence, feminist scholars would do well to examine their own possible infection with the anti-Jewish virus before they point their finger at others. It is often easier to see the speck of anti-Judaism in the eyes of one's sisters than to recognize the beam clouding one's own vision. The issue I seek to raise can be illustrated with a Catholic joke that is an ironic variant of the story of the wo/man caught in adultery, who according to John 7:53–8:11 was brought before Jesus. After Jesus replies to her accusers, "Whoever is without sin may cast the first stone," he bends down and writes in the sand. Suddenly the first stone is thrown, barely missing Jesus' head. Startled, Jesus looks up and moans: "Mother, how could you?"[6]

In the feminist anti-Judaism discussion, the stone throwing seems not to stop. The reason for this appears to be the need to prove one's own innocence. It is the politics of niceness, whiteness, and correctness that fuels much of the finger pointing. By indicting others but not themselves for anti-Judaism, I suggest, Christian feminists reenact the kyriocentric script of the "white lady." Feminist-theological discourses occupy the structural kyriarchal position of the "white lady" when they insist that they are without blemish, pure, innocent, and unbiased. Wo/men in kyriarchal situations must repeatedly stress their innocence and purity in order to show that they are different from tainted others such as feminists, lesbians, blacks, Jews, heretics, pagans, or atheists.

Renate Nestvogel has pointed to the danger of needing to prove one's innocence:

> The fear of scholars to discover their own racism, in my observation, is neutralized, rejected, eliminated, or rationalized in and through an especially intensive interrogation and critique of the racism of others.

---

[6] For those readers who are not familiar with Catholic dogma: Mary is believed to have been conceived without sin.

To learn to admit one's own failings would be the first step to work through such sentiments. . . . If we do not do this, our selective view will always suspect others of such feelings, oppose them, and produce hostile stereotypes and thereby participate in the warlike, aggressive and violent forms of this society, which in one way or the other we have internalized.[7]

While many of the discussions of anti-Judaism claim to be feminist, they often neglect to elaborate what makes their interpretations of biblical texts about wo/men feminist. Antifeminism in biblical scholarship is often not recognized or is justified with the argument that either the feminist interpretation is anachronistic or that everything written by wo/men can be regarded as feminist. More recently, postfeminism, which "struggles for a gender anti-apartheid community of believers and biblical scholars alike," seems to have come into vogue and is often not recognized as actually being antifeminist.

Consider, for instance, the following definition of a postfeminist hermeneutics by the editor of the newest book on "Jesus and Women":

A post-feminist hermeneutics presupposes a feminist hermeneutics and is not possible where feminism has not yet taken root and where the liberation of women from patriarchal structures has not yet taken place. A postfeminist hermeneutics goes a step further and transcends gender boundaries. It implies the voicing of women without the silencing of men.[8]

Ingrid Rosa Kitzberger seems not to realize that her definition of feminism as silencing men and staying within gender boundaries repeats wellworn stereotypes of feminism. Moreover, she appears not to recognize that according to her own definition one cannot move toward "postfeminism" because the "eschaton" clearly has not yet arrived and the "liberation of women from patriarchal structures" in no way has been accomplished.

I raise the antifeminism question not because I want to deflect from the grave injustice of Christian anti-Judaism; rather I want to point out that much of what is considered to be feminist anti-Judaism is simply Christian anti-Judaism internalized by wo/men. What is missing in the midst of all the stone throwing is an investigation of how anti-Judaism, colonialist

---

[7] Renate Nestvogel, "'Fremdes' oder 'Eigenes'? Freiräume zwischen Ausgrenzung und Vereinnahmung," in *"Fremdes" oder "Eigenes"? Rassismus, Antisemitismus, Kolonialismus, Rechtsextremismus aus Frauensicht*, ed. Renate Nestvogel (Frankfurt: IKO-Verlag für Interkulturelle Kommunikation, 1994), 50.

[8] Ingrid Rosa Kitzberger, "Synoptic Women in John: Interfigural Readings," in *Transformative Encounters: Jesus & Women Re-viewed*, ed. Ingrid Rosa Kitzberger (Leiden: Brill, 2000), 80 n. 11.

racism, and antifeminism are part and parcel of the same kyriarchal system of interlocking oppressions and ideological prejudices. If wo/men scholars were aware of how much anti-Judaism, antifeminism, and racism are intermeshed, they would be much more hesitant to label as anti-Jewish feminist work that explicitly takes a stance against interlocking oppressions.

It is sometimes argued that Christian feminist theology has to engender two paradigm shifts: a shift from a patriarchal-sexist to a feminist paradigm, on the one hand, and, on the other, a shift from an anti-Jewish to a pro-Jewish or pro-Israel paradigm, a shift that can both acknowledge that Christian theology owes its existence to Judaism and respect the independence and integrity of Jewish faith and life.[9] However, it seems that feminist biblical studies have a difficult time accomplishing both paradigm shifts. In my view this is the case because this dual paradigm shift is envisioned as happening sequentially rather than simultaneously.

I do not want to be misunderstood: I am not arguing here for a feminist paradigm shift over a pro-Jewish one or vice versa. Rather I want to argue that anti-Judaism and antifeminism are two sides of one and the same kyriarchal coin. Therefore their eradication must go hand in hand. Texts cannot be anti-Jewish without also being antifeminist, and they cannot be anti-feminist without also at the same time being anti-Jewish because some wo/men are Jews and some Jews are wo/men. If one defines as feminist an interpretation that asks whether a text or reading is in the interest of wo/men (my definition of the feminist question), one always already advocates an interpretation that is also pro-Jewish, insofar as some wo/men are Jews. Hence, in Christian feminist theology the feminist paradigm shift must entail the pro-Jewish paradigm shift and vice versa. However, we will be able to bring about such a simultaneous feminist paradigm shift that overcomes anti-Judaism and misogyny only if and when feminist scholars become conscious and critical of the entanglement of anti-Jewish and antifeminist Christian theological knowledge that we have unwittingly internalized in and through religious socialization and academic or ministerial education.

In short, the critical feminist discussion of the structural prejudice of Christian anti-Judaism must not reinscribe and perpetuate either anti-

---

[9] Eveline Valtink, "Feministisch-christliche Identität und Antijudaismus," in *Von der Wurzel getragen: Christlich-feministische Exegese in Auseinandersetzung mit Antijudaismus,* ed. Luise Schottroff and Marie Theres Wacker (Leiden: Brill, 1996), 1–24, quotation from p. 23, with reference to Siegele-Wenschkewitz's work.

Judaism or antifeminism by indicting other feminists for anti-Judaism without also purging one's own work. Furthermore, this discussion must positively insist that feminist scholars do everything in our power to replace scholarly and popular anti-Jewish discourses of dehumanization with critical-feminist discourses of affirmation, respect, and appreciation.

To illustrate my thesis that the present feminist anti-Judaism discussion not only is fueled by the need to prove oneself innocent, but also has unintended antifeminist functions, I want to analyze two specific examples. In doing so I wish to explore the methodological and hermeneutical issues at stake in the accusation of anti-Judaism that is leveled by (Christian) feminists against other (Christian) feminists, without at the same time indicting anti-Judaism in malestream biblical scholarship, where it still has its home.

## IN DEFENSE OF PROTESTANT HERMENEUTICS

The need to prove oneself more orthodox is one of the reasons that seems to fuel the accusation of anti-Judaism in Christian feminist discussions. Susanne Heine, for instance, has indicted not just my work but all of feminist theology for anti-Judaism. She has accused other feminist theologians of "defaming and slandering Jews" but has not searched her own work for the pitfalls of anti-Judaism. Heine distinguishes between two different feminist arguments in modernity. One is the emancipatory "equality discourse" of the Enlightenment; the other is the essentialist "femininity" or "true womanhood" discourse of post-Enlightenment romanticism. The latter "femininity" or "true womanhood" discourse, which celebrates a special nature and essence of wo/men, in Heine's view is responsible for engendering anti-Judaism.

*In Memory of Her* clearly belongs to the "emancipatory discourse" rather than the "femininity discourse" classification. Since Heine is bent on construing it as anti-Jewish, however, she is compelled to misread the book and to squeeze it into the procrustean bed of romanticism. In order to be able to classify *In Memory of Her* as "romantic," although it clearly does not advocate "the femininity discourse," she must alienate it from its Catholic matrix and construe it in terms of the "myth of the golden age," which informs Protestant reconstructions of Christian origins. Like others before her, she misunderstands my reconstructive historical model as a "model of decline" rather than as a "model of ongoing conflict and struggle" between kyriarchal domination and radical democratic structures and world-views—a struggle that runs squarely through ancient and modern history. With the color-coded racist headline, "White Jesus on Black Background," Heine argues that I portray Jesus, the itinerant preacher, in a "bright light" in order to contrast him with the patriarchal darkness of the Jewish society of his day. I allegedly see Jesus not just as an inner-Jewish critic but as fundamentally overcoming Judaism.[10] A few pages later Heine maintains that *In Memory of Her* leaves out the "faith dimension" together with "G*d, revelation and christology" insofar as it is allegedly concerned only with the history of wo/men as the people of G*d.[11]

As to this second charge, Heine goes on to mistake my reconstructive historical model for a theological model that lacks belief in divine revelation. Consequently she maintains that this model proves *In Memory of Her* to be representative of the kind of liberal theology whose apologetic image of

> Jesus always has been what the present demands. It has described Jesus as an Enlightenment figure in the context of an unenlightened Judaism, which is usually characterized as primitive and hopelessly patriarchal. The reason for this negative portrayal of Judaism is the fact that it still believes "in G*d's revelation in the Torah."[12]

Thus Heine accuses *In Memory of Her* not just of anti-Judaism but also of unorthodoxy, insofar as the book allegedly indicts Judaism because of its faith in the divine revelation of the Torah.

How is it possible that a theologian who prides herself on being scientific, objective, and accurate permits herself to engage in such a parody of a colleague's work? A check of all her references to *In Memory of Her* indicates that her caricaturing misreading is triggered not so much by my alleged anti-Judaism as by my critical-feminist hermeneutics, which she deems no longer to be Christian. It seems that the accusation of anti-

---

[10] Susanne Heine, "Die feministische Diffamierung von Juden," in *Der Feministische "Sündenfall"? Antisemitische Vorurteile in der Frauenbewegung*, ed. Charlotte Kohn-Ley and Ilse Korotin (Vienna: Picus, 1994), 15–59, especially 22. Her article is part of the documentation of a symposium sponsored by the Jewish Institute for Adult Education that took place in 1993 in Vienna. Her article is framed and corrected by the essay of Hannelore Schröder entitled "Otto Weinigers Antifeminismus und Antisemitismus." Schröder convincingly shows that anti-Semitism and antifeminism are two sides of the same reactionary "coin." It is also corrected through the balanced contribution of Anita Natmessnig entitled "Antisemitismus und feministische Theologie."

[11] Heine, "Die feministische Diffamierung," 25.

[12] Ibid., 26.

Judaism is used here instrumentally as a weapon against my alleged anti-Christianism, which seems to be the predominant problem for apologetic feminists. Again and again Heine points out that I locate revelation and truth neither in the Lutheran "canon-within-the-canon" principle nor in the scientific objectivism of malestream biblical scholarship but rather in the *ekklēsia* of wo/men and its scriptural prototype. Hence, the accusation of anti-Judaism seems to be triggered by a feminist-hermeneutical model that offends Heine's Protestant theological understanding of revelation with its insistence on *sola scriptura*.

However, in her book *Frauen der frühen Christenheit*, which appeared two years after *In Memory of Her*, Heine did not accuse me of anti-Judaism. Rather she correctly observed that the "present and not the past praxis of (women) Church testifies to what is decisive for it."[13] This notwithstanding, even though she emphasizes that the "canon is not a book of doctrines," she goes on to insist that "the New Testament is the measuring rod for what it means to be Christian." The Christian Testament's "contemporary significance for women as well as for theology and church must be measured or corrected" with this canon.[14]

According to Heine, the baptismal formula of Gal. 3:28, "There is neither Jew nor Greek, slave nor free, male and female in Christ Jesus," constitutes such a "canon within the canon." Heine claims that the gist of this verse comes from Jesus himself. Moreover, she maintains that, without question, "the baptismal formula of Gal. 3:28 represents already in the Jesus group something like a *specificum Christianum* which reflects the authentic praxis of Jesus." From here one need only make a small step in order to contrast Judaism negatively with the extraordinary and unique praxis of Jesus.

> The history of Christianity begins with the confession to Jesus' praxis which is opposed to the hegemonic life praxis of his Jewish context. Jesus himself understands it as the praxis of the reign of God, in which the difference between the sexes does not play a role as a matter of principle. The praxis of Jesus cannot be deduced either from the Jewish or from the Hellenistic praxis of the relation between the sexes.[15]

I need to stress once more that I am not interested in accusing Heine of intentional anti-Judaism. Rather I seek to inquire why Heine, in her accu-

---

[13] Susanne Heine, *Frauen der frühen Christenheit*, 14 (translated by John Bowden as *Women and Early Christianity: A Reappraisal* [Minneapolis: Augsburg, ©1987, 1988]).
[14] Heine, *Frauen in der frühen Christenheit*, 59.
[15] Ibid., 163f.

sation of anti-Judaism in feminist theology, does not problematize her own hermeneutical framework, which stresses the uniqueness of the praxis of Jesus and introduces Gal. 3:28 as a scriptural principle that can be traced back to Jesus himself. While she accuses others, Heine in no way reflects critically on how her own scholarly work reinscribes the structural anti-Judaism of malestream biblical and theological scholarship, which paints Judaism as the negative contrasting image to Christianity and underscores the uniqueness of Jesus. Moreover, Heine insists on the value-neutrality and objectivity of scientific scholarship;[16] hence she is not able to critically elucidate how hegemonic scientific biblical scholarship and its methods reinscribe and perpetuate anti-Jewish thought patterns. The absence of a critical reflection on christology and Christian identity formation has the same effect.

Like others before her, Heine argues that it was not Jesus but christology that led to the separation of Christianity from Judaism in the first century. It was the "belief in Christ's divine nature that initiated this separation process and produced anti-Judaism which would become the stain or blemish of Christian culture."[17] Since she locates the stain of anti-Judaism in christology and Christian culture rather than in the Christian Testament, she is not able to critically reflect on how high christology and hostile anti-Judaism are intertwined at the roots. Instead she maintains that "christology is neither implicitly nor explicitly anti-Jewish, even though it was interpreted in such a way throughout the centuries."[18] Heine does not deny "the global judgments against 'the Jews' inscribed in New Testament Scriptures," but she insists over and against the majority of exegetes that they are found "specifically in the later writings, when no direct contact existed any longer with Jewish communities."[19] Christianity and Judaism are two independent religions that are nevertheless somewhat interdependent. Although Judaism does not share in christology, Christianity remains obligated to the Torah and its ethical-moral functions.

Moreover, in Heine's view religion in its essence cannot be oppressive but can only be misused to oppress. With Gordon Alpert she defines religion "not as self-justification, self-aggrandizement, but as humility, self-

---

[16] See Susanne Heine, "Brille der Parteilichkeit: Zu einer feministischen Hermeneutik," *Evangelische Kommentare* 23 (1990): 354–57, where she rejects my criticism of positivism and objectivism in malestream biblical studies as unscientific.

[17] Heine, "Die feministische Diffamierung," 26.

[18] Ibid., 43f.

[19] Ibid., 41.

abrogation, and love for the neighbor."[20] This definition determines the notion of religion very much in Christian (romantic, feminine) terms and reinscribes into the essence of religion the old anti-Jewish opposition between justice and love. Since Heine does not problematize the interwovenness of christology with anti-Judaism and its devastating consequences, she falls victim to the same romantic essentialist thinking promoted by the romantic "femininity feminism" she criticizes.

Since Heine's essentialist theological concept of religion is unable to critically reflect on its historical roots and diverse forms, she is forced to separate an essentialist kernel from contingent historical discourses in order to "purify" the innermost essence of religion. Just as Heine's argumentative strategy seeks to free christology and religion from their historical responsibility for dehumanizing injustice and domination, so also "femininity feminism" attempts to absolve wo/men from their historical responsibility for injustice and prejudice. Both "femininity feminism" and Heine's emotional polemic against it are funded by an unhistorical essentialist philosophy that, as Plaskow, Heschel, and others have elucidated, remains a fecund nurturing ground for anti-Judaism. In contrast to such an ahistorical theological essentialist hermeneutical approach, the kyriarchal analytic that I have developed is capable of showing why essentialist discourses again and again engender dehumanizing ideologies for legitimizing structures and mind-sets of domination.

Heine's critique of "femininity feminism" fails to recognize that the romantic femininity discourse or, as I would dub it, the ideology of the "white lady," has not been invented by feminists but has been produced by hegemonic structures of domination. Wo/men are not simply victims of this discourse but they participate in it insofar as they actively appropriate the subject position of domination it offers. The cultural feminine roles into which they are slotted by kyriarchal structures are mediated ideologically through education, schools, and cultural media. Euro-American white wo/men had and still have the task within this system not just to mediate kyriarchal knowledge, culture, and religion but also to control other wo/men in the interest of the hegemonic cultural system of domination.

In short, Heine's indictment of other feminist work for anti-Judaism is inspired both by her Protestant hermeneutics of *sola scriptura* and by her polemic against "femininity feminism." While I agree with the latter, I

[20] Ibid., 45.

obviously do not subscribe to the former. Moreover, Heine does not realize that both follow the same cultural essentialist logic that has engendered
not only the "myth" of pristine early Christian origins based on *sola scriptura* but also the cultural discourses on femininity and true womanhood
as the discourses of the "white lady."

### AGAINST THE PROTESTANT MYTH OF CHRISTIAN ORIGINS

The need to distance oneself from one's religious background and
upbringing is another reason for charging others with anti-Judaism. Kathleen Corley's essay entitled "The Egalitarian Jesus," which was published in
*Forum*, the in-house publication of the Jesus Seminar, in turn seems to
derive its logic from her pathos against the scholarly "myth of pristine
Christian origins," which was first indicted by her teacher Burton Mack.
This "myth" of pristine origins is related to the Protestant decline thesis
and its attendant anti-Judaism. But whereas Mack's critique rightly points
to the functions of this myth in maintaining Christian relations of domination, Corley applies it to marginal feminist voices that resist domination. In this essay she continues her polemic against "the feminist myth" of
Christian origins, as she labels an egalitarian reconstructive model of the
early Christian movements—a polemic that she first published in the
Festschrift for Burton Mack. While at first glance it is not clear why Corley
goes out of her way to attack "egalitarianism," a careful rhetorical analysis
can elucidate the kyriarchal anti-Jewish implications of this attack, since
one can easily show that egalitarianism is intrinisic to many forms of
Judaism.

Since Corley comes from a Protestant evangelical tradition, her primary
goal is to lay to rest the Protestant "myth" of pristine radical egalitarian
Christian origins. Thus, her target of criticism is the same as that of Heine
though she does not refer to Heine's work. In the first part of the article
Corley discusses the methods used to establish the "egalitarian Jesus," who,
according to her, is at the center of the myth of pristine Christian origins.
She asserts that the portrayal of the "egalitarian Jesus" needs Judaism as its
negative foil without considering my argument that the opposite is the
case: Jesus can only be understood as egalitarian if at least some strands of
Judaism in antiquity were egalitarian. Corley is not able to consider this
point because her thesis identifies egalitarianism as the crux of the anti-
Jewish myth of origins.

Hence, she goes on to repeat the by now familiar argument that most

books on "Jesus and wo/men" paint a graphic picture of the desolate status of Jewish wo/men as negative "background" to the positive relationship
of Jesus to wo/men. After having done so, scholars go on to compare Jewish wo/men with Hellenistic and Roman wo/men, who also suffered a bad
lot but were much better off than Jewish wo/men of the time. Over against
this negative cultural and anti-Jewish "background" depiction, scholars
then portray the liberating revolutionary figure of Jesus. This observation
has been amply proven to be correct, but Corley does not problematize it
further by investigating the politics of meaning that needs a negative construction of Judaism as its foil. If she had focused on an analysis of the
hegemonic "myth" of pristine Christian origins and its function for contemporary churches, rather than on an assumed "feminist egalitarian
myth," she might have been able to recognize the generative force of Christian anti-Judaism that is at work in the Christian discourses on "Jesus and
wo/men."

Corley seems to take it for granted that her postulated feminist myth of
origins leads to a negative portrait of Judaism because Jesus is seen as
"egalitarian." She does not consider that one cannot simply construct a
feminist "myth" as identical with the hegemonic myth of origins because
its politics of meaning asserts Christian supersessionism and the superiority of Christianity over and against Judaism but certainly not egalitarianism.

It is not egalitarianism, I contend, but the need to assert the superiority
of Christianity over and against feminists as well as over and against other
religions that engenders Christian anti-Judaism. In order to maintain such
Christian supremacy, which is thrown into question by feminist criticism,
apologetic writers maintain that Christianity is superior to Judaism because
it allegedly has improved the dismal status of Jewish and Greco-Roman
wo/men.

Corley with many others rightly argues against such an apologetic contention, that the "situation of revolutionary radical beginnings" did not
last but was rapidly reversed either by "the reassertion of Jewish tradition,"
or by "the encroachment of pagan or Hellenistic conservatism," or by "the
threat of gnosticism which offered more roles for wo/men," so that "by the
second or third centuries the reversal was complete."[21] Yet Corley does not
take her argument to its logical conclusion, that anti-Judaism ceased when

---

[21] Kathleen Corley, "The Egalitarian Jesus: A Christian Myth of Origins," *Forum New
Series* 1–2 (1998): 295.

the situation of pristine egalitarian beginnings ceased—an argument she obviously cannot make historically. Hence, she cannot recognize that it is not egalitarianism but the alleged "decline" into structures of domination that spawned anti-Judaism.

Instead, with Jonathan Z. Smith, Corley indicts the rhetorics of a radical egalitarian Jesus movement and the critique of its decline into an institutionalized hierarchical church as Protestant "anti-Catholic apologetics."[22] However, Corley does not pause to ask whether the critique of hierarchalism in the name of egalitarianism is actually anti-Catholic and would be seen as such by Catholic feminists. Nor does she question the underlying assumption that Protestantism and not Catholicism was at its roots egalitarian.

In a third section of her article Corley seeks to correct this by now familiar analysis of pristine origins and rapid decline with an elaboration of the situation of Jewish wo/men in the first century C.E.,[23] which she correctly asserts was not different from that of their Gentile compatriots. This part of her essay brings together the rich fruit of feminist research on the situation of wo/men in the first centuries C.E., which in the past two decades has become a field of study in its own right, a field which *In Memory of Her* pioneered. While individual studies may differ in their results, this research has documented that, without question, wo/men were active and sometimes leading participants in the diverse forms of Judaism in and outside of Palestine in the first centuries C.E. But if this was the case, why Corley's polemic against egalitarianism?

Although Corley documents the broad and exciting results of this new field of historical Wo/men's Studies, she does not discuss the theoretical framework that allows her to select and valorize some studies and not others. Moreover, she does not ask why no full-fledged *feminist* historical reconstruction of the diverse formations of first-century Judaism exists, a reconstruction that would provide a different historical framework able to unseat the topical androcentric approach that determines the studies of "wo/men in Judaism." One must ask whether such a lack of a feminist reconstructive framework is due to the fact that the field remains caught up in the "add wo/men and stir approach" of malestream reconstructive

---

[22] Ibid., 296.
[23] For a critical review of research on Jewish wo/men in the Second Temple period, see Tal Ilan, *Mine and Yours Are Hers: Retrieving Women's History from Rabbinic Literature* (Leiden: Brill, 1997), 1–50.

models. Or, one might ask, is Corley not interested in this question because she is bent on debunking feminist egalitarianism? Instead of reflecting on what a feminist egalitarian reconstruction of early Judaism would look like and showing how it would differ, for instance, from my own reconstruction of the Jewish Jesus movement, Corley chooses once more to find the "speck" of anti-Judaism in my theoretical vision. Although she acknowledges that I was the first to take a stance against anti-Jewish assumptions in early Christian studies and that I have again and again clarified my reconstructive model in order to defend against its anti-Jewish misreading, she nevertheless claims that, despite my good intentions, "[t]he reconstruction of Jesus' movement in *In Memory of Her* still functions to reinforce the 'Jesus the feminist' model that preceded her."[24] In order to support her case, Corley makes a number of allegations that I will briefly address.

According to Corley, I allegedly set Jesus apart from his environment in order to establish a foundation for modern feminist theology. This is a curious argument in two ways: first, it assumes that Jesus' Jewish environment could not possibly have been egalitarian, and second, it implies that to point out the theological significance of the Jesus movement for contemporary Christian feminists is by definition anti-Jewish.

Corley further maintains that I do not identify a comparable Jewish renewal movement, although I claim that the Jesus movement was one among several Jewish emancipatory movements. This objection is simply disingenuous, because *In Memory of Her* not only follows standard scholarship in outlining the Jewish "sectarian" movements known primarily through the work of the Jewish apologist Flavius Josephus but also asks for the first time, to my knowledge, about the participation of wo/men in these movements. Not only is Corley well aware of the scarcity of sources on alternative movements within Judaism. She also knows that the available information on such sects or movements is treated differently by different scholars. Tal Ilan characterizes this research situation as follows:

> Second Temple Judaism was undoubtedly characterized by a strong schismatic tendency. Sects abounded, each with its own unique interpretation of Scripture and each with its own theology. Their Jewishness was demonstrated by their adherence to a more or less similar corpus of holy books . . . and by a profession of monotheism. Otherwise they were mutually exclusive, each claiming to represent the only correct Judaism, while denying its

[24] Corley, "Egalitarian Jesus," 302.

sister a similar claim. . . . Thus the Jesus movement was just one other option in the colourful array of religious, social and political affiliation options available to the Palestinian Jew [sic] during the first century C.E.[25]

*In Memory of Her* not only points to the lack of sources for pre-70 Judaism but also carefully discusses the scarce information on wo/men's equality and leadership in general, and on Jewish wo/men in particular, that was available at the time. Moreover, with the story of Judith I proposed that wo/men were Pharisees and lived according to the Pharisaic ethos, a suggestion that was sternly rejected by Susanne Heine but has been positively affirmed by Tal Ilan.[26]

Corley further claims that I still "juxtapose [sic] Jesus over and against Judaism" by emphasizing that Jesus preached the "wholeness[27] of all" in contrast to "the holiness of the elect." However, in order to make her point, she needs to quote out of context. After elaborating the vision that the Jesus movement shared with the diverse Jewish movements of the time, I commented on its particularity as follows:

> The Jesus movement in Palestine does not totally[28] reject the validity of Temple and Torah as symbols of Israel's election but offers an alternative interpretation of them by focusing on the people itself as the locus of G*d's power and presence. By stressing the present possibility of Israel's wholeness, the Jesus movement integrates prophetic-apocalyptic and wisdom theology insofar as it fuses eschatological hope with the belief that the G*d of Israel is the creator of all human beings, even the maimed, the unclean, and the sinners. . . . Wholeness spells holiness and holiness manifests itself precisely in human wholeness.[29]

Corley concedes in places that even if Jesus had preached an egalitarian message, this would "not make him necessarily anti-Jewish." But she hastens to add that it is not likely that Jesus advocated an "egalitarian program directed toward women as women, although his message addressed issues important to women (as to men)." Yet at no place did *In Memory of Her*

[25] Tal Ilan, "In the Footsteps of Jesus: Jewish Wo/men in a Jewish Movement," in *Transformative Encounters*, ed. Kitzberger, 123–24.

[26] Heine, "Brille der Parteilichkeit," 354–57; Tal Ilan, "The Attraction of Aristocratic Jewish Women to Pharisaism," *Harvard Theological Review* 88 (1995): 1–33.

[27] Today I would problematize the expression "wholeness" as inadequate on feminist theoretical grounds and speak of "well-being."

[28] I would now strike this word as misleading since the next sentence makes clear that I do not speak of rejection but of a different interpretation.

[29] Schüssler Fiorenza, *In Memory of Her*, 120.

suggest that Jesus directed a program to *women as women*. Instead, it focused on the question of whether we still can detect egalitarian elements in the earliest Jesus traditions that challenge kyriarchal structures and mind-sets.

Whereas Corley claims that an egalitarian ethos and praxis of the Jesus movement is improbable and anti-Jewish to boot, she nevertheless explains its decline. She unproblematically assumes that conservative trends in society from the first to the third centuries led to the subsequent changes of wo/men's role in early Christianity rather than, as I supposedly hold, that "the encroachment of Greco-Roman social institutions" led to the decline in the status of early Christian wo/men. However, as she herself recognizes, I do not work with a model of "decline" from pristine egalitarian beginnings to kyriarchal institutionalization but with a model of ongoing struggles between egalitarianism and kyriarchy. I trace this struggle by reading the so-called household code texts as kyriarchal texts advocating the ethos of domination and submission, an ethos which since the time of Plato and Aristotle has been used over and against an egalitarian democratic ethos.

In sum, Corley seems to be agitated by my reconstruction of Jesus as a Sophia-inspired prophet who fostered "a new egalitarian movement of social equality." She simply refuses to recognize that it is in her (mis)reading of my text that the egalitarian movement becomes "new" and that "Jesus remains without peer in Palestine in his teaching of egalitarian reform." One wonders what is so threatening for her in the idea of an egalitarian movement as the root of Christianity (and in my view also of Judaism albeit in a different sociotheological form) that she cannot avoid such misreadings.

I can understand when such attacks against my egalitarian feminist ideology come frequently from malestream conservative scholars and churchmen, but it is difficult to see why a wo/man scholar who claims to be a feminist is bent on debunking the possibility of an egalitarian ethos in the first century. Is it because she cannot imagine that some formations of early Judaism could have been egalitarian? Or is it that she cannot assert an equal standing or even decisive leadership either for Jewish wo/men or for feminist scholars who assert such equality? Several clues or symptoms in Corley's text indicate that the latter is the case. Perhaps it is this that inhibits her historical imagination of the former.

*First,* Corley observes that some malestream and feminist biblical scholars agree on the egalitarian ethos of the Jesus movement. She notes that

Crossan, Horsley, and Borg have been influenced by my ideas,[30] but she does not ask whether they have co-opted them in the process or whether they have seriously discussed my framework and method especially with respect to anti-Judaism. One would have expected that after having established the dangers of the "Jesus the feminist" model, she then would have gone on to investigate the work of these scholars as to its anti-Jewish tendencies. Instead she chastises only my work for anti-Judaism although, as she herself acknowledges, I have done everything I can to avoid it.

*Second,* when discussing *Jesus: Miriam's Child, Sophia's Prophet,* Corley notes that I maintain "a critical distance from mainstream" biblical studies and postmodern criticism because I fear that feminist work is in danger of being co-opted by "'malestream' academic theories."[31] Here, she makes clear that she distances herself from the descriptive feminist term "malestream," which I have taken over from feminist theorists not only because it more adequately characterizes the "mainstream" tradition but also because "mainstream" reinscribes the de facto "malestream" biblical and Western cultural traditions as central and wo/men's and other subaltern traditions as marginal. She claims that by maintaining this distance from postmodern criticism I thereby

> discourage the work of both historical-critical feminist scholars, on the one hand, and postmodernist feminist scholars on the other, in favor of a feminist scholarship that must by its nature be defined as theological, in order to be considered feminist. In doing this Schüssler Fiorenza creates a dichotomy between "good feminists" who follow her method of theological reconstruction and "bad feminists" (so-called "gender feminists"[32]) who do not.[33]

Those familiar with my work will recognize that this statement entails several inaccurate and inadequate insinuations. Corley's accusation is bolstered by reference to *The Postmodern Bible* but does not mention my critical reply to it in *Sharing Her Word.*[34] Moreover, my point has been not that *only* certain feminist work but that *all feminist work* including my own is

[30] Corley, "Egalitarian Jesus," 291f.
[31] Ibid., 304.
[32] I have distinguished "gender feminists," that is, feminists who use an essentializing dualistic gender framework, from liberationist feminists, who work with a multiplex analysis of domination on *theoretical* but not on theological grounds.
[33] Corley, "Egalitarian Jesus," 304.
[34] Elisabeth Schüssler Fiorenza, *Sharing Her Word: Feminist Biblical Interpretation in Context* (Boston: Beacon Press, 1998), 15–21.

open to co-optation by the kyriarchal powers that are. Hence, it is Corley who creates a "false dichotomy" between feminist scholars.

Relatedly, Corley maintains that I am "inimical to the use of biblical critical methods by feminists (except for the theological method)." She does not mention, however, that I have criticized only certain kinds of biblical (positivist) and postmodern (ludic, i.e., playful) studies but not biblical criticism or postmodern scholarship *tout court*. How could I do so, since my work is firmly rooted in historical and rhetorical biblical method as well as feminist theory?

Moreover, I have never argued that theological feminist scholarship is superior to other feminist scholarship, as Corley claims, although I have consistently maintained that because of the nature of its object of study, biblical scholarship must investigate not just the philological, historical, archaeological, or literary features of biblical texts but also their theological rhetoric. True, I have always acknowledged that I am socially located in the Catholic tradition and as a "connected critic" do my work for wo/men belonging to this and other biblical traditions and communities. This, however, does not mean to argue that feminist scholarship must be theological in order to be feminist.[35] Rather, it means that feminist scholarship must remain engaged with and accountable to a feminist movement for change.

*Finally*, Corley maintains not only that I am suspicious of critical biblical methods but also that I am inconsistent because I myself use such "malestream" methods for my own historical reconstructions. She mentions as a specific example my critique of John Dominic Crossan and the Jesus Seminar for relying on the particular stratigraphy of Q while I myself presuppose the hypothesis of Q. Admittedly, I have criticized Crossan and the Jesus Seminar but I have done so for different reasons. I have critically questioned the Jesus Seminar not because it presupposes the hypothesis of Q—which I also presuppose in my work—but because the Jesus Seminar's polling method uses a reductionist consumer approach derived from market research, insofar as scholars cast votes to decide whether Jesus texts are authentic or secondary.

Since the literary stratigraphy of John Kloppenborg is often connected to tradition and redaction criticism and espouses the sociological-cultural understanding of the Jesus movement as a Cynic movement, it operates

---

[35] See my interview with Alice Bach, "Feminist Biblical Method: Interview with Alice Bach," *Biblicon* 3 (1998): 27–44.

within a liberal "de-Judaizing" framework. Richard Horsley and Jonathan Draper's study of Q shows that this framework, as it is elaborated, for instance, by Burton Mack is anti-Jewish.[36] Why then does Corley indict me for allegedly prohibiting other feminists from using the scientific method of stratigraphy but not criticize Mack (her teacher) and the Jesus Seminar (publisher of her article) for anti-Judaism? Does Corley point out the speck in her feminist colleagues' eyes in order not to see the beam in that of her brother teachers and colleagues? Is she really not so much troubled by anti-Judaism as by the claim to egalitarianism, as the title of her article indicates?

The feminist anti-Judaism debate seems so damaging (and so depressive) because it remains within and reinscribes the Christian hermeneutical framework and approach that through positivistic readings of kyriocentric texts marginalizes both wo/men and Jews by valorizing Jesus as the liberated man, and by deprecating Judaism as patriarchal. If I understand Corley correctly, she seems to think that one can undermine this framework by refusing to see the Jesus movement as egalitarian. She seems to believe that a reading of the Jesus movement as egalitarian is by definition anti-Jewish, whereas an interpretation that stresses its nonegalitarian character is pro-Jewish.

Several points can be made against such a hermeneutical assumption, which apparently mistakes as feminist the framework of conservative and liberal theology that insists, over and against Judaism, on the singularity of Jesus the great man and hero. *In Memory of Her,* together with all of my feminist work, has sought to counteract this anti-Jewish interpretive model. First, I have decentered Jesus, making him a member, albeit a crucial one, of a Jewish emancipatory movement. Second, I have sought to destabilize the positivistic historical method of Jesus research, which reinscribes androcentric and anti-Jewish source texts as historical evidence. Instead, third, I have argued that scholars must stand accountable for the historical and rhetorical models determining their historical reconstructions. It is on this methodological level that historical and theological claims must be negotiated and accounted for. Fourth, I have sought to undermine the *criterion of dissimilarity* and radical difference between Jews and the Jesus movement(s), as well as between the past and the present, that underlies malestream and feminist anti-Jewish reconstructions of the Jesus movement.

---

[36] Richard A. Horsley with Jonathan A. Draper, *Whoever Hears Me: Prophets, Performance, and Tradition in Q* (Harrisburg, Pa.: Trinity Press International, 1999).

In conclusion—to tease out the logic of the argument: If one were, on the one hand, to set out—as most malestream Historical-Jesus scholarship has done until very recently and still does in some quarters today—to reconstruct the Jesus movement as part and parcel of its allegedly patriarchal-kyriarchal Jewish society and culture, one would not diminish but would strengthen the discourses stereotyping Judaism as patriarchal. On the other hand, if one would want to promote the Christian feminist claim that the "real" Jesus was not tainted by patriarchalism, one would be logically compelled to construct aspects of Judaism as egalitarian. Such an egalitarian Christian feminist reconstruction of the Jesus movement would no longer need to insist that Jesus was un-Jewish because he was egalitarian. Hence, such a reading would cease to reinscribe the allegedly patriarchal ethos of Judaism as inimical to Jewish and all other wo/men. In other words, it was and is my contention that only if one recognizes the egalitarian forces in Judaism can one avoid reinscribing the vilification of Jewish wo/men and argue that Jesus as a Jew was egalitarian.

## THE ANTI-JUDAISM DEBATE
## IN JEWISH FEMINIST WRITINGS

The problem of Christian anti-Judaism has been treated differently by different Jewish feminist scholars, and I can mention here only a few crucial contributors. First, an apologetic hermeneutics seems to be operative in the work of the Jewish scholar Ross Shepard Kraemer, who investigates the participation of Jewish wo/men in the Jesus movement. In a recent article Shepard Kraemer also starts by responding to the Christian hermeneutics that pits "Jesus the feminist" over and against depraved Judaism and presents Jewish wo/men as "subordinate and disadvantaged by virtue of being wo/men."[37] Rather than rejecting this construction with its anti-Jewish and androcentric assumptions on theological grounds, she sets out to document that it cannot be "proven" by the "evidence" we have. To do so she adopts the positivist statistical method of prosopography, counting the passages on wo/men in the gospels and reading them as "data" in the androcentric minimalist way that marginalizes wo/men. The outcome is, as one might expect, very similar to malestream Christian interpretations.

---

[37] Ross Shepard Kraemer, "Jewish Women and Christian Origins: Some Caveats," in *Women and Christian Origins,* ed. Ross Shepard Kraemer and Mary Rose D'Angelo (New York: Oxford University Press, 1999), 35–49, especially 42.

After a careful scrutiny of the textual evidence on Jewish wo/men who are said to have joined the Jesus movement, Shepard Kraemer concludes:

> The actual number of wo/men represented by the texts as participating in the Jesus movement who are identifiable as Jews is fairly small. As I have pointed out in several earlier studies, these women are almost always represented as anomalous in some respect, often with regard to ancient cultural constructions of gender. . . . Though I do not want to downplay the complex reasons women, both Jewish and non-Jewish, may have had for joining the movement centered on Jesus and his teachings, I think it is unwise to ignore the potential implications of these observations. Missing among the women portrayed as Jesus' close disciples and supporters are married women with husbands and children. . . . Missing are also aristocratic women comparable in social class and status to the non-Jewish wo/men who populate the pages of Acts.[38]

Moreover, appealing to the scientific authority of the Jesus Seminar's polling practices, Shepard Kraemer declares all gospel texts on women to be inauthentic. Although she deliberately refrains from any critical investigation of the authenticity of the texts on wo/men, she expresses "serious doubts that any of these episodes go back to Jesus himself."[39] One is tempted to ask, what is new? Until it was challenged by feminist interpretation, malestream Christian scholarship has always "known" that wo/men did not and do not count. Rather than challenging the androcentric-kyriocentric tenets of such scholarship, Shepard Kraemer confirms its basic assumption that wo/men are and always have been marginal. In so doing she continues to focus on the positivist method of Historical-Jesus research and fails to mine the rich feminist scholarship on the gospel texts she discusses.

At the end of her article Shepard Kraemer herself also recognizes the pitfalls of the apologetic approach that defends against the "Jesus the feminist" model and the danger of perpetuating its ideological functions without critically discussing the positivist methods and ideological frameworks of its constructions.

---

[38] Ibid., 44f.

[39] Ibid., 41. The corroborating n. 24, however, does not distinguish between sayings and narratives when it refers to the Jesus Seminar: ". . . it is interesting to note that the members of the self-designated 'Jesus-Seminar' consider none of these sayings authentic to Jesus. Rather they are all printed in black, denoting the seminar's consensus that Jesus said none of them, and that each is the work of later tradents or authors" (p. 48).

In the desire to combat feminist Christian anti-Judaism, there is always the danger that we may unwittingly allow Christian scholarship and theological concerns to dictate the reconstruction of Jewish women's lives.[40]

I could not agree more. Feminists must never relax their vigilance against anti-Judaism so that we do not perpetuate unwittingly anti-Jewish and anti-Semitic racist and misogynist prejudices. Racist and sexist ideas such as anti-Judaism that are produced by institutions and acted out by people not only can kill but have killed in the name of G\*d. However, this caveat applies not just to theological but to all scholarship that is not critically aware of the interconnections of knowledge and power.

Second, although, like Shepard Kraemer, the Israeli scholar Tal Ilan focuses on Jesus the individual and uses a somewhat positivist method "for procuring historical data," her study "In the Footsteps of Jesus: Jewish Wo/men in a Jewish Movement" comes to different results.[41] This is the case, I suggest, because she does not adopt an apologetic approach to the question. Rather she seeks to decenter "the feminist Jesus" by first placing Jewish wo/men in antiquity at the center of attention and then seeing Jesus in light of their situation. She points to three central features in the materials about Jesus: his healing activity, his understanding as a prophet, and the accusation against him of possession by evil power. All three reflect the powers of the marginalized who cannot derive their authority from the established institutions of the day.

"If Jesus was primarily a healer," Tal Ilan suggests, "he could have received some formal education in a professional guild of healers, many of which were wo/men,"[42] because wo/men were considered to be the first healers and sorcerers in antiquity. Moreover, utilizing the sectarian model developed by R. R. Wilson,[43] Ilan argues that Jesus understood himself as a prophet and after his death "an outburst of prophetic uttering could be heard in the emerging Christian movement. Not surprisingly some of them [the prophets] were women."[44] Finally, she points out that prophecy and Spirit-possession are intertwined.

The prophet Jesus not only expelled demons but also was accused of being possessed by evil spirits, an accusation of witchcraft that has always been leveled against wo/men. To make her point, Ilan quotes the rabbis as

[40] Kraemer, "Jewish Women," 46.

[41] See n. 25 above.

[42] Ilan, "Footsteps," 129.

[43] R. R. Wilson, *Prophecy and Society in Ancient Israel* (Philadelphia: Fortress Press, 1980).

saying, "most witchraft is found in wo/men" and points out that Rabbi Simeon ben Shatah executed eighty wo/men at Ashkelon. These wo/men are identified by the Palestinian Talmud as witches, whose hanging is interpreted as crucifixion.[45] Thus she reads Jesus' fate in terms of Exod. 22:18: "You shall not suffer a sorceress to live."

In short, all three characterizations place Jesus on the same level with Jewish wo/men, Ilan posits, and hence may account for the attractiveness of the Jesus movement to them.

> My main argument is, in conclusion, that the powers and authority Jesus claimed for himself derived not from the main bodies of power of his time such as the Temple, the priesthood, even the Torah and its study, but rather from the peripheral, charismatic fringes. . . . Jesus is thus to be found in typical feminine [wo/men's] settings and accused of typical feminine [female] transgressions. His message, even when entirely not feminist in character, would be understood by wo/men, because he spoke in a familiar language and went through familiar motions.[46]

While one may be concerned about the adopted social-scientific anthropological model of interpretation, Tal Ilan's reconstruction nevertheless shows that the replacement of the anti-Jewish "Jesus the feminist" interpretive model with a wo/men-centered one, rather than the apologetic defense against it, results in a fresh reading of the texts about Jesus. Tal Ilan's article points the way to a methodological reconceptualization of Second Temple Judaism as well as to a different handling of the Jesus–and–anti-Judaism debate in feminist terms. By placing Jewish wo/men as historical agents into the center of her historical reconstruction she opens up a new approach not only to the gospels but also to other Jewish source texts.

Third, in a recent article Amy-Jill Levine seeks to move the feminist discussion of anti-Judaism in biblical and theological studies in a different direction, although at first glance she seems to reinscribe the terms of the discussion with a vengeance. In a painstaking, sometimes scathing review of Christian wo/men's literature that has appeared in the past decade, Levine shows that despite all feminist criticism of and serious attempts to avoid Christian anti-Judaism, it continues to flourish especially in liberationist popular studies of 2/3 World wo/men.[47]

---

[44] Ilan, "Footsteps," 133.
[45] Ibid., 136.
[46] Ibid.,135.
[47] Levine points to several contributions in *Searching the Scriptures,* where despite our

Levine, however, does not react defensively and reject or minimize the egalitarianism and contributions of either the Jesus movement or of Jewish wo/men in the first century,[48] though she narrowly focuses on scholarship by wo/men and does not go on to point out anti-Judaism in malestream Jesus scholarship and hermeneutics. She refuses to blame the "2/3 world" wo/men, who because of their lack of detailed knowledge of Judaism unwittingly perpetuate anti-Judaism with their "skewed comparisons." Rather, Levine places the blame squarely at the doorstep of biblical scholarship where it rightly belongs. She points out that anti-Judaism seems to be absent in non-Western, nonacademic wo/men's interpretations but does not think that this is

> occasioned by the women's lack of biblical literacy.... The absence is rather caused to a great extent by the women's lack of access to, or interest in, biblical scholarship. In other words, the problem of anti-Judaism can in great measure be laid at the feet of "us," the scholars. We Western feminists imbibed anti-Judaism as the mother's [father's?] milk of our own academic training; we took what we were taught in many of our "New Testament" classes and what we read in mainstream "New Testament scholarship," and extended the argument to women's concerns.[49]

Levine diagnoses here—in my view correctly—the structural roots of and impulse for the continuing flourishing of anti-Judaism in feminist discourses, and thereby opens up a new way for Jewish and Christian feminists to discuss it. As she correctly observes, it is the kyriarchal function of educated wo/men or, more accurately, the function of the "white lady," to mediate and to transmit malestream knowledge and hegemonic scholarship that produce and legitimate noxious prejudices such as anti-Judaism. Only if we recognize this structural kyriarchal role and function as wo/men scholars, will the feminist discussion of Christian anti-Judaism be able to stop looking for the speck in the eye of the "other wo/man" and turn its creative energies to develop and teach a different kind of biblical knowledge and scriptural interpretation.

Like Levine, I have insisted in this chapter that the focus of the feminist anti-Judaism discussion must shift to a critical investigation of our own

---

vigilance and many demands for correction, some anti-Jewish traces seem to have still survived. This project taught me how deep-seated unconscious anti-Judaism still is.

[48] Cf. Bernadette Brooten, "Jewish Women's History in the Roman Period: A Task for Christian Theology," *Harvard Theological Review* 79 (1986): 22–30.

[49] Amy-Jill Levine, "Lilies of the Field and Wandering Jews: Biblical Scholarship, Women's Roles, and Social Location," in *Transformative Encounters*, ed. Kitzberger, 348.

social location and function in the structural position of the "white lady." However, we may not stop there but rather must turn our critical focus to hegemonic malestream scholarship on Christian anti-Judaism before we can spell out wo/men scholars' complicity with it. Otherwise the discussion will continue to reinscribe antifeminism, while not being able to obliterate the deadly virus of anti-Semitism and heal the kyriarchal symptoms caused by it and vice versa.

The following hermeneutical theses and ideology-critical prescriptions seek to complement the historical-critical methodological ones underlying *In Memory of Her.* I hope that both sets of theses together will initiate a wider discussion on finding the right medicine to effectively rid feminist discourses of the kyriarchal virus of anti-Judaism:

1. Feminist scholars must constantly scrutinize texts and traditions for kyriarchal ideologies, be they anti-Judaism, misogyny, racism, ethnocentrism, or homophobia. Hence, it must become a matter of course to acknowledge first the "beam" of prejudice in one's own work before one points out the "speck" in the writings of others. Otherwise feminist scholars continue unwittingly to perform the mediating functions of the "white lady."

2. Instead of just bemoaning the contagion of anti-Judaism we must create communities of discourses, conferences, teaching materials, web sites and a critical but supportive climate of exchange that cultivate knowledge about and respect for the other. Levine's suggestion of mutual criticism before we publish our work is an important step in this direction.

3. Our goal must be to reduce rather than increase anti-Jewish mindsets and assumptions. Hence we need to be careful to point out how texts can be read in a pro-Jewish way rather than insinuate that they must be read in an anti-Jewish way when we don't agree with their theoretical or hermeneutical positions and methods. For instance, when teaching *In Memory of Her,* one needs to point out not only how some of its statements can be and have been read in an anti-Jewish way but also teach how the same passages might be read with a pro-Jewish lens. Otherwise anti-Judaism will be reinscribed in and through the critique of anti-Judaism.

4. Critiques of anti-Judaism must at one and the same time point out the traces of antifeminism in anti-Jewish discourses. For instance, when discussing the myth of "Jesus the feminist" one must point out not only its anti-Jewish ramifications but also explore its antifeminist implications. To place "Jesus the feminist" in opposition to Judaism engenders anti-Jewish

prejudice. However, it also leads to the further "immasculation" (to borrow an expression from Judith Fetterly) of wo/men readers who internalize religiously their dependence on elite men. Such self-alienation and elite male identification in turn opens the door to internalized contempt for wo/men, who become the "others." Thus anti-Judaism and antifeminism go hand in hand.

5. The feminist anti-Judaism discussion will not be successful unless and until malestream scholarly works and ecclesiastical teachings become the focus of attention and are scrutinized with the same zeal as feminist works are now. If we criticize feminist discourses for anti-Judaism but do not at the same time identify and indict the anti-Judaism of malestream biblical scholarship that produces it—both popular and scholarly—anti-Judaism together with all the other kyriarchal ideologies will continue to affect negatively the spiritual, mental, and physical health of wo/men and the ethos of the discipline. Susannah Heschel's work has been pathbreaking in identifying and naming the anti-Semitic arguments of German biblical scholarship during the time of National Socialism.[50] However, similar feminist studies on colonialism in British or imperialism in American biblical scholarship are lacking.

6. Anti-Judaism in feminist writings must be discussed not only on a historical but also on a theological level. Just as Jews invoke the Torah, so Christians appeal to Jesus over and against unjust structures and dehumanizing oppressions. "Jesus the feminist" is often a powerful weapon in the hands of marginalized and powerless Christian wo/men arguing against racist institutions or misogynist ecclesiastics. Their readings of the gospels figure Jesus as a feminist but the scribes, Pharisees, and priests of his day in negative terms not because they intend to make an anti-Jewish argument but in order to deploy "Jesus" against oppressive power and the kyriarchal clerics of today.

---

[50] For instance, she has shown that the contrast "Galilee of the Gentiles" and "Jerusalem of the Jews" is part and parcel of the argumentation of National Socialist biblical scholarship. See, e.g., her essay "Nazifying Christian Theology: Walter Grundmann and the Institute for the Study and Eradication of Jewish Influence on German Life," in *Church History* 63 (1994): 587–605, in which she discusses the arguments of the influential German exegetes Ernst Lohmeyer (*Galiläa und Jerusalem* [Göttingen, 1936]) and Walter Grundmann (*Jesus, der Galiläer, und das Judentum* [Leipzig, 1940]) that Jesus' racial identity was not Jewish because he descended from alien immigrant peoples who lived in Galilee and numbered among them also Arians. See also the very important article by Wolfgang Stegemann, "Das Verhältnis Rudolf Bultmanns zum Judentum: Ein Beitrag zur Pathologie des strukturellen theologischen Antijudaismus," *Kirche und Israel* 5 (1990): 26–44.

Such a typological rhetoric must not be mistaken for the historical, positivist, factual one of biblical science, as is often the case. For instance, in Catholic wo/men's writings the negative understanding of purity laws is not fueled by a disrespect for Jewish orthodox wo/men who cherish the laws of *niddah*, but is engendered by the knowledge that until the reforms of Vatican II these laws were church laws barring wo/men from the sanctuary. Although the negative theological arguments and church laws for the cultic exclusion of Catholic wo/men ostensibly have been rejected, the papal "femininity theology" is still affected by them. Hence, it is crucial that one analyze the rhetorical contexts in which allegedly anti-Jewish arguments are made.

7. Last but not least, the most difficult issue to be raised is the question of what constitutes a feminist interpretation and argument. Is a study feminist just because it is written by a wo/man? Is a work feminist if it raises just the issue of wo/men or gender discrimination but does not consider all the other kyriarchal structures of marginalization and domination? In a time of neoliberal pluralism where everything goes as long as it appeals to consumers, we must set some standards for what it means to produce feminist work. Otherwise the market will continue to dictate the terms. In the discussions of Christian feminist anti-Judaism it is often assumed that works like that of Leonard Swidler or Ben Witherington III are feminist. But what makes them so?

Conversely, much of the new scholarship on wo/men does not define itself as feminist. However, if the discussion of anti-Judaism in feminist work has taught us anything, it is the insight that not everything written about or by wo/men or in the name of feminism is in the interest of wo/men and other second-class citizens in society, academy, and religious communities. As long as we do not have a clear understanding of what feminism is and how it is addressing all structures of domination and prejudice affecting the lives of wo/men, the anti-Judaism discussion will continue to be used for antifeminist ends. In the concluding chapter I therefore will once more attempt to constructively articulate a feminist critical approach to the Historical-Jesus syndrome and its christological ramifications.

# 5

# TO REALIZE THE VISION
## Feminist Jesus Discourses

AFTER EXPLORING THE IMPACT OF SCIENTIFIC HISTORICAL-JESUS research on feminist Jesus discourses in the preceding chapter, I want now to look critically at feminist christological discourses on Jesus, and I will do so by first identifying four crucial problem areas: the maleness of Jesus, the controversy around Sophia-Wisdom, anti-Judaism in Christian feminist Jesus discourses, and the problem of racism in white feminist discourses. In a second step I sketch out my own proposal for the reconstruction of the Jewish Jesus movement as an emancipatory *basileia* movement.

## CONTROVERTED ISSUES
### The Maleness of Jesus

The focus on the *maleness* of Jesus in feminist Jesus discourses must be seen in the context of contemporary feminist political struggles. On the religious Right, for example, the combination of Protestant revival methods with the cultural romance narrative—Jesus loves me so!—seeks to secure the loyalty of Christian wo/men. Jesus becomes commodified and commercialized in terms of heterosexuality and wo/men's desire for the perfect man, the knight in shining armor who will rescue and truly love them. The following experience at a meeting of a Christian right-wing wo/men's group called "Grace 'N Vessels," described by Donna Minkowitz, illustrates this:

> On the stage, Alicia, a twenty-two-year-old with long hair and a voice like Debby Gibson, starts singing about Jesus as though he were a perfect

boyfriend: "'Tis so sweet to trust in Jesus, / Just to take him at his word. / Just to rest upon his promise" . . . she cheeps endless variations on this happy theme: song after song about how he's going to come and make her whole again, fulfill all her yearnings, free her from everything that isn't beautiful. By this fifth ballad, women are looking up at God with private smiles. "Jesus, Jesus, how I trust him," Alicia warbles, "How I trust him night and day." Women start to jump and holler, as though they had just remembered a steamy date. "Oh, she really gets me on fire!" Gina says when she takes over from the singer. Gina, who's a professional cosmetologist with a ravenous air, gets the atmosphere even hotter. "He is so madly in love with you," she croons.[1]

At the same time, as Minkowitz points out, this celebration of romantic love for Jesus has a homoerotic and sado-masochistic (S/M) subtext:

. . . [T]he language of the ritual gets more inflamed and sexual by the second: "Fill her, Lord Jesus," Gina cries, as the throng surrounds a fifty-five-year-old black woman. "Fill her! Fill her! Fill her, Lord! Fill her right now!" . . . "You're gonna stay and melt her, melt her, melt her, Lord Jesus melt her." . . . Women pitch and totter as Gina invites Jesus to enter them ("In Jesus' name! In Jesus' name. Oh God, fill her, fill her, fill her, in Jesus' name!") invokes S/M imagery [sic] ("Oh, I pray you bring the harness upon her, Lord!"). . . .

But it is Grace who carries the erotic banner furthest. She hoots for our attention, comes to the center of the room, and starts singing at the top of her lungs, "Ain't nobody do me like Jesus!" She gets the audience to respond antiphonally, "No, / Ain't nobody do me like Jesus" while a teenager kicks her legs like a Rockette to the beat. Grace grabs two of the youngest children in the audience, girls about five or six years old, and makes them dance and sing with her in a little circle. . . . The girls smile unctuously and warble, Ain't nobody do me like Jesus!" Can't nobody do me like Jesus!" and I feel abruptly nauseous.[2]

The political function of the tangible power of language expressing such a cultural romance and erotic longing for Jesus, the Man, is neglected by Carter Heyward, who, in her book *Saving Jesus from Those Who Are Right*, does not change but reinscribes masculine language for Jesus.[3] Such masculine inclusive language does not affirm the "brothers," but reinscribes discourses of cultural romance.

[1] Donna Minkowitz, *Ferocious Romance: What My Encounter with the Right Taught Me about Sex, God and Fury* (New York: Free Press, 1998), 151f.

[2] Ibid., 169f.

[3] Carter Heyward, *Saving Jesus from Those Who Are Right: Rethinking What It Means to Be a Christian* (Minneapolis: Fortress Press, 1999).

On the other side, in my own church, Roman Catholicism, christology has been and still is used to deny wo/men's sacred powers and full citizenship.[4] In May 1994, a papal Apostolic Letter *Ordinatio Sacerdotalis* arrived, stating that the church has no authority whatever to confer priestly ordination on wo/men, although many Christian churches that are reading the same scriptures have claimed the authority to ordain wo/men. In the face of such silencing, Catholic feminists have continued to indict the hierarchy for sexism and to argue, "if you don't ordain women, don't baptize them."

Hence, in 1998 a new papal decree made its way into the press trying to teach the faithful with legal intimidation. Under threat of heavy censure and punishment the *motu proprio, Ad Tuendam Fidem,* seeks to eliminate the remnants of "the lawful freedom of inquiry and of thought and the freedom to express it" that the Second Vatican Council had promised. The prohibition of euthanasia and prostitution, as well as the exclusion of women from ordination, are the prime examples of authoritative teachings that may not be questioned. It is obvious that this most recent papal decree attempts to silence once and for all women's claim to full "ekklesial" citizenship.

Since both Protestant evangelicalism and Roman Catholic authoritarianism in different ways construct discourses on Jesus' maleness, it is not surprising that the problem of how to understand Jesus, the Man, has taken center stage in feminist theology.[5] Just like other christological reflections, feminist discussions of Jesus center on questions that arise either from a doctrinal, theological, or positivist historical framework.[6] They often seek either to answer or to displace arguments against wo/men's full citizenship with reference to scripture in general and to the historical Jesus in particular. Feminist christological debates, for instance, have focused on the theological problem posed by the maleness of the historical Jesus and have problematized the centrality of a male savior figure. Rosemary Radford Ruether has aptly summed up this feminist debate in the question: "Can a male savior redeem and save wo/men?"[7] An articula-

[4] See Elisabeth Schüssler Fiorenza and Hermann Häring, eds., *The Non-Ordination of Wo/men and the Politics of Power* (Concilium; Maryknoll, N.Y.: Orbis Books, 1999).

[5] For the discussion, see chapter 2 of my book *Jesus: Miriam's Child, Sophia's Prophet: Critical Issues in Feminist Christology* (New York: Continuum, 1994).

[6] See my book *Rhetoric and Ethic: The Politics of Biblical Studies* (Minneapolis: Fortress Press, 1999).

[7] See the discussion between Rosemary Radford Ruether and Daphne Hampson, "Is There a Place for Feminists in a Christian Church?" *Blackfriars* (January 1987): 1–12.

tion of the central feminist christological problem that concentrates on the maleness of Jesus and its import for incarnation and salvation is conditioned by both its dogmatic and its historical-political location in the struggle of wo/men for rights and liberation.

In the last century suffragists insisted that Christendom would tumble like a house of cards if the misogynist doctrinal trump card of original sin were pulled out from under it. The Christian doctrine of redemption is so deleterious for wo/men, they argued, because it teaches not only that a wo/man has brought sin into the world but also that wo/men must be saved by a male savior. I quote Elizabeth Cady Stanton:

> Take the snake, the fruit tree and the woman from the tableau, and we have no fall, no frowning Judge, no Inferno, no everlasting punishment—hence no need of a Savior. Thus the bottom falls out of the whole Christian theology. Here is the reason why in all the biblical researches and higher criticisms, the scholars never touch the position of women.[8]

Whereas in the last century female sinfulness and male salvific power have occupied center stage, in this century the theological significance of Jesus' male gender is pivotal to feminist theological debates. This shift in emphasis points to a shift in the cultural-political contextualization of christological discourses. Today, the misogynist theology of the last century that underscored wo/man's sinfulness, cunning, and weakness no longer has the same persuasive power as in the past. In a sociopolitical context in which wo/men's equal rights and dignity are accepted, at least in theory if not in practice, arguments against wo/men's ordination, for instance, can no longer resort to the dogma of wo/man's sinfulness because it no longer has persuasive power in Western cultures. To regain such cultural power of persuasion the religio-political arguments for wo/men's exclusion from church leadership have had to shift. This shift in argument has firmly anchored christological debates within sociocultural discourses on gender difference and gender complementarity.

Since Western cultural gender[9] discourses naturalize masculinity and femininity as biological givens and "commonsense" facts, their persuasive power is culturally very potent. Hence ecclesiastics can use the maleness of Jesus as a primary christological argument for wo/men's exclusion from

---

[8] As quoted by Mary Daly, *Beyond God the Father: Toward a Philosophy of Women's Liberation* (Boston: Beacon Press, 1973), 69.

[9] See my article "Gender," in *The Encyclopedia of Politics and Religion* (Washington, D.C.: Congressional Quarterly Books, 1998), 290–94.

church leadership as well as for their essential difference and differing roles in church and society. Such a politics of gender—advocated not only by the Vatican—argues that wo/men and men are of equal worth but that they are essentially different by nature. Masculinity and femininity have different but complementary symbolic functions in society and religion.

This politics of gender[10] understands masculine and feminine gender difference either as natural fact or as metaphysical essence or as socially constructed gender roles that are allegedly rooted in biological sex. Yet such an ideological framework obscures and mystifies that the notion of two sexes is a sociocultural construct for maintaining wo/men's second-class citizenship rather than a biological given or innate essence.

This gender framework is asymmetrical and hierarchical, insofar as the dominant language and society have produced and still produce elite maleness as generic manifestation of being human, and they have done so in the interest of domination. In an unjust society the construction of natural gender is routinized in and through language. Grammatical gender becomes naturalized and "commonsense." Such a gender framework informs and determines scientific knowledge, religious symbol systems, and everyday experience. It makes us forget that until very recently class and racial differences also were considered to be natural biological givens or to be ordained by G*d.

As long as this ideological cultural gender politics, which makes gender difference appear to be "natural," "commonsense," and "G*d-given," remains operative even in feminist-christological discourses, it functions as an (often unconscious) religious framework in which the masculine gender of Jesus cannot but remain the central focus and problem for feminist christology. Such a concentration of christology on the masculine gender of Jesus or on the theological maleness of incarnation and redemption can only be relativized, I submit, when its hegemonic gender frame is critically investigated as to its systemic cultural-linguistic presuppositions and sociopolitical implications.

## Wisdom-Sophia

The second point of controversy is feminist Wisdom theology. Feminist christological discourses that understand Jesus as a child and prophet of

---

[10] For a discussion of the sex/gender system, see my book *But She Said: Feminist Practices of Biblical Interpretation* (Boston: Beacon Press, 1992).

Divine Wisdom or as Sophia incarnate not only offer possibilities for a new Christian biblical self-understanding and feminist solidarity, but also are a controverted site of struggle over the politics of interpretation. Although the feminist scholarly search for the footprints of Wisdom-Sophia in biblical writings encounters a host of historical-theological problems, it is nevertheless commonly accepted that the biblical image of Sophia has integrated Goddess language and traditions.[11] Hence, the divide between feminist biblical theologians and Goddess thealogians, I suggest, can be bridged by a hermeneutics of desire that searches for female images of the Divine.

Whereas the biblical Wisdom literature generally has been seen as kyriocentric literature[12] written by and for elite educated men,[13] more recent feminist studies have argued[14] that postexilic wo/men in Israel and Hellenistic Jewish wo/men in Egypt have conceived of Divine Wisdom as prefigured in the language and image of Goddesses such as Isis,[15] Athena, or

[11] It is interesting to note that Jewish feminists have elaborated not the figure of Chokmah-Sophia but that of the Shekinah representing Divine Presence. See also Susan Starr Sered, "Jewish Women and the Shekinah," in *In the Power of Wisdom: Feminist Spiritualities of Struggle,* ed. Elisabeth Schüssler Fiorenza and Maria Pilar Aquino [Concilium 5; forthcoming (2000)].

[12] See, e.g., W. C. Trenchard, *Ben Sira's View of Women* (Chico, Calif.: Scholars Press, 1982); Claudia V. Camp suggests that Ben Sira's "shrill, sometimes virulent instructions on women" are due to stress generated by two social forces: "One is the loss of control that the sage experienced in the larger social realm, which may have translated into an obsession for control in the closer sphere, specifically his sexuality and his household. The second is the conflict of social values which stress exacerbates" ("Understanding a Patriarchy: Women in Second Century Jerusalem through the Eyes of Ben Sira," in *"Women Like This": New Perspectives on Jewish Women in the Greco-Roman World,* ed. Amy-Jill Levine [Atlanta: Scholars Press, 1991] 1–40, quotation from p. 38).

[13] See Carol A. Newsom, "Woman and the Discourse of Patriarchal Wisdom: A Study of Proverbs 1-9," in *Gender and Difference in Ancient Israel,* ed. Peggy L. Day (Minneapolis: Fortress Press, 1989), 142–60. Here she concludes her study with a helpful methodological insight: "Having learned from the father how to resist interpolation by hearing the internal contradictions in discourse, one is prepared to resist the patriarchal interpolation of the father as well. For the reader who does not take up the subject position offered by the text, Proverbs 1-9 ceases to be a simple text of imitation and becomes a text about the problematic nature of discourse itself" (p. 159).

[14] See especially Silvia Schroer, *Die Weisheit hat ihr Haus gebaut: Studien zur Gestalt der Sophia in den biblischen Schriften* (Mainz: Grünewald, 1996), with extensive references to the literature on Chokmah-Sophia-Wisdom.

[15] James M. Reese, *Hellenistic Influences on the Book of Wisdom and Its Consequences* (Analecta Biblica 41; Rome: Biblical Institute Press, 1970); John S. Kloppenborg, "Isis and

Dike.[16] Like the Goddess Isis, Divine Wisdom is represented as using the proclamatory "I am" style for announcing her universal message of salvation. According to a very well known prayer, all the different nations and people use divine titles derived from their own local mythologies when they call on the Goddess Isis. They do so in the full knowledge that Isis is one, but encompasses all. Similarly, like the widespread Isis cult and mythology, the variegated Sophia-Wisdom discourses of postexilic Palestinian wo/men elaborate the image and figure of Divine Chokmah as the "other name" of G*d. In the image of Sophia, Hellenistic Jewish wo/men hold together belief in the "one" G*d of Israel with a cosmopolitan ethos that can respect local particularities without giving up claims to universality.

Since both Jewish and Christian texts present and simultaneously obfuscate Divine Wisdom with kyriocentric theological language, some feminist scholars have asked whether it is possible at all for feminist interpretation to transform the obscured female figure of Wisdom-Sophia in such a way that she can once again develop her imaginative power. Other feminist scholars have argued to the contrary that one must reject the traditions of Divine Wisdom as kyriarchal male traditions that are misogynist and elitist.

In my view, Jewish and Christian discourses on Divine Wisdom are significant today not only because they are a rich resource for female language for G*d but also because they provide a framework for developing a feminist ecological theology of creation. Moreover, they embody a religious ethos that is not exclusive of other religious visions but can be understood as respecting them. The earliest Sophia-traditions that still can be traced in the margins of early Christian works intimate a perspective that combines Jewish prophetic and sophialogical *basileia* traditions in a political, open-ended, and cosmopolitan religious vision of struggle and well-being for everyone.

In recent years scholarship and texts about Divine Wisdom-Sophia-Chokmah have received intensive feminist attention because of the female gender of Chokmah-Sophia-Wisdom. Feminists in the churches have

---

Sophia in the Book of Wisdom," *Harvard Theological Review* 75 (1982): 57–84, for review of the literature.

[16] Hermann von Lips, "Christus als Sophia? Weisheitliche Traditionen in der urchristlichen Christologie," in *Anfänge der Christologie: Festschrift Ferdinand Hahn*, ed. Cilliers Breytenbach and Henning Paulsen (Göttingen: Vandenhoeck & Ruprecht, 1991), 75–96.

translated the results of biblical scholarship on early Jewish and Christian Wisdom discourses into the idiom of song, poem, and liturgy. This practical and creative feminist attention to the divine female figure of Wisdom has brought the results of scholarship on biblical wisdom literature to public attention.

For instance, in 1993 Protestant feminists sponsored a conference in Minneapolis that not only featured lectures on Divine Sophia but also invoked and celebrated her in prayer and liturgy. This *Re-Imagining* Conference was allegedly the most controversial ecumenical event in decades. Conservatives claimed that it challenged the very foundations of mainline Protestantism in the United States. The reaction of the Christian Right to this conference was so violent that one high-ranking woman lost her church job and others have run into grave difficulties.[17] This struggle indicates the significance of Divine Sophia-Wisdom for contemporary Christian self-understanding.

German biblical scholar Luise Schottroff, however, has raised serious historical and theological objections to feminist attempts at recovering the earliest Sophia discourses in order to valorize "Woman Wisdom."[18] She argues that the fascination of feminist theologians with Sophia christology is misplaced because Wisdom speculation is at home in Israel's elite male circles and bespeaks their elite interests.

I disagree with Schottroff, however, that the reflective christology of the earliest Jesus groups emerged from the rarefied atmosphere of elite Wisdom schools. I suggest, to the contrary, that such sophialogical reflection was forged in a deliberative communal process of Jewish wo/men in the *basileia* movement, which sought to make sense out of the execution of Jesus within a sapiential-apocalyptic framework. In the everyday life of Galilean villagers and townspeople, "folk wisdom" was widespread and treasured. Moreover, divine female figures were in all likelihood well known. Hence, it is quite possible to argue that Jesus could have been re-remembered as one of the prophets whom Divine Sophia had sent, who was executed, and who was experienced by Galilean wo/men as the Living One. Finally, in this reflective meaning-making of the Jesus movement, a creative interaction between Wisdom theology and *basileia* proclamation could have taken place that had the power to transform both of these traditions.

---

[17] See Nancy J. Berneking and Pamela Carter Joern, eds., *Re-Membering and Re-Imagining* (Cleveland: Pilgrim Press, 1995).

[18] Luise Schottroff, "Wanderprophetinnen: Eine feministische Analyse der Logienquelle," *Evangelische Theologie* 51 (1991): 322–34.

Rather than exploring the possibility of an integration of Wisdom and *basileia* discourses, Schottroff insists to the contrary that the Sophia tradition is permanently suspect not only as an elite male, kyriocentric tradition but also as one that, in a dualistic fashion, plays the "good" wo/man Wisdom against the "strange" and "evil" woman.[19] Such a misogynist tradition cannot be concerned with justice at all. Silvia Schroer has rightly objected to such a negative evaluation of the Wisdom traditions.[20] Not only has she pointed out that Wisdom discourses are permeated with the teachings of Woman Justice,[21] but she also agrees with me that in the first century, prophetic-apocalyptic and sapiential traditions were intertwined, integrated, and changed.

In addition, Schroer argues that the Wisdom traditions had been democratized in the first century and that much of the sapiential tradition of the gospels reflects folk wisdom that very well could have been articulated by and for wo/men. Finally, Schroer points out that Schottroff's exegetical-historical objection to the feminist regeneration of Divine Chokmah-Sophia-Wisdom may also be due to her different confessional location[22] and indebtedness to neo-orthodox theology.[23]

## *Anti-Judaism*

Since in the last chapter I have elaborated anti-Judaism in academic and feminist Historical-Jesus studies, I mention the problem here only in passing. It is the Jewish theologian Judith Plaskow who again and again has pointed to such anti-Jewish inscriptions in malestream[24] and feminist christological discourses:

[19] However, in fairness to the Wisdom traditions it must be pointed out that the prophetic or apocalyptic traditions are equally suspect because they are also permeated by kyriocentric bias.

[20] Silvia Schroer, "Jesus Sophia: Erträge der feministischen Forschung zu einer frühchristlichen Deutung der Praxis und des Schicksals Jesu von Nazareth," in *Vom Verlangen Nach Heilwerden,* ed. Strahm and Strobel (Fribourg: Exodus, 1991), 112–28.

[21] See also Claudia V. Camp, *Wisdom and the Feminine in the Book of Proverbs* (Bible and Literature Series 14; Sheffield: Almond, 1985).

[22] Whereas Schroer and I are Catholic, Schottroff and Dorothee Soelle, who is equally opposed to feminist Wisdom theology, are Lutherans. Since most of the Wisdom writings are part of the Catholic canon, Schroer conjectures that Catholic wo/men are more inclined to work with them. Fortunately, such a confessional divide has not emerged in the U.S. context.

[23] See Schoer, *Die Weisheit,* 138–39.

[24] For instance, Luke T. Johnson, in "The New Testament's Anti-Jewish Slander and the

I find it especially disturbing, that the tendency to define Jesus as unique over and against Judaism remains even in feminists who do not make use of the Jesus-was-a-feminist-argument, who are quite aware of Christian anti-Judaism, who are freely critical of Christian sources, who have gone very far in deconstructing Jesus' divinity. . . . It seems as if the feminist struggle with patriarchal christologies leads back into the trap of anti-Judaism. . . . Can Christians value Jesus if he was just a Jew who chose to emphasize certain ideas and values in the Jewish tradition but did not invent or have a monopoly on them?[25]

The obstinate persistence of veiled or explicit anti-Judaism in Christian arguments for the liberatory uniqueness of Jesus raises two sets of epistemological questions: the first one is *historical,* the second *theological* or ideological. The first set of questions asks not only *what* we can know historically about first-century Judaism and the relations between Jesus and wo/men but also *how* we know what we know, *who* has produced this knowledge, and to *what ends.* The second set of questions explores what kind of theological interests compel Christian anti-Jewish reconstructions of the Historical-Jesus.

## *Racism*

Similar questions could be asked with respect to racism in general. The African American theologian Jacquelyn Grant has criticized "white" femi-

---

Conventions of Ancient Polemic," *Journal of Biblical Literature* 108, no. 3 (1989): 419–41, cavalierly solves the problem of anti-Judaism in the Christian Testament by pointing out that such slanderous behavior was common in the first century. He seems not to have read anything I have written when he characterizes my approach as liberationist censorship, "which is frequently based on the premise that texts should reflect our liberated self-understanding and practice. If they offend our sensibilities, they are dispensable" (p. 421). In a footnote (n. 4) he credits Rosemary Radford Ruether for having defined the "basic liberationist approach" and me for having extensively developed it in *In Memory of Her.* He probably would justify such a sloppy but politically expedient scholarly procedure that still seems to be widespread in biblical studies today!

[25] Judith Plaskow, "Feminist Anti-Judaism and the Christian God," *Journal of Feminist Studies in Religion* 7, no. 2 (1991): 106. For her early critique, see eadem, "Christian Feminism and Anti-Judaism," *Cross Currents* 33 (1978): 306–9; for her most recent contribution, see "Anti-Judaism in Feminist Christian Interpretation," in *Searching the Scriptures,* vol. 1, *A Feminist Introduction,* ed. Elisabeth Schüssler Fiorenza (New York: Crossroad, 1993), 117–29, quotation from p. 118; see also Susannah Heschel, "Jüdisch-feministische Theologie und Antijudaismus in christlich-feministischer Theologie," in *Verdrängte Vergangenheit,*

nist christological discourses as tainted by racism.[26] She distinguishes between biblical or evangelical feminists, feminist liberation theologians, and rejectionist feminists, who repudiate biblical tradition and faith. Grant argues that all three directions in feminist theology adopt a white racist frame of reference insofar as they universalize the experience of white wo/men in articulating feminist christology, and insofar as they do not take the experience of wo/men of color or poor wo/men into account. Although liberation theologians such as Letty Russell, Carter Heyward, and Rosemary Radford Ruether analyze racism and classism, in Grant's judgment they nevertheless remain caught up in the dualistic gender framework of malestream scholarship. This theoretical framework seems to compel them to structure the Christian feminist dilemma in terms of gender difference where "male" and "female" are seemingly unified catebories. Grant summarizes the position of Russell and Radford Ruether as follows:

> The historical Jesus was a man, but men do not have a monopoly upon Christ, and Eve was a woman but women do not have a monopoly on sin. For "Christ is not necessarily male, nor is the redeemed community only women, but new humanity, female and male".... The maleness of Jesus is superseded by the Christness of Jesus. Both Russell and Ruether argue that the redemptive work of Jesus moves us toward the new humanity which is in Jesus Christ. But whereas Russell still holds to the unique Lordship of Jesus, Ruether raises the possibility that this Christ can be conceived in nontraditional ways,—as in sister.[27]

I am not interested here in assessing whether Grant's reading is correct but in highlighting its methodological implications for feminist theology. Grant formulates two important criteria for the evaluation of feminist christological arguments. First, she insists that all theoretical frameworks of white feminist christology must be scrutinized for whether they employ a one-dimensional gender analysis or whether they develop a multi-systemic analysis of sexism, racism, and class exploitation. Second, Grant

---

*die uns bedrängt: Feministische Theologie in der Verantwortung fur die Geschichte,* ed. Leonore Siegele Wenschkewitz (Munich: Kaiser, 1988), 54–103; and also Susannah Heschel, "Anti-Judaism in Christian Feminist Theology," *Tikkun* 5, no. 3 (1990): 26–28.

[26] Jacquelyn Grant, *White Women's Christ and Black Women's Jesus* (Atlanta: Scholars Press, 1989); see also Kelly Brown Douglas, *The Black Christ* (Maryknoll, N.Y.: Orbis Books, 1994); and Delores Williams, *Sisters in the Wilderness: The Challenge of Womanist God-Talk* (Maryknoll, N.Y.: Orbis Books, 1993).

[27] Grant, *White Women's Christ,* 144.

argues that feminist christology must emerge from the experience and situation of the least, because "Jesus located the Christ with the outcast."[28] Therefore, she insists that the experience of black wo/men must become the second norm with which the limitations of feminist theological perspectives must be judged.

Like other 2/3 World wo/men before her, Grant challenges white European and American feminists to abandon their dualistic gender analysis. Responding to this challenge, I have developed an analytic of kyriarchy conceptualized as an interstructured pyramid of multiplicative oppressions. The neologism "kyriarchy," which connotes the rule and domination of the lord/master/father/husband, is a more apt analytical tool than patriarchy,[29] which in white feminist theory has been understood as the domination of all men over all wo/men equally. Whether one looks at feudal, late capitalist, monarchical, democratic, national, or global systemic forms of kyriarchy, its structures of domination and exploitation always are determined by male elites and affect different wo/men differently.

A critical analysis of systemic kyriarchy allows one to trace not only the historical roots of domination and exploitation but also their ideological mystifications such as anti-Judaism and white supremacy. The ideological mystification of Western systems of domination is already found in classical philosophy. Greco-Roman philosophy has legitimated elite male domination and the subordination of marginalized wo/men. This ideological argument has found its way into the Christian canon in the form of the so-called Neo-Aristotelian household code texts.[30] Their claim to divine rev-

---

[28] Ibid., 6.

[29] *Patriarchy* in the "narrow sense" is best understood as "father-right and father-might." However, this translation overlooks that the father as the head of household was in antiquity also lord, master, and husband. Consequently, patriarchy/patriarchal connotes a complex system of subordination and domination. Moreover, the patriarchal system of the household also was the paradigm for the order of society and state. For a review of the common feminist understanding of patriarchy, see V. Beechey, "On Patriarchy," *Feminist Review* 3 (1979): 66–82; Gerda Lerner, *The Creation of Patriarchy* (New York: Oxford University Press, 1986), 231–41; C. Schaumberger, "Patriarchat als feministischer Begriff," in *Wörterbuch der feministischen Theologie* (Gütersloh: Mohn, 1991), 321–23 with literature. For Roman patriarchal structures, see W. K. Lacey, "Patria Potestas," in Beryl Rawson, ed., *The Family in Ancient Rome: New Perspectives* (Ithaca, N.Y.: Cornell University Press, 1986), 121–44.

[30] See Klaus Thraede, "Zum historischen Hintergrund der 'Haustafeln' des Neuen Testaments," in *Pietas: Festschrift B. Kötting* (Münster: Aschendorff, 1980), 359–68; D. Lührmann, "Neutestamentliche Haustafeln und antike Ökonomie," *New Testament Studies* 27 (1980–81): 83–97; David L. Balch, *Let Wives Be Submissive: The Domestic Code in 1 Peter*

elation has determined subsequent Christian theology and practice decisively. Although this ideological-religious legitimization of the Western system of domination has continued throughout Christian history, it has never been total, since alternative voices and egalitarian visions advocating a domination-free world and church have also been codified in Hebrew and Christian scriptures.

Such a systemic analysis of kyriarchy provides a different hermeneutical lens for feminist Jesus studies. It does not compel one to position feminist Jesus research theoretically within the patriarchal sex-gender system but rather allows one to situate it within wo/men's historical-religious experience of domination and their feminist struggles for liberation. Whether black or white, rich or poor, lesbian or married, Christian wo/men until very recently have been excluded from church leadership and have been silenced and marginalized by law and custom. Although all wo/men have been marginalized and silenced by kyriarchal theology, such marginalization and exploitation have affected wo/men differently depending on their social location within the kyriarchal pyramid.[31]

The full oppressive power of kyriarchy is manifested in the lives and struggles of the poorest and most oppressed wo/men, who live on the bottom of the kyriarchal pyramid. The feminist movement has not yet succeeded as long as the oppression of wo/men continues who suffer under multiple interlocking exploitative structures. Although wo/men may experience moments of liberation in the struggles for survival in and transformation of kyriarchal structures, no wo/man is free and liberated unless all wo/men are full citizens in society and church.

In contrast to Jacquelyn Grant, however, I do not seek to derive the criterion and norm of feminist Christian theology from the option of the his-

---

(Chico, Calif.: Scholars Press, 1981); idem, "Household Codes," in *Greco-Roman Literature and the New Testament*, ed. David E. Aune (Atlanta: Scholars Press, 1988), 25–50; see also chapter 4 in my *Bread Not Stone: The Challenge of Feminist Biblical Interpretation* (Boston: Beacon Press, 1985); Clarice Martin, "The 'Haustafeln' (Household Codes) in African American Biblical Interpretation: 'Free Slaves' and 'Subordinate Women,'" in *Stony the Road We Trod: African American Biblical Interpretation*, ed. Cain Hope Felder (Minneapolis: Fortress Press, 1991), 206–31, for feminist/womanist discussion of and literature on the household code texts; Susan Moller Okin, *Women in Western Political Thought* (Princeton: Princeton University Press, 1979), 15–98; and Elizabeth V. Spelman, *Inessential Woman: Problems of Exclusion in Feminist Thought* (Boston: Beacon Press, 1988), 19–56.

[31] For a feminist discussion of the interplay between language and identity, see, e.g., the contributions in *Women and Language in Transition*, ed. Joyce Penfield (Albany: State University of New York Press, 1987).

torical Jesus for the poor and the outcast. Being poor and outcast does not as such manifest G\*d's[32] grace and liberation. Rather I seek to ground this norm in the emancipatory historical struggles for the transformation of kyriarchal relations of domination. Scripture, tradition, theology, and Jesus research are to be critically analyzed and tested as to their ideological-political functions in legitimating or subverting muliplicative kyriarchal structures of domination. They are to be judged on whether and how much they articulate Christian identity and faith in terms of kyriarchal dehumanization or in terms of emancipatory subversion.

## STRUGGLE AND VISION: SOJOURNER TRUTH

Such a struggle-oriented feminist hermeneutical perspective was articulated already in the last century, although its theoretical implications have not yet been fully reflected or explicated. I think here of the often-quoted speech of Sojourner Truth, an African American wo/man and a former slave, who could not read or write. Sojourner Truth gave this speech in 1852 at a mostly European-American suffrage gathering in Akron, Ohio. It owes its historical transmission to the collaboration between a black woman and a white wo/man.[33] Since I do not want to reduce Sojourner Truth's very particular experience and its paradigmatic articulation to mere abstraction, I quote it here extensively:

> That man over there say
> a woman needs to be helped into carriages

[32] As noted earlier, in order to mark the inadequacy of our language about G\*d, I have adopted this writing of the word G\*d.

[33] In her Marion Thomson Wright Lecture, given on February 20, 1993, at Rutgers University, Nell Irvin Painter pointed out that Frances Dana Gage published this speech twelve years after the event as a response to Harriet Beecher Stowe's profile article "Sojourner Truth, the Libyan Sibyl," which had appeared in the *Atlantic Monthly*. See Nell Irvin Painter, "The Writing and Selling of Sojourner Truth," in her study packet "An Introduction to Black Women's Studies" (Princeton University, Fall 1993). For further discussion and bibliography, see Nell Painter, "Truth, Sojourner (c. 1799–1885)," in *Black Women in America: A Historical Encyclopedia*, ed. Darlene Clark Hine (Brooklyn: Carlson, 1993), 1172–76, and her biography of Truth, *Sojourner Truth: A Life, a Symbol* (New York: W. W. Norton, 1996); see also *Narrative of Sojourner Truth*, ed. Margaret Washington (New York: Vintage, 1993), especially the introduction; and Karen Baker Fletcher, "Anna Julia Cooper and Sojourner Truth: Two Nineteenth Century Black Interpreters of Scripture," in *Searching the Scriptures*, vol. 1, ed. Schüssler Fiorenza, 41–51.

and lifted over ditches
and to have the best places everywhere.
Nobody ever helped me into carriages
or over mud puddles
or gives me best place. . . .
And ain't I a woman?
Look at me!
Look at my arm!
I have plowed and planted
and gathered into barns
and no man could head me. . . .
And ain't I a woman?
I could work as much
and eat as much as a man—
when I could get it—
and bear the lash as well,
and ain't I a woman?
I have borne 13 children
and seen most all sold into slavery
and when I cried out a mother's grief
none but Jesus heard me. . . .
and ain't I a woman?
That little man in black there say
a woman can't have as much rights as a man
cause Christ wasn't a woman.
Where did your Christ come from?
From God and a woman!
Man had nothing to do with him!
If the first woman God ever made
was strong enough to turn the world
upside down all alone
together women ought to be able to turn it
right-side up again.[34]

My theoretical elaboration of this statement is not so much interested
in the answer to "ain't I a woman?" as in its methodological implications
for feminist Jesus studies and christology. This address contains several
important hermeneutical insights. Unlike the feminist critique of christology put forward by Elizabeth Cady Stanton, for instance, Sojourner Truth
does not apply her critique directly to the doctrinal christological system

---

[34] Erlene Stetson, ed., *Black Sister: Poetry by Black American Women 1746–1980* (Bloomington: Indiana University Press, 1981), 24f.

but to those who have articulated it. She points to the political interests of those who are the theoreticians not only of the myth of "true womanhood" but also of kyriarchal christology. She confronts them with her own concrete experience of slavery. Confronted with the experiences of a slave, the myth of the "eternal feminine" and its concomitant sex-gender theology turn out to proclaim the ideal of the "white lady" that is promulgated by white elite educated men. In other words, I do not argue that the question "ain't I a woman?" serves to elicit white feminist identification with Sojourner Truth, as the productive misreading of Karen Trimble Alliaume claims.[35] Rather, I argue that it unmasks the ideology of elite white femininity.

The myth of "true womanhood"[36] promotes not only sexist but also cultural, racist, and classist interests. This Western ideological construct of femininity cannot be fully recognized within the framework of gender theory but only within a complex theory of interlocking kyriarchal structures. The experience of the former slave Sojourner Truth underscores that the theoretical construction of gender difference is not primarily anthropological, but social. It serves to maintain kyriarchal relations of domination. Consequently, Sojourner Truth sees christology as enmeshed in the societal and ecclesial web of kyriarchal structures. She explicates the interconnection between the ideology of the "white lady" and christology by pointing out that elite clergy men ("That man over there say"; "The little man in black there say") continue to produce such kyriarchal theology in order to maintain the status quo ("woman can't have as much rights as a man / because Christ wasn't a woman"). Over against such kyriarchal christological claims Sojourner Truth appeals to her own experience as a hard-working slave and mother whose children were sold into bondage. Her experience of exploitation and domination compels her to formulate the following two arguments, and she does so with reference to the Bible, which she herself could not read because of kyriarchal prohibitions.

On the one hand, Sojourner Truth points out that the incarnation of Christ must be correctly understood as the collaboration of G*d and a

---

[35] Karen Trimble Alliaume, "The Risks of Repeating Ourselves: Reading Feminist/Womanist Figures of Jesus," *Cross Currents* 48, no. 2 (1998): 198–218.

[36] For the elaboration of this expression, see Hazel V. Carby, "On the Threshold of Women's Era: Lynching, Empire and Sexuality," in *Race, Writing, and Difference,* ed. Henry L. Gates (Chicago: University of Chicago Press, 1986), 301–28. See also the article by Kwok Pui-Lan, "The Image of the White Lady: Gender and Race in Christian Mission," in *The Special Nature of Women,* ed. Anne Carr and Elisabeth Schüssler Fiorenza (Philadelphia: Trinity Press International, 1991), 19–27.

wo/man. On the other hand, she stresses that redemption from sinful structures can only be experienced when wo/men come together for turning the "world right-side up" again. Truth accepts the claim of kyriarchal theology and traditional doctrine that wo/man caused original sin, but draws a different conclusion from it. Exactly because a wo/man was implicated in and collaborated in the original fall, wo/men cannot continue to understand themselves as innocent victims but must get together to make right the perversion of the world wrought by oppression and domination. Taken together, both arguments articulate a theological norm which locates G*d in wo/men's struggles for "mending creation"—to use a focal expression of Letty Russell.[37]

Like white suffragists, Sojourner Truth sees incarnation and redemption as intrinsic elements of doctrinal christology which perpetuate the marginality and oppression of wo/men. However, she understands the christological system as intertwined with the cultural system of essential or natural gender difference. She understands wo/men not simply as oppositional "others" of men or as innocent victims who can disassociate themselves from responsibility for kyriarchy. Rather she sees wo/men as deeply implicated in generating and sustaining the kyriarchal perversion of the world.

In short, Sojourner Truth does not advocate a new feminist christological principle or system as normative for Christian experience and identity, nor does she appeal to the historical Jesus. Rather, by pointing to her own concrete experiences of dehumanization, she unmasks kyriarchal christology as a rhetorical construction of male clerics. However, it is not her personal spiritual experience of Jesus but her call for wo/men to get together in order to "turn the world right-side up again" that provides the theoretical breakthrough that I have in mind. Neither Sojourner herself nor even Jesus is the *locus* of liberation and salvation but rather wo/men's movements for change and transformation. In my view, her speech pioneers a theological approach that locates G*d, Christ, and the possibility of salvation in a wo/men's movement concerned with justice and well-being for all. To misread such a theological move as a move from Jesus Christ to the *ekklēsia of wo/men* is to seriously misread it.[38]

---

[37] See, e.g., her *Household of Freedom: Authority in Feminist Theology* (Philadelphia: Westminster Press, 1978), 71f., and *The Church in the Round: Feminist Interpretation of the Church* (Louisville: Westminster/John Knox Press, 1993).

[38] Carter Heyward (*Saving Jesus*, 60) seems not to understand that the difference in our two approaches exists in that for me the matrices of all feminist theology are social visions and political struggles for the survival and well-being of all without exception, whereas for

By invoking the theological argument of Sojourner Truth, I do not want to canonize her nor uncritically subscribe to her point of view. Nor do I want to suggest that feminists who call themselves Christians must express their liberation experience in similar terms. I do not want to use Sojourner as a Jesus figure. I also do not celebrate her as an *academic* theologian, as Karen Trimble Alliaume suggests.[39] Rather, I want to lift her up as a *feminist* theologian, who, like many wo/men, does theology from her own daily experience of struggle. Hence, I see her neither as a spokeswo/man for the least of the oppressed nor as representing them, nor as their or white feminists' surrogate. Instead, I see her as an Africana feminist[40] theologian who calls on every wo/man who is implicated in structures of oppression to get together with other wo/men for righting the wrongs. Since Sojourner's call is not limited to a specific group of wo/men, but nevertheless is rooted in her particular experience of oppression, it can claim universal significance.

Rather than reinterpret the historical maleness of Jesus in humanist,[41] trickster,[42] transvestite,[43] or feminine terms, I have argued, feminist theology must join Sojourner Truth in insisting on the wo/men's movement for change as the space where G*d and liberation are to be located. Hence, it must reject the hegemonic cultural gender framework of the scientific quests for the Jesus of history as well as the belief that Christian identity

---

her it is metaphysical and ontological mutuality. That she does not comprehend my theoretical framework comes to the fore in her assertion that I have been "critical of many women theologians on this very question of whether we make our claims strongly enough for the universal validity of our work" (p. 218). However, the claim to universality has never been my concern—postmodern critiques make it impossible to do so. Instead, I have critically interrogated feminist theoretical frameworks of mutuality and relationality as not being able to coherently articulate a feminist critical political theology or christology of liberation.

[39] Alliaume, "Risks of Repeating Ourselves," 211.

[40] I thank Cynthia Johnson for the expression "Africana feminist." See her senior thesis, "Leaving Her Water Jar: Africana Feminist Perspectives in Biblical Interpretation" (Harvard College, 1996).

[41] See Rosemary Radford Ruether, *Sexism and God-Talk: Toward a Feminist Theology* (Boston: Beacon Press, 1983), 137. See also Mary Hembrow Snyder, *The Christology of Rosemary Radford Ruether: A Critical Introduction* (Mystic, Conn.: Twenty Third Publications, 1988).

[42] Donna Haraway, "Ecce Homo, Ain't (Ar'n't) I a Wo/man, and Inappropriate/d Others: The Human in a Post-Humanist Landscape," in *Feminists Theorize the Political*, ed. Judith Butler and Joan W. Scott (New York: Routledge, 1992), 90.

[43] Eleanor McLaughlin, "Feminist Christologies: Re-Dressing the Tradition," in *Reconstructing the Christ Symbol: Essays in Feminist Christology*, ed. Maryanne Stevens (Mahwah, N.J.: Paulist Press, 1993), 118–49.

must remain contingent upon the scientific reconstructions and dogmatic constructions of the divine maleness of Jesus. This is not to say, however, that Christian feminist scholars must eschew all historical reconstruction of their own theological and historical roots.

## AN EGALITARIAN RECONSTRUCTIVE MODEL

My work has sought to spell out an alternative reconstructive model to that of gender. This model seeks not only to address the question raised by decades of Historical-Jesus research but also to make explicit its own hermeneutical perspective and theological framework. As I have pointed out, popular and scholarly discussions of the *topos* "Jesus and wo/men"[44] tend to adopt the objectivist value-detached postures of historical criticism and the androcentric categories of the social sciences in order to justify the kyriarchal cultural or ecclesial status quo that marginalizes or excludes wo/men. Christian feminist assertions about "Jesus and wo/men" in turn are often seen as apologetic attempts to challenge the dominant positivist historical and theological constructions of Jesus and his movement. Yet such arguments collaborate with hegemonic kyriarchal ones when on exegetical grounds they seek to show that Jesus was the exception to the patriarchal rule.

Although such malestream and feminist apologetic arguments today are generally formulated on historical grounds, they nevertheless remain caught up in the doctrinal paradigm of interpretation that utilizes the scriptures as a storehouse of proof texts for furthering kyriarchal Christian identity and an exclusivist historical imagination. Rather than begin with a kyriarchal model of historical reconstruction that assumes wo/men's marginality or absence as historical agents, a critical feminist historical reconstructive model, as my work has developed it, begins with the assumption of wo/men's presence and agency rather than with the kyriarchal preconstructed discourse of their marginality and victimization.[45]

---

[44] For a fuller discussion, see my book *Jesus: Miriam's Child, Sophia's Prophet*, 67–88.

[45] Since *In Memory of Her* appeared, several important works on Jewish women in the Greco-Roman world have been published. See, e.g., Judith Romney Wegner, *Chattel or Person? The Status of Women in the Mishnah* (New York: Oxford University Press, 1988); Amy-Jill Levine, ed., *"Women Like This": New Perspectives on Jewish Women in the Greco-Roman World* (Atlanta: Scholars Press, 1991); Cheryl Ann Brown, *No Longer Be Silent: First Century Jewish Portraits of Biblical Women* (Louisville: Westminster/John Knox Press, 1992); Ross Shepard Kraemer, *Her Share of the Blessing: Women's Religions Among Pagans, Jews and*

Such a contention shifts "the burden of proof" to malestream biblical scholarship, which assumes that Jewish wo/men were *not* active and present in the development of early Christian life and theology. Only the presumption of the historical and theological agency of wo/men—slaves and freeborn, rich and poor, black and white—I argue, will allow us to read the slippages, ambiguities, gaps, and silences of androcentric, that is, grammatically masculine, texts,[46] not simply as properties of language and text but as the inscribed symptoms[47] of historical struggles.

Feminist christological reconstruction must not limit itself, I have argued, to an investigation of texts about wo/men and Jesus or simply focus on gender relations. Rather, it must conceptualize early Judaism and early Christianity in such a way that it can make marginalized wo/men visible as central agents who have shaped Jewish and Christian history and religion. This requires a reconsideration of the theological framework that —as Rosemary Radford Ruether has put it —has produced Christian anti-Judaism as the left hand and divine masculinism as the right hand of christology. In short, only an emancipatory feminist model of historical and theological reconstruction can do justice both to our common struggles for transforming religious kyriarchy and to our particular historical struggles and religious identity formations that are different.

Such a change of theoretical framework or hermeneutical "lenses" makes it possible to understand Jesus and early Christian beginnings as shaped by the agency and leadership of Jewish, Greco-Roman, Asian,

---

*Christians in the Greco-Roman World* (New York: Oxford University Press, 1992); Sally Overby Langford, "On Being a Religious Woman: Women Proselytes in the Greco-Roman World," in *Recovering the Role of Women: Power and Authority in Rabbinic Jewish Society,* ed. Peter J. Hass (South Florida Studies in the History of Judaism 59; Atlanta: Scholars Press, 1992), 113–30; and especially the work of the Israeli scholar Tal Ilan, *Mine and Yours Are Hers: Retrieving Wo/men's History from Rabbinic Literature* (Leiden: Brill, 1997).

[46] Dennis Baron, *Grammar and Gender* (New Haven: Yale University Press, 1986); Robert H. Robins, *A Short History of Linguistics* (London: Longmans, 1979); Casey Miller and Kate Swift, *Words and Women: New Language in New Times* (New York: Doubleday, Anchor Books, 1977); Gloria A. Marshall, "Racial Classifications: Popular and Scientific," in *The "Racial" Economy of Science: Toward a Democratic Future,* ed. Sandra Harding (Bloomington: Indiana University Press, 1993), 116–27; for a comparison of sexist and racist language, see also the contributions in *Sexist Language: A Modern Philosophical Analysis,* ed. Mary Vetterling-Braggin (Littlefield: Adams & Co., 1981), 249–319.

[47] For the elaboration of such a "symptomatic reading" approach, see especially the work of Rosemary Hennessy, *Materialist Feminism and the Politics of Discourse* (New York/London: Routledge, 1993).

African, free and enslaved, rich and poor, elite and marginal wo/men. Those who hold the opposite view, that, for instance, slave wo/men were not active shapers of early Christian life, would have to argue their point. If one shifts from a kyriarchal preconstructed frame of reference to that of a discipleship of equals, one no longer can hold, for instance, that wo/men were not members of the communities that produced the hypothetical Sayings Source Q.[48] If one cannot show definitely that wo/men were not members of this early Christian Jewish group, so my argument goes, one needs to give the benefit of the doubt to the textual traces suggesting that they were. Rather than take the kyriocentric text at face value, one must unravel its politics of meaning.

The objection that this is a circular argument applies to all hermeneutical practices. For instance, as I have argued in chapter 3, social-scientific studies that presuppose the "preconstructed"[49] dualistic opposition of "honor and shame" as given "facts" of Mediterranean cultures will read early Christian texts "about wo/men" within this theoretically "preconstructed" kyriocentric frame of reference.[50] Their narratives, however, appear to be more "realistic" and "objective" than feminist ones, only because kyriocentric discourses function as ideologies, that is, they mystify the "constructedness" of their account of reality. Therefore such hegemonic narratives of how the world of early Christianity "really was" are considered to be "commonsense," objective, "scientific" historical accounts, although they are as much a "construction" as feminist ones are.

[48] Amy-Jill Levine, "Who Caters the Q Affair? Feminist Observations on Q Paraenesis." *Semeia* 50 (1990): 145–61.

[49] For this concept, see Michel Pécheux, *Language, Semantics, and Ideology* (New York: St. Martin's Press, 1975). In any discursive formation the "preconstructed" produces the effect of an "always already given," the "commonsense" meaning, or "what everyone already knows."

[50] See, e.g., Bruce Malina, *The New Testament World: Insights from Cultural Anthropology* (Atlanta: John Knox, 1981); and Bruce Malina and Jerome H. Neyrey, "First-Century Personality: Dyadic, Not Individual," in *The Social World of Luke-Acts: Models for Interpretation*, ed. Jerome H. Neyrey (Peabody, Mass.: Hendrickson, 1991), 67–96. For a critical assessment, see Mary Ann Tolbert, "Social, Sociological, and Anthropological Methods," in *Searching the Scriptures*, vol. 1, ed. Schüssler Fiorenza, 255–72 and chapter 3 above. For a critical evaluation of the anthropological construct of "the Mediterranean," see especially the articles by Michael Herzfeld, "The Horns of the Mediterranean Dilemma," *American Ethnologist* 11 (1984): 439–55, and "'As in Your Own House': Hospitality, Ethnography, and the Stereotype of the Mediterranean Society," in *Honor and Shame and the Unity of the Mediterranean*, ed. David Gilmore (Washington, D.C.: American Anthropological Association, 1987).

Undergirding my reconstructive model are four basic theoretical assumptions:

*First,* the hermeneutical practice of anti-Judaism is contrary to a Christian feminist theology of liberation because this assumption does not recognize that Jesus and his first followers were Jewish wo/men. They were *not Christian* in our sense of the word. Rather, as Jewish Galilean wo/men they gathered together for common meals, theological reflection, and healing events. They did so because they had a "dream" and followed a vision of liberation for every wo/man in Israel.

*Second,* who Jesus was and what he did can *only* be glimpsed in the interpretations and memory of the Jesus movement understood as a first-century Jewish movement. Therefore the Jesus movement must not be separated methodologically from other messianic movements in first-century Judaism. Moreover, one must keep in mind that just as there was no unified early Christianism, neither was there an "orthodox" singular Judaism in the first century C.E.[51] Orthodox Judaism, like orthodox Christianity, emerged only in subsequent centuries.

*Third,* this emancipatory movement of Galilean Jewish wo/men must be seen as a part of the variegated *basileia* and holiness movements that in the first century sought the "liberation" of Israel from imperial exploitation. The concrete political referent of these movements was the colonial occupation of Israel by the Romans. Hence, it is no accident that in this political context they invoked the covenant promise of Exod. 19:6. Some of them, such as the Pharisees or Essenes, stressed the notion of "priesthood and holy nation." Others, such as the apocalyptic prophetic movements— among them the Jesus movement—stressed the political notion of the *basileia* (empire/commonweal) of G*d as counterterm to the Roman empire.

*Fourth,* the emerging, variegated, predominantly Galilean Jesus movement understood itself as a prophetic movement of Divine Sophia-Wisdom.[52] That it named itself after Jesus, the Christ, was probably due to

[51] See Bruce Chilton and Jacob Neusner, *Judaism in the New Testament: Practices and Beliefs* (New York: Routledge, 1995), 10–18, for a critique of E. P. Sanders's (*Judaism 63 BCE –66 CE: Practice and Belief*) construct of a single unitary Judaism attested by a coherent canon.

[52] Elisabeth Schüssler Fiorenza, "Jesus—Messenger of Divine Wisdom," *Studia Theologica* 49 (1995): 231–52.

the conviction that had emerged after Jesus' execution that he was the Anointed One who is now the Vindicated or Resurrected One. This conviction, I have argued in *Jesus: Miriam's Child, Sophia's Prophet*, had its base in the wo/men's tradition of the "empty tomb," which centered on the proclamation "that Jesus is *going ahead* of you to Galilee," the site where the antimonarchical prophetic traditions of the northern kingdom were still alive. This tradition manifests the self-understanding of the Jewish Galilean *basileia*-(empire/commonweal)-of-G*d movement as an ongoing and inclusive movement of prophets and messengers sent to Israel by Divine Wisdom. The *basileia* movement is thus best understood as a Wisdom/Sophia movement in which Jesus is *primus inter pares*, first among equals.

Such an egalitarian reconstructive model, I submit, is able to place the beginnings of the Galilean prophetic-wisdom *basileia* movement within a broader universalizing historical frame of reference. This frame allows one to trace the tensions and struggles between emancipatory understandings and movements in antiquity inspired by the democratic logic of equality, on the one hand, and the dominant kyriarchal structures of society and religion, on the other.

Ancient movements of emancipatory struggle against kyriarchal relations of exploitation do not begin with the Jesus movement. Rather, they have a long history in Greek, Roman, Asian, and Jewish cultures.[53] The emancipatory struggles of biblical wo/men must be seen within the wider context of cultural-political-religious struggles. Such a historical model of emancipatory struggle sees the historical Jesus and the movement that has kept alive his memory not over and against Judaism but over and against kyriarchal structures of domination in antiquity.

Such a reconstructive frame of reference, I submit, is able to conceptualize the emergent Jesus movement and its diverse articulations as participating in popular movements of cultural, political, and religious resistance. To variegate Bultmann's well-known scholarly dictum: Jesus did not just rise into the kerygma as a "dangerous memory." Rather, he is "going ahead" in the emancipatory struggles for a world of justice, liberation, and freedom from kyriarchal oppression. He is "going ahead" in wo/men's struggles to "mend the world."

---

[53] See Barbara H. Geller Nathanson, "Toward a Multicultural Ecumenical History of Women in the First Century/ies CE," in *Searching the Scriptures*, vol. 1, ed. Schüssler Fiorenza, 272–89.

Yet, to speak about the Jesus movement as an inner-Jewish renewal movement, as I have done in *In Memory of Her,* still provokes several misunderstandings between Jews and Christians. Jacob Neusner has rightly pointed out that the notion of "renewal" still carries traces of supersessionism insofar as it suggests that Christianity is a "better" form of Judaism. In other words, the notion of a reform movement still can be made to fit into the hegemonic Christian construct of the *Judeo-Christian* tradition, which posits a supersessionist continuity between Judaism and Christianity.[54] Only if one explicitly acknowledges that Judaism and Christianity are two different religions which have their roots in the Hebrew Bible and in the pluriform religious matrix of first-century Israel can one avoid reading "renewal movement" in a supersessionist fashion. As Alan Segal has aptly put it: Early Judaism and Christianism are Rebecca's children, twin siblings of the same mother.[55]

Moreover, to speak about the Jesus movement as an inner-Jewish renewal movement of the first century can be and has been further misread as implying that the Jesus movement was the *only* reform movement at the time and that Jewish or Greek wo/men who did not join this movement suffered from a "false consciousness."[56] Furthermore, if read in a preconstructed frame of meaning that maintains the uniqueness of Jesus, the expression "renewal movement" suggests not only Christian particularity and exceptionality but also superiority. For that reason, I cannot stress enough that the Jesus movement must be understood as *one among several prophetic* movements of Jewish wo/men who struggled for the liberation of Israel. As a result, I have replaced the notion of "renewal movement" with the concept of the Jesus movement as an emancipatory movement.

### THE CENTRAL VISION OF *BASILEIA*

The central symbol of this movement, the *basileia* of G\*d,[57] expresses a Jewish religious-political vision that spells freedom from domination and

---

[54] Jacob Neusner, *Jews and Christians: The Myth of a Common Tradition* (Philadelphia: Trinity Press International, 1991). See also Arthur Cohen, *The Myth of the Judeo-Christian Tradition* (New York: Harper & Row, 1969).

[55] Alan Segal, *Rebecca's Children: Judaism and Christianity in the Roman World* (Cambridge, Mass.: Harvard University Press, 1987).

[56] For such a [deliberate?] misreading, see Ross Kraemer's reviews of *In Memory of Her* in *Religious Studies Review* 11, no. 1 (1985): 107, and in *Journal of Biblical Literature* 104, no. 4 (1985): 722. See also my response to her in the introduction to the tenth anniversary edition of the book.

[57] For a comprehensive review of the meaning of this expression in contemporary

is common to all the different movements in first-century Israel. As I have already pointed out, it is difficult to translate the Greek term *basileia* adequately because it can either mean kingdom, kingly realm, domain or empire, or it can be rendered as monarchy, kingly rule, sovereignty, dominion, and reign. In any case the word has not only monarchic but also masculinist overtones.

According to G. Dalman, the Hebrew equivalent of *malkuth* when applied to G*d always means kingly rule and has never had the territorial sense of kingdom. Following him, most exegetes translate *basileia* with "kingly reign" and understand it as G*d's all-overpowering initiative and sovereign ruling. Moreover, most reviews of scholarship on the meaning of the expression *basileia* of G*d do not even discuss its political significance in a context where people must have thought of the Roman empire when they heard the word.

To lift the political meaning of *basileia* into consciousness, I suggest that the expression is best translated with words such as "empire, domain, or commonweal." Such renderings of the word *basileia* underscore linguistically the oppositional character of the empire/commonweal of G*d to that of the Roman empire. Since such a translation is generally not understood in an oppositional sense, however, but as ascribing to G*d imperial monarchic power, I have tended *not* to translate the Greek word *basileia* but to use it as a tensive symbol that evokes a whole range of theological meanings and at the same time seeks to foster a critical awareness of their ambiguity. The translation of the term as "kindom," which has been suggested by Ada María Isasi-Díaz also loses the political overtones of *basileia*. By not translating the Greek term, I seek to bring to the fore its political impact and eschatological significance in the first century C.E. while at the same time problematizing its kyriarchal politics of meaning.

Exegetes agree that the Roman form of imperial domination signified

---

Judaism, see Anna Maria Schwemer, "Gott als König und seine Königsherrschaft," in *Königsherrschaft Gottes und himmlischer Kult in Judentum, Urchristentum und in der hellenistischen Welt*, ed. Martin Hengel and Anna Maria Schwemer (Tübingen: J. C. B. Mohr, 1991), 45–118. For the discussion of the *basileia* discourse in early Christianity, see Helmut Merkel, "Die Gottesherrschaft in der Verkündigung Jesu," ibid., 119–61. See also Marinus de Jonge, "The Christological Significance of Jesus' Preaching of the Kingdom of God," in *The Future of Christology: Essays in Honor of Leander E. Keck*, ed. Abraham J. Malherbe and Wayne A. Meeks (Minneapolis: Fortress Press, 1993), 7: "Notwithstanding the intrinsic difficulties in reconstructing Jesus' message concerning the kingdom, there is a surprising consensus" in understanding it as meaning "the time and place where God's power and kingly rule will hold sway."

by the term *basileia* has determined the world and experience of all Jewish movements in the first century, including that which named itself after Jesus. Jesus and his first followers, wo/men and men, sought for the emancipation and well-being of Israel as the people of G*d, a kingdom of priests and a holy nation (Exod. 19:6). They announced the *basileia* (commonweal/empire) of G*d as an alternative to that of Rome.

The *basileia*/commonweal of G*d is a *tensive* religious symbol[58] not only of ancestral range proclaiming G*d's power of creation and salvation. This term is also a political symbol that appealed to the oppositional imagination of people victimized by the Roman imperial system. It envisions an alternative world free of hunger, poverty, and domination. This "envisioned" world is already anticipated in the inclusive table-sharing, in the healing and liberating practices, as well as in the domination-free kinship community of the Jesus movement, which found many followers among the poor, the despised, the ill and possessed, the outcasts, prostitutes, and sinners.[59]

The story of the Jesus movement as emancipatory *basileia*-of-G*d movement is told in different ways in the canonical and extracanonical gospel accounts. These accounts have undergone a lengthy process of rhetorical transmission and theological edition. The gospel writers were not concerned with antiquarian historical transcription but with interpretive remembrance and rhetorical persuasion.

They did not simply want to write down what Jesus said and did. Rather, they utilized the Jesus traditions which were shaped by Jesus' first followers, wo/men and men, for their own rhetorical interests and molded them in light of the political-theological debates of their own day. As a result, what we can learn from the rhetorical process of gospel transmission and redaction is that Jesus as we still can know him must be remembered, contextualized, discussed, interpreted, questioned, or rejected not only within an intertheological and interfaith debate, but also within a political-cultural debate.

However, one must be careful not to construe the Jesus movement as free from conflict and kyriarchal tendencies, lest in so doing one idealize it as the very "other" and positive counterpart of Judaism understood nega-

---

[58] For this expression, see Norman Perrin, *Jesus and the Language of the Kingdom* (Philadelphia: Fortress Press, 1976).

[59] For a similar account, see also Alan F. Segal, "Jesus, the Jewish Revolutionary," in *Jesus' Jewishness: Exploring the Place of Jesus Within Early Judaism,* ed. James H. Charlesworth (New York: Crossroad, 1991), 212–14.

tively. From the very beginnings of the Jesus movement differences, divisions, and conflicts existed, as the variegated if not contradictory articulations of the extant gospels indicate. For instance, the varicolored *basileia* sayings tradition that surfaces in Mark 10:42–45 and 9:33–37 par. is an anti-kyriarchal rhetorical tradition that contrasts the political structures of domination with those required among the disciples.[60] Structures of domination should not be tolerated in the discipleship of equals, but those of the disciples who would-be-great and would-be-first must become slaves and servants[61] of all. While this tradition advocates non-kyriarchal relationships in the discipleship of equals, its grammatical imperative simultaneously documents that such relationships were not lived by everyone. Especially, the would-be "great" and "first" seem to have been tempted to reassert kyriarchal social and religious status positions. The argument of the Syrophoenician wo/man, which has given *But She Said* its name, provides another example for such debates, since this story criticizes the ethnic bias of Jesus himself.

One also must not overlook that all four gospel accounts reflect the controversies with and separation anxieties from hegemonic forms of Judaism. Consequently, they all reinscribe Christian identity as standing in conflict with Judaism. A good example of this kyriocentric process of anti-Jewish and anti-wo/man inscription can be found when one traces the transmission history of the story about the wo/man who anointed Jesus as the Christ. The gospel of Mark places this story at the beginning of the narrative about Jesus' execution and resurrection.[62] Here Mark probably takes up a traditional story that knows of a wo/man anointing Jesus' head and

---

[60] Schüssler Fiorenza, *In Memory of Her*, 148.

[61] Jacquelyn Grant, "The Sin of Servanthood and the Deliverance of Discipleship," in *A Troubling in My Soul: Womanist Perspectives on Evil and Suffering*, ed. Emily M. Townes (Maryknoll, N.Y.: Orbis Books, 1993), 199–218, and I have problematized servanthood and emphasized discipleship in very similar ways, although we come from quite different social and religious backgrounds. Since Grant does not refer to my theoretical analysis (see my article "'Waiting at Table': A Critical Feminist Theological Reflection on Diakonia," *Concilium* 198 [1988]: 84–94, and my book *Discipleship of Equals: A Critical Feminist Ekklesia-logy of Liberation* [New York: Crossroad, 1993], 290–306), I feel justified in surmising that a comparable multiplicative analysis of kyriarchy results in coinciding theoretical proposals.

[62] See Robert Holst, "The Anointing of Jesus: Another Application of the Form-Critical Method," *Journal of Biblical Literature* 95 (1976): 435–46; Claus-Peter März, "Zur Traditionsgeschichte von Mk 14,3-9 und Parallelen," *New Testament Studies* 67 (1981–82): 89–112; for a general bibliography on the passion narratives, see Raymond E. Brown, *The Death of the Messiah* (New York: Doubleday, 1994), 94–106.

thereby naming him as the Christ, the Anointed One.[63] A revelatory word of Jesus links her prophetic sign-action with the proclamation of the gospel in the whole world.[64] The community that retells this story after Jesus' execution knows that Jesus is no longer in their midst. They do no longer "have" Jesus with them.

Either in the course of the transmission of this story or at the editorial stage three kyriocentric interpretations of the wo/man's prophetic sign-action are introduced. First, the objection and debate with the male disciples introduce a kyriarchal understanding that sees "the poor" no longer as constitutive members of the community but as "the others," as people who deserve alms. The second interpretation construes the unnamed wo/man's sign-action in feminine kyriocentric terms: She does what wo/men are supposed to do, prepare the bodies of the dead for burial.[65] Finally, the third interpretation reframes the story as an ideo-story or example story that counterposes the action of the wo/man to that of Judas, the betrayer of Jesus.[66]

Insofar as the wo/man disciple remains unnamed whereas the male disciple who betrays Jesus is named Judas, the text evokes not only an androcentric response that, contrary to the word of Jesus, does not comprehend the significance of the wo/man's prophetic naming. By underscoring that the name of the betrayer is Judas, a name that linguistically reminds one of "Jew/Judaism," it elicits an anti-Jewish response that is intensified in the course of the passion narrative. Thus, we still can trace the gospels' anti-Jewish rhetoric in the reinterpretations of the anointing story, a story that was potentially a politically dangerous story. The depoliticizing rhetoric which comes here to the fore has engendered not only anti-Jewish inter-

---

[63] See, e.g., the fresco at Dura Europos for the importance of prophetic anointing. See Warren G. Moon, "Nudity and Narrative: Observations on the Frescoes from the Dura Synagogue," *Journal of the American Academy of Religion* 40 (1992): 587–658.

[64] For a discussion of Mark's account, see Marie Sabin, "Women Transformed: The Ending of Mark Is the Beginning of Wisdom," *Cross Currents* 48 (1998): 149–68; Monika Fander, *Die Stellung der Frau im Markusevangelium unter besonderer Berücksichtigung kultur- und religionsgeschichtlicher Hintergründe* (Altenberge: Telos Verlag, 1989), 118–35; for Matthew, see the excellent analysis of Elaine M. Wainwright, *Towards a Feminist Critical Reading of the Gospel According to Matthew* (Beihefte zur Zeitschrift für die neutestamentliche Wissenschaft 60; Berlin: Walter de Gruyter, 1991), 252–83.

[65] Vernon K. Robbins, "Using a Socio-Rhetorical Poetics to Develop a Unified Method: The Woman who Anointed Jesus as a Test Case," in *Society of Biblical Literature 1992 Seminar Papers*, ed. Eugene H. Lovering (Atlanta: Scholars Press, 1992), 311.

[66] James Brownson, "Neutralizing the Intimate Enemy: The Portrayal of Judas in the Fourth Gospel," in *Society of Biblical Literature 1992 Seminar Papers*, ed. Lovering, 49–60.

pretations of Jesus' suffering and execution but also has forged Christian political adaptation to Roman imperial structures that with its apologetic defense of the Roman authorities opened the door to the co-optation of the gospel in the interest of domination.

Since the process of the kyriarchal reinterpretation of the story in the gospels has produced the "preconstructed," by now, commonsense, kyriocentric frame of meaning that marginalizes wo/men and vilifies Jews, it is necessary to dislodge our readings from such a preconstructed frame of reference and to reconfigure the Christian Testament discourses about Jesus. Constructing the Jesus movement as one among many *emancipatory movements* in the first century, I have argued here and elsewhere, provides such a different historical frame of reference. It allows for a Christian self-understanding that is neither articulated over and against Judaism nor remains intertwined with theological masculinism. Such a christological rereading does not need to relinquish the quest for its historical Jewish roots nor end in Christian supremacy and exclusivism. It does not tie Christian self-identity to its previous stages of formation and their socio-cultural contexts but remains obligated to the messianic *basileia*-vision of G*d's alternative world of justice and salvation.

In sum, a feminist Christian identity is to be articulated again and again within the emancipatory struggles for the vision of G*d's *basileia,* which spells well-being and freedom for all in the global village. Similarly, a Jewish feminist identity is to be articulated within the emancipatory struggles for the "restoration of the world," of *tikkun olam*[67] as the social, political, and religious transformation of kyriarchal structures of injustice and domination. The one biblical G*d of Jews, Christians, and Muslims today still calls wo/men of faith to engage in the prophetic-messianic vision of justice, freedom, love, and salvation that has inspired our ancestors in their religious-political struggles for a more just world.

By focusing not on the Historical-Jesus as the great (male) individual and charismatic leader but on the vision and praxis of the movement gathered in his name, such a reconstructive model not only aims to make anti-Judaism harder to import but also seeks to avoid the cultural romantic trap of wo/men's sado-masochistic attachment to the man Jesus. Just like all other Historical-Jesus discourses, I have argued here, feminist Jesus discourses also must constantly be scrutinized for their possible functions in

---

[67] "*Tikkun*—to mend, repair and transform the world" is the programmatic motto of the progressive Jewish journal *Tikkun,* published by the Institute for Labor and Mental Health.

strengthening or undermining relations of domination. For, as Michelle Russell has recognized more than twenty years ago:

> The question is this: How will you refuse to let the academy separate the dead from the living, and then yourself declare allegiance to life? As teachers, scholars and students, how available will you make your knowledge to others as tools for their own liberation. This is not a call for mindless activism, but rather for engaged scholarship.[68]

[68] Michelle Russell, "An Open Letter to the Academy," *Quest* 3 (1977): 77f.

# INDEX